THE INTERACTIVE CASEBOOK SERIES™

LEGAL WRITING

A Contemporary Approach

———————

by

Ann Sinsheimer
PROFESSOR OF LEGAL WRITING
UNIVERSITY OF PITTSBURGH SCHOOL OF LAW

Teresa Kissane Brostoff
PROFESSOR OF LEGAL WRITING
UNIVERSITY OF PITTSBURGH SCHOOL OF LAW

Nancy M. Burkoff
ASSOCIATE PROFESSOR OF LEGAL WRITING
UNIVERSITY OF PITTSBURGH SCHOOL OF LAW

———————

WEST
ACADEMIC
PUBLISHING

Mat #40880387

Interactive Casebook Series is a trademark registered in the U.S. Patent and Trademark Office.

© 2014 LEG, Inc. d/b/a West Academic

    444 Cedar Street, Suite 700
    St. Paul, MN 55101
    1-877-888-1330

West, West Academic Publishing, and West Academic are trademarks of West Publishing Corporation, used under license.

Printed in the United States of America

ISBN: 978–0–314–90672–4

Dedication

Thank you, Marvin, for patiently listening to every idea.

A.S.

I dedicated this book with love to my first and best teachers, my Dad,
Jack Kissane, and to the warm and lovely memory of my mom, Helen Kissane.

T.K.B.

Dedicated with love to John, my husband, mentor, and best friend,
and to our family.

N.B.

Acknowledgments

We would like to thank the many people who helped and supported us in writing this book. First, we would like to thank our deans, past and present, Mary Crossley and William Carter who supported us during the writing process. We also owe Louis Higgins at West Academic a debt of gratitude for inviting us to write this text and for his kindness and patience throughout an extended drafting period. Many students helped us research and/or donated some of their work to help future law students. They are (in no particular order): Ed SanFillipo, Clems Weygandt, Jennifer McCreery, Julie Vanneman, Jamie Reese, Jennifer St. Preux, Leigh Argentieri, Sarah Kashusbski-Chips, Stephen Zumbrun, Rebecca Grinstead, Nikolay Markov, Kate Langford, Maria Salvatori, Elie Freedman, Lauren Laing, Endia Vereen, Rodney and Angela Miller, Sean Kerr, Amy Hewitt, Molly Q. Campbell, Adrienne Lester-Fitje, Joe Lodico, and Ken Ludlum. We extend a special thanks to our first year students (class of 2016) at the University of Pittsburgh School of Law who so patiently helped us to tune our drafts. John Williams and Professor Vivian Curran gave us expert advice on two legal issues addressed in student exercises. Dr. Marilyn Freedman graciously provided her lovely illustration for our Puppy Putters exercise. Linda Tashbook helped us with international research. Phil Zarone supplied us with advice and sample client letters. We thank Kalypa Acharya Adam Lobel for his generous guidance and teaching that inspired the Mindful Lawyering chapter. The professionals who work in our Document Technology Center were a wonder. They made each chapter look beautiful and were patient and calm with our many formatting questions. They are: LuAnn Driscoll, Phyllis Gentille, Karen Knochel Darleen Mocello, and Barb Salopek. Our editors at Red Line, Megan Anderson and Laura Kruse made everything easy for us, and we thank them.

Most importantly, we thank our families for their love and support while writing this book and in all things.

Table of Contents

Table of Cases

CHAPTER 1

Introduction

Welcome to Law School and to a new way of thinking, solving problems, and writing. Legal writing serves as both an analytical tool and a form of communication. It also plays a fundamental role in creating and shaping the law. In the legal profession, the ability to write well to express ideas is extremely valuable. This text primarily examines this analytical process and the role of written communication in the field of law.

Legal Analysis and Writing is a language and culture course, specifically a course on the language and culture of law. This book covers the forms of writing commonly associated with legal practice, including the predictive writing styles found in legal memoranda and the persuasive writing and styles found in trial and appellate court briefs and court opinions. The book will introduce you to the language and culture of law and provide a foundation for work in the legal profession. Most immediately, this book will help you to successfully navigate the first year of law school by providing practice in analyzing and writing about the law and applying the law to solve legal problems. You will also prepare for legal practice by strengthening problem solving and communication skills.

Specifically the book will enable you to:

- Accurately assess a legal problem, evaluate potential solutions, and communicate conclusions in verbal and written form.
- Predict the potential outcome of a legal dispute and construct a persuasive legal argument.
- Recognize and apply principles of professional communication (audience, purpose, organization, style, flow, and presentation) as they appear in various types of texts associated with the legal profession.
- Examine how writing is used within legal culture.
- Assess your own strengths and weaknesses in legal analysis and writing particularly as you are forming your professional identity.

This text first focuses on predictive or objective writing. You will discover how to find, synthesize, and apply sources of law such as judicial opinions and statutes to solve legal problems. You will develop problem-solving skills as you predict the outcome of simulated legal disputes and evaluate solutions that will help to resolve these disputes. Through a series of client-focused exercises such as presentations, memos, and client communications, you will develop listening, speaking, and writing skills.

After completing the predictive section of this book, you will be able to:

- Read cases and determine the law.
- Synthesize this information and analyze legal problems; make a prediction and prove that the prediction is sound.
- Write effectively, meaning clearly and concisely.
- Learn to edit your own work and to write and organize information for other readers.

The text also focuses on persuasive speaking and writing, and applying the skills learned in the work world that follows law school. You will focus on persuading an audience that a certain perspective on the law is "correct" or the one that a court or other reader or listener should adopt. Appreciating the nature of the audience for persuasive speaking and writing is very important and documents and presentations are closely tailored in form and function to the nature of the audience. This portion of the text teaches the art of persuasion in many different contexts, and allows you to draft documents with different purposes and to different audiences. It also shows examples of well-written student work and professionally drafted documents. The text also addresses the challenges of entering the work world of legal professionals by providing tools for managing stress and examples of documents and work habits that legal settings may require.

After completing the persuasive section of this text, you will be able to:

- Identify the use of persuasive language and techniques in the documents they read.
- Use persuasion in its many forms to assure readers of the correct foundation and reasoning of their legal position.
- Produce professionally drafted documents using the proper rules and format for each document.
- Address a court or tribunal to give a professional, clear and persuasive oral argument.
- Understand how to manage the stress of legal practice.
- Understand some of the additional documents and techniques that legal practice requires.

Lawyers in the United States, a common law system, should be aware that most of the world's countries use a civil law system of law and government. Therefore, this text also has an international focus. Throughout the chapters, there are references to the civil law approach to lawyering tasks, analysis and problem solving. Most lawyers, even those with a purely domestic practice, will encounter some questions that involve understanding international or civil law. You will place U.S. law and legal reasoning in a world context, rather than viewing it as the dominant international view of the law. You will also understand some of the basic differences between common law and civil law practice.

Finally, this text has online links to important and useful information and examples. Accessing this information will deepen and expand your knowledge of the material in the text. We hope you enjoy this added feature, and we wish you well in law school and in your chosen profession.

CHAPTER 2

The United States Legal System

When beginning to study the law, law students must first understand the legal structures of government and how each functions as a source of law. Understanding the source of law and how each law interacts with others and with legal decision-makers makes easier the task of reading cases and statutes. In fact, law students will be much more specific when referring to the law. Each type of law has a specific name. In the U.S. common law system, these consist primarily of constitutions, statutes, cases, rules and regulations.

Go Online

See examples of these types of laws at these sites. <u>Constitutions</u>, <u>statutes</u>, <u>cases</u>, and <u>rules and regulations</u>.

This chapter will introduce you briefly to the United States Legal System as a structure of government and as sources of law. It will also briefly introduce the **civil law**'s view of legal systems as sources of law.

What's That?

<u>Civil Law</u>

The United States Constitution

<u>The United States Constitution</u> enumerates the powers granted to the federal government and dictates its structure. It provides broad, yet limited, power to the central federal government and reserves other powers to the states and the people. In addition, the Constitution gives substantive and procedural rights to the citizens. As the United States has a federalist system of government, each state also has a written constitution, some predating the U.S. Constitution: <u>http://www.dos.state.ny.us/info/constitution.htm</u>. The U.S. government and each state's government are divided into three branches, the Executive, Legislative and Judicial branches, each of which functions independently and interdependently with the others within its system. The constitutions in each system define the powers allocated to each branch of government.

The Executive Branch

The Executive Branch is empowered through Article II, section 1 of the U.S. Constitution. Its duty is to implement and enforce the law. The chief executive is the President of the United States. He or she is the Commander-in-Chief of the Armed Forces and makes the ultimate decisions regarding domestic policy, law enforcement and international affairs. The President also has the power of appointment regarding many actors within several branches of government, including his cabinet and the heads of agencies. These actors are part of the Executive Branch as are the departments headed by the members of the President's cabinet, as well as administrative agencies. This is a link to an administrative agency: http://www. fda.gov/.

These agencies are the primary source of law from the Executive Branch because they **promulgate** rules and regulations, such as the cigarette labeling regulation. Rules and regulations implement the language of statutes and instruct those using the statutes on how to enforce the statutory language. Usually the statute itself will authorize an agency to make the regulations and rules.

What's the Verb?

Promulgate is the verb most commonly associated with the formation of regulations.

The U.S. legal system is often said to be a system of checks and balances where no one branch of government is all-powerful. The Executive Branch can interact with other branches of government to insure that neither the Legislative nor Judicial branches become too powerful. For the Legislative Branch, the President can introduce legislation to Congress as in this legislation—a jobs bill from early September 2011 and can also **veto** legislation that has been passed by Congress. In addition, the vice president is the President of the Senate and has the power to cast a tie breaking vote there. For the Judicial Branch, the President through the power of appointment can influence judicial decisions as the President appoints all federal judges, United States Attorneys and Federal Public Defenders.

What's the Verb?

Veto

The Legislative Branch

Article I, section 8 empowers the federal legislature. In both federal and in most state governments, the legislature is bicameral, comprised of a House of Representatives http://www.house.gov/ where the number of representatives is determined by the population of each state and the Senate where each state has two Senators. http://www.senate. gov/ Congress **enacts** statutes as the primary source of law to come from the Legislative Branch. The Legislative Branch has the power to lay and col-

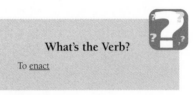

What's the Verb?

To enact

lect taxes, borrow and spend money, regulate interstate commerce, declare war and ratify treaties.

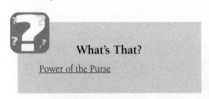

What's That?

Power of the Purse

The Legislative Branch also plays a role in the system of checks and balances. It can influence the Executive Branch by funding or refusing **to fund** initiatives or by refusing to enact legislation proffered by the President. The Congress can also override a Presidential veto with a two-thirds majority vote in both houses. In addition, the Senate must offer its advice and consent on all Presidential nominees before they can assume their posts. Lastly and very rarely, the legislature can impeach, convict and remove the President from office. For the Judicial Branch, the legislature can overturn judicial decisions through legislation. If constitutional, these statutes will take priority over inconsistent case or common law.

The Judicial Branch

The Judicial Branch is the court system. As with the other branches of government, each state has its own court system, coexisting with the federal court system. Courts decide cases. As the United States is a common law system, judges make law with case decisions and opinions. This is called

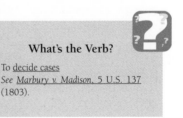

What's the Verb?

To decide cases
See Marbury v. Madison, 5 U.S. 137 (1803).

common law. Courts also interpret statutes and regulations and constitutions. This is called case law. Courts must wait for the parties to bring a controversy or case to them before they have the power to resolve that legal issue on the particular facts of the parties' dispute.

The courts also are part of the system of checks and balances. Courts influence the legislature by interpreting statutes and deciding whether a statute is constitutional. Courts may also interpret the language of regulations or even disregard them when interpreting a statute, influencing the Executive Branch. In addition, because of their lifetime tenure on the bench, judges can develop their own judicial philosophies and become independent of the President who appointed them.

Diagram of Federal Government

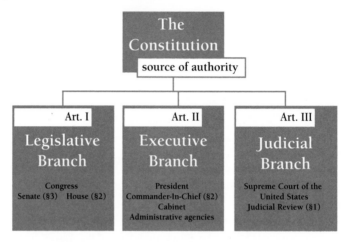

Diagram of State Government

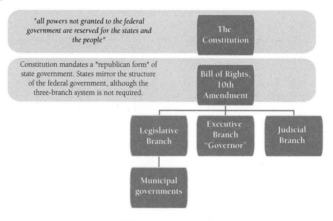

The U.S. Court System

Both the state and federal court systems are hierarchical. This means there are several levels of courts. In the federal and most states jurisdictions, there are three main levels of court. In general, these levels are the trial court, the intermediate appellate court and the highest court. In the federal system, the courts are named the <u>United States District Court</u>, the United States Courts of Appeals, e.g. <u>Ninth Circuit Court</u>, and the <u>Supreme Court of the United States</u>.

The district courts are named for the state in which they sit. An example is the <u>U.S. District Court for the Western District of Pennsylvania</u>. The intermediate appellate courts are named by Circuit of which there are eleven numbered circuits, the DC and the Federal Circuits. A Circuit is usually comprised of several geographically close states.

The trial court is the lowest level of court. It is here that most lawsuits or criminal prosecutions begin. One judge presides over the proceedings. The parties are called the plaintiff and defendant in civil cases or the prosecution and criminal defendant in criminal cases. Cases can be resolved through pre-trial motions, mediation or negotiation, or a case can go to trial. The judge always decides the law of the case and rules on any questions of law. The judge can also decide the facts of the case. If the judge decides law and facts, the trial is called a **bench trial**. However, a jury can also decide the facts of the case. A jury is usually composed of 12 persons who sit through the trial and hear all the evidence and ultimately decide the facts of the case. The jury will then come to a **<u>verdict</u>** by applying the law as the judge has instructed them to the facts of the case as they have found them.

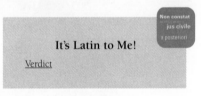

It's Latin to Me!

<u>Verdict</u>

A case will move to the intermediate appellate court if one or more of the parties is dissatisfied with the outcome of the case. Every party is entitled to one appeal at the intermediate appellate court level, an "appeal as of right." The parties are called the **appellant** and **appellee**. To present the appeal, the appellant must demonstrate an error of law or a contested legal issue. The facts are only decided in the trial court and cannot be the subject of appeal to correct them.

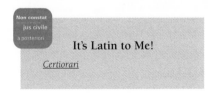

It's Latin to Me!

<u>Certiorari</u>

The highest court has **discretionary review**, which means that the court can choose the cases it will hear. In the U.S. Supreme Court, the petitioner must file a petition for a writ of **_certiorari_** with the petitioner trying to persuade the Court of the merits of the case. The respondent will usually oppose the petition. If the Court decides to accept the case, the writ of *certiorari* is granted. The Court receives many thousands of petitions, but will usually accept about one hundred cases or less each year.

As the United States has a common law legal system, cases are important parts of the law. Courts follow the doctrine of **_Stare Decisis_** meaning they follow the cases that have been decided previously on that legal issue.

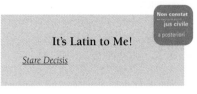

It's Latin to Me!

Stare Decisis

If the highest court decides an issue, that decision is considered binding on the lower courts. The system of precedent guides the courts in their decision-making, and provides consistency and predictability in the law. Decisions of the highest court and the intermediate courts set precedent which other courts will follow. However, the highest court may change precedent as changing conditions or circumstances demand.

The Federal Court System

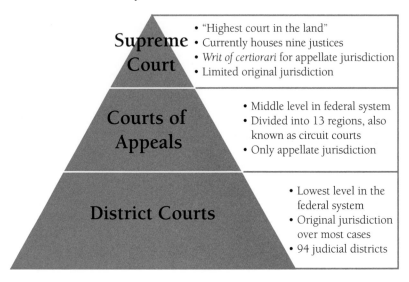

Supreme Court
- "Highest court in the land"
- Currently houses nine justices
- *Writ of certiorari* for appellate jurisdiction
- Limited original jurisdiction

Courts of Appeals
- Middle level in federal system
- Divided into 13 regions, also known as circuit courts
- Only appellate jurisdiction

District Courts
- Lowest level in the federal system
- Original jurisdiction over most cases
- 94 judicial districts

Play The Corpus Juris Game

Brief Overview of Civil Law Legal Systems

Most countries in the world follow the Civil Law tradition descended from Roman Law while the United States has a Common Law tradition descended from English Law. Civil Law systems of government follow a similar pattern of Executive, Legislative and Judicial branches; however, only the legislative branch is a source of law. The law is contained in a series of Codes on various legal subject matters. The legislative branch in many of these countries tends to be the most powerful branch with the Ministers in the legislature or parliament making the law and the Prime Minister leading the government. In these systems, the President may be the head of the country, but he or she may have no law-making power.

The courts apply the codes, but their decisions do not bind subsequent courts to reach similar decisions and are not considered law unto themselves. In the civil law trial, the judge has the primary inquisitorial role rather than the attorneys. Typically, there are no juries present in the trial court. Therefore, the judge decides all questions of law and fact. While some countries are moving to having lay judges, they are usually experts in a particular field rather than a group of people drawn from the general population. There is no system of precedent or principle of *stare decisis*, and the facts of each case do not influence how the court will apply the section of the code in the next case. In fact, the work of scholars is generally more influential to courts making their decisions than the decisions of prior courts.

For More Information

See *A Primer on the Civil Law System* by James G. Apple and Robert Deyling.

For More Information

Read a U.S. Supreme Court case and a case from the European Court of Justice and notice differences in form based on the differences in common law and civil law. Notice, however, that there are some similarities in legal reasoning.
Example—Compare these cases:
The Queen v. Immigration Appeal Tribunal et Surinder Singh, ex parte Secretary of State for Home Department
And
Knauff v. Shaughnessy, 338 U.S. 537 (1950)

However, in recent years, there has been some merging of traditions with civil law courts reading and trying to reconcile their decisions with those of the appellate courts. While the courts are not bound to do this, they may do it for consistency in the law and to avoid be overturned on appeal when a decision contradicts an earlier one of the appellate courts.

CHAPTER 3

Understanding Cases as a Source of Law

In the common law legal system, judicial opinions are a source of law so lawyers must read these opinions to identify the controlling law. The power of the courts is narrow—judges may resolve cases and controversies, which means that the judicial branch resolves disputes between parties. Whereas the legislature can research an area where a law will be needed and enact very broad legislation, judges must wait until a case is brought to them. Judges can only decide the issues that the parties bring to them, so while they may want to decide certain issues or to make policy in an area, they must wait until that dispute is before them. The law they provide is fact sensitive and governs particular parties, but when these decisions are compared and read as a group or a body of law they create legal doctrine or common law.

When judges issue their decisions, they issue them in the form of legal opinions—written pieces of advocacy that introduce a rule of law and form a body of law in particular subject areas. Through these decisions, courts create precedent—which means that court decisions, collectively and individually, are used to decide future cases and to predict how future cases should be resolved. The higher the court making the decision, the greater the weight it has as authority or precedent. If the decision is from the highest court in the jurisdiction, it is considered binding precedent or mandatory authority and must be followed by the lower courts in that jurisdiction.

Lawyers and future lawyers read judicial opinions because they help us to: 1) determine how a dispute was resolved in the past; 2) understand what the law governing a current dispute is; and 3) predict the outcome of future disputes. These opinions, or "cases," are our tools. Additionally, judicial opinions provide insight into the legal system and the way in which lawyers are taught to think about a problem. The text of a judicial opinion provides clues about legal culture and legal conventions. For example, a judicial opinion is typically organized in a particular manner and contains particular information that reveals how legal professionals are taught to think about problems. An opinion includes an articulation of the issue before the court, a discussion of the controlling law in the case, and an application of legal precedent to the facts of the case. As you read a case, you should try to identify this information so that you can uncover the crucial information in an opinion.

The following case is annotated so you can see what form this information might take.

COMMONWEALTH of Pennsylvania, Appellee, *Caption of the case*

v.

Barbara GOSSELIN, Appellant.

Superior Court of Pennsylvania. *Court deciding the case*

Argued Aug. 31, 2004.
Filed Nov. 5, 2004.

Background: Defendant was convicted in *Criminal case* the Court of Common Pleas, Schuylkill County, Criminal Division, No. S03-1528, Dolbin, J., of unlawful taking or possession of game or wildlife. Defendant appealed.

Holdings: The Superior Court, No. 1978 *Summary of the case* MDA 2003, Hudock, J., held that: *written by the publisher*

(1) defendant's taking and domestication of squirrel from South Carolina was lawful, and

(2) trial court could not rely on statute governing importation, sale and release of wildlife to support judgment of con-

COM. v. GOSSELIN

Cite as 861 A.2d 996 (Pa.Super. 2004)

Pa. **997**

Official Reporter Citation

viction for unlawful taking or possession of game or wildlife as charged in citation.

Sentence reversed; citation dismissed.

Headnotes: helpful research tool but not authorized by the court.

1. Criminal Law ⊙ 1019

The Commonwealth Court of Pennsylvania is conferred with jurisdiction over appeals from criminal prosecutions brought pursuant to the Game and Wildlife Code.

2. Statutes ⊙ 188

The basic tenet of statutory construction requires a court to construe the words of the statute according to their plain meaning.

3. Game ⊙ 7

Defendant's taking of squirrel from South Carolina was lawful, and thus, defendant could not be prosecuted under statute prohibiting unlawful taking or possession of game or wildlife outside Commonwealth, where South Carolina did not prohibit taking and domestication of squirrels and had no statutory provisions for tagging and marking squirrel. 34 Pa. C.S.A. § 2307(c).

4. Criminal Law ⊙ 255.4, 260.11(6)

Trial court's reference to statute prohibiting importation or possession of wildlife held in captivity to sustain defendant's conviction under separate statute prohibiting unlawful taking or possession of game or wildlife was reversible error, as citation charged only unlawful possession offense under latter statute, which was different from importation offense, and defendant received no notice of potential for conviction under importation statute. 34 Pa. C.S.A. § 2307(a); 58 Pa.Code § 137.1(a); Rules Crim.Proc., Rule 403(A)(6), 42 Pa. C.S.A.

Dirk S. Berger, Pottsville, for appellant.

Andrew J. Serina, Asst. Dist. Atty., Pottsville, for Com., appellee.

BEFORE: HUDOCK and KLEIN, JJ., *Judges hearing the case* and McEWEN, P.J.E.

OPINION BY HUDOCK, J.: *Authoring judge*

¶ 1 This appeal revolves around the life and times of Nutkin the squirrel.

¶ 2 Nutkin's early life was spent in the *Facts* state of *ferrae naturae*, in the state of South Carolina, and, as far as we can tell, in a state of contentment. She apparently had plenty of nuts to eat and trees to climb, and her male friends, while not particularly handsome, did have nice personalities. Life was good.

¶ 3 Then one day tragedy struck: Nutkin fell from her tree nest!

¶ 4 But fate was kind. Nutkin was found and adopted by Appellant and her husband who, at that time, were residents of South Carolina. Appellant lovingly nursed Nutkin back to health, and Nutkin became the family pet. A large room-sized enclosure was built so Nutkin had plenty of room to run and climb. Life was good again.

¶ 5 Nutkin's captivity and domestication were perfectly legal in South Carolina, possibly a reflection of that state's long tradition of hospitality to all.

¶ 6 In 1994, Appellant and her husband moved to Pennsylvania and brought Nutkin with them. Life was full of promise.

¶ 7 Dark clouds began to gather, however, in November, 2002, when Appellant's husband phoned the Pennsylvania Game Commission concerning a hunter whom he and Appellant believed was hunting near an area on their property where they had set out food for deer. In response to that complaint, a Wildlife Officer appeared at Appellant's property to investigate. At that time the Officer became aware that a deer had been illegally shot on Appellant's property and dragged to a neighboring property. Appellant and her husband requested that the Game Officer further investigate the poaching of the deer. The Officer refused to do so, but when he spotted Nutkin in her room-sized enclosure, he advised Appellant that it was a violation of the law to keep Nutkin in this manner. The Game Officer acknowledged that the squirrel was too old and too tame to be released to the wild (A situation akin to that of an old appellate judge, like the undersigned, attempting to return to the boiling cauldron of the trial court after being tamed by years of peace and quiet above the fray. Chances of survival of both species are poor.) He offered to forgo citing Appellant if she would relinquish Nutkin to his control. Appellant and her husband refused.

¶ 8 The reasons for this refusal are not apparent of record, but familial ties no doubt played a part in the decision. (At oral argument, our esteemed colleague, Judge Klein, alluded to the possibility of "squirrel stew", but there is insufficient evidence to support this horrific supposition.)

¶ 9 Nutkin would then learn the shocking truth that the cheery Pennsylvania slogan "You've got a friend in Pennsylvania" did not apply to four-legged critters like Nutkin. On December 2, 2002, the Wildlife Conservation Officer issued a citation directed to Appellant's husband for violating section 2307(a) of the Game and Wildlife Code, entitled "Unlawful taking or possession of game or wildlife".[1] For some unexplained reason, this citation was withdrawn and a new citation alleging the same violation was directed to Appellant.

Procedural history

¶ 10 Appellant had become known to the Pennsylvania Game Commission by appearing to testify before the Game and Fisheries Committee of the Pennsylvania House of Representatives in September, 2001. In this testimony, the Appellant complained about the enforcement proceedings of the Pennsylvania Game Commission, and particularly complained of the fact that every year "bubba" hunters showed up in the woods near their house to drive out the deer and the hunters were guilty of various other displays of bad hunting manners. Stipulation of Facts, 8/5/03, Exhibit C. She further testified to her opinion that the Game Commission is "against any landowner who posts their property." *Id.*

¶ 11 While there is no explicit claim of retaliatory prosecution, the stipulated facts show an interesting temporal relationship between Appellant's complaints both to the Game Commission and the General Assembly and her present difficulties.

[1] ¶ 12 In any event, Appellant was convicted of the offense before a district justice and again before the common pleas court in a trial *de novo* based upon stipulated facts. She was fined $100.00 plus the costs of prosecution. While the trial court did not file an opinion, it did provide the following reasoning in support of its decision in a footnote to the order finding Appellant guilty:

*To sustain this finding, reference must be had to the PA Code Title 58 Chapter 137 in which it is provided at 137.1(a), "unless otherwise provided in this section or the Act, it is unlawful for a person to … possess … (9) game or wildlife taken alive from the wild or (10) game or wildlife held captive or game or wildlife held in captivity or captive bred

---

1. 34 Pa.C.S.A. § 2307(a).

in another state." Also, 137.31(b) a person violating this subchapter will be subject to the penalties provided in 2307 of the Act (relating to unlawful taking or possession of game o[r] wildlife).

Order dated 11/21/03. This timely appeal followed.[2]

Issues ¶ 13 Two issues are raised on appeal:

    A. Whether, based on the exception set forth in 34 Pa.C.S.A. § 2307(c), the trial court erred in convicting [Appellant] for violating 34 Pa.C.S.A. § 2307(a)[?]

    B. Whether the trial court, in convicting [Appellant] for violating 34 Pa.C.S.A. § 2307(a) improperly applied 58 Pa.Code § 137.1[?].

Appellant's theory of the case Appellant's Brief at 6 (emphasis deleted). The essence of Appellant's arguments is that her possession of Nutkin is permitted pursuant to the language of 34 Pa.C.S.A. section 2307(c). Appellant contends that the trial court not only failed to consider this provision, but, rather convicted her for violating a provision of the Pennsylvania Code (58 Pa.Code section 137.1) with which she was not charged.

Standard of review ¶ 14 Our standard of review of a trial court's adjudication entered following a *de novo* trial on a summary offense has been summarized as follows:

    [An appellate court's review of a] *de novo* trial on a summary offense is limited to whether the trial court committed

an error of law and whether the findings of the trial court are supported by competent evidence. The adjudication of the trial court will not be disturbed on appeal absent a manifest abuse of discretion. An abuse of discretion exists when the trial court has rendered a judgment that is manifestly unreasonable, arbitrary, or capricious, has failed to apply the law, or was motivated by partiality, prejudice, bias, or ill will.

Commonwealth v. Parks, 768 A.2d 1168, 1171 (Pa.Super.2001) (citations and quotation marks omitted). Moreover, because the issues on appeal concern the interpretation of a statute, it is purely a question of law, over which our review is plenary. *R.M. v. Baxter*, 565 Pa. 619, 624, 777 A.2d 446, 449 (2001).

[2] ¶ 15 This case concerns the interpretation of 34 Pa.C.S.A. section 2307, under which Appellant was charged and convicted. Section 2307 provides, in relevant part, as follows: *Court is reviewing the application of a statute*

§ 2307. Unlawful taking or possession of game or wildlife

    (a) General rule.-It is unlawful for any person to aid, abet, attempt or conspire to hunt for or take or possess, use, transport or conceal any game or wildlife unlawfully taken or not properly marked or any part thereof, or to hunt for, trap, take, kill, transport, conceal,

---

2. The Commonwealth Court of Pennsylvania is conferred with jurisdiction over appeals from criminal prosecutions brought pursuant to the Game and Wildlife Code. *Commonwealth v. Neitzel*, 451 Pa.Super. 1, 678 A.2d 369, 370 n. 2 (1996) (citing *Dickerson v. Commonwealth*, 138 Pa.Cmwlth. 141, 587 A.2d 379, 380–81 (1991)). *See also* 42 Pa.C.S.A. § 762(a)(2)(ii) (providing that the Commonwealth Court has jurisdiction over criminal proceedings for violations of regulatory statutes administered by Commonwealth agencies). However, because oral argument has

already occurred and the parties have not challenged the Superior Court's jurisdiction, we will, in the interest of judicial economy, address the merits of the issues raised in the appeal. *Neitzel*, 678 A.2d at 370 n. 2. *See also* Pa.R.A.P. 741(a) (stating that "[t]he failure of an appellee to file an objection to the jurisdiction of an appellate court ... shall ... operate to perfect the appellate jurisdiction of such appellate court, notwithstanding any provision of law vesting jurisdiction of such appeal in another appellate court").

possess or use any game or wildlife contrary to the provisions of this title.

* * *

(c) Wild Birds and wild animals taken outside Commonwealth.-Nothing in this title shall prohibit the possession, at any time, of wild birds or wild animals lawfully taken outside of this Commonwealth which are tagged and marked in accordance with the laws of the state or nation where the wild birds or wild animals were taken. It is unlawful to transport or possess wild birds or wild animals from another state or nation which have been unlawfully taken, killed or exported.

34 Pa.C.S.A. § 2307(a) and (c). "The basic tenet of statutory construction requires a court to construe the words of the statute according to their plain meaning." *Grom v. Burgoon,* 448 Pa.Super. 616, 672 A.2d 823, 825 (1996) "[W]ords and phrases contained in a statute shall be construed according to rules of grammar and according to their common and approved usage." *R.M.,* 565 Pa. at 626, 777 A.2d at 451; 1 Pa.C.S.A. § 1903(a). "When the words of a statute are clear and free from ambiguity the letter of it is not to be disregarded under the pretext of pursuing its spirit." *Id.* (citing Pa.C.S.A. § 1921(b)).

Court's holding

¶ 16 Our review of the language of section 2307 leads us to conclude that Appellant's interpretation of the statute is consistent with the plain meaning of the text. The language of section 2307 clearly and unambiguously provides that possession of wild animals in this Commonwealth is not prohibited where: (1) the wild birds or wild animals are lawfully taken [3] outside of

this Commonwealth; and, (2) the wild birds or wild animals are tagged and marked in accordance with the laws of the state or nation where the birds or animals were taken.

Rule

[3] ¶ 17 In this instance the parties have stipulated that Nutkin is a wild animal within the meaning of this section. They have further stipulated that in the state of South Carolina the taking and domestication of squirrels is legal and that there are no provisions for tagging or marking animals taken, as contemplated in section (c) of the Pennsylvania statute. Thus, because it is agreed by both parties that Nutkin is a "wild animal", and that she was "taken" outside the Commonwealth in a lawful fashion, the first element of the exception set forth in Section 2307(c) has been established. For the exception in 2307(c) to apply, then it seems that Nutkin must have been tagged and marked in accordance with the laws of the state where she was taken. We then refer to the law of South Carolina to see what the requirements of marking and tagging are. As stated above, it was stipulated that there are no such marking and tagging requirements. Hence, the lack of tagging and marking *is* in "accordance with the laws of the state . . . where the . . . wild animals were taken." Accordingly, we find that both elements of Section 2307(c) have been satisfied and, as such, the exception applies here.

Court's reasoning. Application of law to the facts of case.

¶ 18 Nonetheless, the Commonwealth argues that this interpretation of Section 2307 is erroneous and it points to various sections of Title 58 of the Pennsylvania Code, which it claims prohibits possession of animals taken from the wild, no matter

Appellee's theory of the case

---

3. The word "Take" in the context of the Game and Wildlife Code has been defined as: "[t]o harass, pursue, hunt for, shoot, wound, kill, trap, capture, possess or collect any game or wildlife, including shooting at a facsimile of

game or wildlife, or attempt to harass, pursue, hunt for, shoot, wound, kill, trap, capture or collect any game or wildlife or aiding, abetting or conspiring with another person in that purpose." 34 Pa.C.S.A. § 102.

COM. v. GOSSELIN   Pa. **1001**
Cite as 861 A.2d 996 (Pa.Super. 2004)

where the taking took place. The Commonwealth first points to 58 Pa.Code Sections 131.1 and 131.2 which explain that Title 34 of the Pennsylvania Consolidated Statutes (the Act), which embodies the Game and Wildlife Code, and Title 58 of the Pennsylvania Code are interrelated and shall be construed with reference to each other. Then the Commonwealth alludes to 58 Pa.Code section 137.1(a) which states "[i]t is unlawful for a person to import [and/or] possess . . . (9) [g]ame or wildlife taken alive from the wild . . . [or] (10) [g]ame or wildlife held in captivity or captive bred in another state" and section 137.31 which provides that, "[i]t is unlawful for a person to possess live wildlife taken from a wild state within this Commonwealth", with certain exceptions not relevant here. Thus, the Commonwealth concludes that to interpret 34 Pa.C.S.A. section 2307(c) as Appellant does would render Section 2307(c) and 58 Pa.Code Sections 137.1 and 137.31 incongruent. The difficulty with the Commonwealth's argument is that Section 137.1 specifically provides in subsection (a) the language "[u]nless otherwise provided in this section or the [A]ct, it is unlawful for a person to import, possess," etc. As stated above, the Act itself in 34 Pa.C.S.A. section 2307(c) does provide otherwise. It provides an exception to the otherwise blanket prohibition in section 2307(a) and the regulation.

¶ 19 The Commonwealth in further support of its argument points to 34 Pa.C.S.A. section 2163. Section 2163 provides that "[i]t is unlawful for any person to bring or, in any manner, to have transported into this Commonwealth from any other state or nation, any living game or wildlife . . . the importation of which is prohibited by the commission . . . ." Thus, the Commonwealth contends that because 58 Pa.Code section 137.1 is a regulation of the commission, and it prohibits importation of

wildlife, Appellant is in violation of the regulation. While the regulation of the commission set forth in Section 137.1 on its face seems to prohibit all importation of wildlife, the regulation of the commission cannot conflict with an act of the General Assembly, such as 34 Pa.C.S.A. section 2307(c), which creates an exception. *See Commonwealth v. DeFusco*, 378 Pa.Super. 442, 549 A.2d 140, 145 (1988) (providing that "where . . . there is an apparent conflict between a statute and a regulation promulgated thereunder, the statute must prevail"); *Lookenbill v. Garrett*, 340 Pa.Super. 435, 490 A.2d 857, 861 (1985) (same); *Wernersville State Hospital v. Peters*, 659 A.2d 67, 69–70 (Pa. Cmwlth.1995) (same). *[Rule of law]*

[4] ¶ 20 While our disposition of Appellant's first issue requires a reversal of the conviction, we believe Appellant's second issue also has merit. Rule 403 of the Pennsylvania Rules of Criminal Procedure provides, in relevant part: *[Another basis for decision or potentially dicta]*

Rule 403.   Contents of Citation

A.   Every citation shall contain:

* * *

(6) a citation of the specific section and subsection of the statute or ordinance allegedly violated, together with a summary of the facts sufficient to advise the defendant of the nature of the offense charged[.]

Pa.R.Crim.P. 403(A)(6). The citation in this case charges a violation of section 2307(a), and it is that charge which Appellant was on notice to defend against. The trial court's incorporation of 58 Pa.Code section 137.1(a) in its order charges a new offense in that this latter section prohibits the importation or possession of wildlife held in captivity without any exception for animals taken and marked and tagged in accordance with the law of state where taken. It is obvious that 58 Pa.Code section 137.1(a) is a different offense from the one charged in Appellant's citation. Therefore, Appellant's conviction also must fail on this basis.

Decision/ disposition ¶ 21 Accordingly, for the reasons set forth above, we must reverse the judgment of sentence and dismiss the citation.

¶ 22 Judgment of sentence reversed. Citation dismissed. Fines and costs, if paid, to be returned.

How to Read and Brief a Case

Reading a Case

In your professional life, any time you read, and particularly when you read legal materials, you should try to be an active reader. Read with a purpose in mind. That purpose might be to understand what the case reveals about the law or to prepare to answer questions about the opinion for a class discussion. It might also be to identify how the opinion helps to address a client's concern. However you define your purpose, read critically—look up unfamiliar vocabulary and question the text. Look for the typical categories of information that appear within a judicial opinion:

- the caption;
- procedural and substantive facts;
- issue;
- holding;
- rule;
- rationale; and
- concurring or dissenting opinions.

These categories may or may not be clearly labeled in the opinion, but they are probably included in some form. Think critically too, which means looking closely at the words and taking your time to process the language. Your goal is to develop a solid understanding of what the text means. Think about reading as an interpretative process in which you are trying to make sense of what you are reading. Mark up the text. Note where you have questions. Ask yourself what the text says and try to summarize this meaning in your own words. Be prepared to defend or substantiate your view of the text. To do this, you should annotate the parts of the text that support the meaning you propose.

Consider how you might actively read the *Gosselin* case annotated above. Someone reading *Gosselin* actively might make the following annotations to the text:

COMMONWEALTH of Pennsylvania,
Appellee,

v.

Barbara GOSSELIN, Appellant.

Superior Court of Pennsylvania.

Argued Aug. 31, 2004.

Filed Nov. 5, 2004.

Intermediate
Court of Appeal

Background: Defendant was convicted in the Court of Common Pleas, Schuylkill County, Criminal Division, No. S03-1528, Dolbin, J., of unlawful taking or possession of game or wildlife. Defendant appealed.

Holdings: The Superior Court, No. 1978 MDA 2003, Hudock, J., held that:

(1) defendant's taking and domestication of squirrel from South Carolina was lawful, and

(2) trial court could not rely on statute governing importation, sale and release of wildlife to support judgment of con-

COM. v. GOSSELIN Pa. **997**

Cite as 861 A.2d 996 (Pa.Super. 2004)

viction for unlawful taking or posses-sion of game or wildlife as charged in citation.

Sentence reversed; citation dismissed.

1. Criminal Law O 1019

The Commonwealth Court of Pennsyl-vania is conferred with jurisdiction over appeals from criminal prosecutions brought pursuant to the Game and Wildlife Code.

2. Statutes O 188

The basic tenet of statutory construc-tion requires a court to construe the words of the statute according to their plain meaning.

3. Game O 7

Defendant's taking of squirrel from South Carolina was lawful, and thus, de-fendant could not be prosecuted under statute prohibiting unlawful taking or pos-session of game or wildlife outside Com-monwealth, where South Carolina did not prohibit taking and domestication of squir-rels and had no statutory provisions for tagging and marking squirrel. 34 Pa. C.S.A. § 2307(c).

4. Criminal Law O 255.4, 260.11(6)

Trial court's reference to statute pro-hibiting importation or possession of wild-life held in captivity to sustain defendant's conviction under separate statute prohibit-ing unlawful taking or possession of game or wildlife was reversible error, as citation charged only unlawful possession offense under latter statute, which was different from importation offense, and defendant received no notice of potential for convic-tion under importation statute. 34 Pa. C.S.A. § 2307(a); 58 Pa.Code § 137.1(a); Rules Crim.Proc., Rule 403(A)(6), 42 Pa. C.S.A.

Dirk S. Berger, Pottsville, for appellant.

Andrew J. Serina, Asst. Dist. Atty., Pottsville, for Com., appellee.

BEFORE: HUDOCK and KLEIN, JJ., and McEWEN, P.J.E.

OPINION BY HUDOCK, J.:

¶ 1 This appeal revolves around the life and times of Nutkin the squirrel.

¶ 2 Nutkin's early life was spent in the state of *ferrae naturae*, in the state of South Carolina, and, as far as we can tell, in a state of contentment. She apparently had plenty of nuts to eat and trees to climb, and her male friends, while not par-ticularly handsome, did have nice personal-ities. Life was good.

¶ 3 Then one day tragedy struck: Nut-kin fell from her tree nest!

¶ 4 But fate was kind. Nutkin was found and adopted by Appellant and her husband who, at that time, were residents of South Carolina. Appellant lovingly nursed Nutkin back to health, and Nutkin became the family pet. A large room-sized enclosure was built so Nutkin had plenty of room to run and climb. Life was good again.

¶ 5 Nutkin's captivity and domestication were perfectly legal in South Carolina, possibly a reflection of that state's long tradition of hospitality to all.

¶ 6 In 1994, Appellant and her husband moved to Pennsylvania and brought Nut-kin with them. Life was full of promise.

¶ 7 Dark clouds began to gather, howev-er, in November, 2002, when Appellant's husband phoned the Pennsylvania Game Commission concerning a hunter whom he and Appellant believed was hunting near an area on their property where they had set out food for deer. In response to that

Squirrel fell from nest. Wild in S. Carolina, nursed back to health & domesticated; family moved with Squirrel to Pennsylvania.

Defendant's/ Appellant's husband reported illegal hunting to Pa. Game Commission (an executive agency).

Agent sent to investigate, but refused to report poaching; instead issued a citation for unlawfully taking possession of wildlife (aka Nutkin).

complaint, a Wildlife Officer appeared at Appellant's property to investigate. At that time the Officer became aware that a deer had been illegally shot on Appellant's property and dragged to a neighboring property. Appellant and her husband requested that the Game Officer further investigate the poaching of the deer. The Officer refused to do so, but when he spotted Nutkin in her room-sized enclosure, he advised Appellant that it was a violation of the law to keep Nutkin in this manner. The Game Officer acknowledged that the squirrel was too old and too tame to be released to the wild (A situation akin to that of an old appellate judge, like the undersigned, attempting to return to the boiling cauldron of the trial court after being tamed by years of peace and quiet above the fray. Chances of survival of both species are poor.) He offered to forgo citing Appellant if she would relinquish Nutkin to his control. Appellant and her husband refused.

¶ 8 The reasons for this refusal are not apparent of record, but familial ties no doubt played a part in the decision. (At oral argument, our esteemed colleague, Judge Klein, alluded to the possibility of "squirrel stew", but there is insufficient evidence to support this horrific supposition.)

¶ 9 Nutkin would then learn the shocking truth that the cheery Pennsylvania slogan "You've got a friend in Pennsylvania" did not apply to four-legged critters like Nutkin. On December 2, 2002, the Wildlife Conservation Officer issued a citation directed to Appellant's husband for violating section 2307(a) of the Game and Wildlife Code, entitled "Unlawful taking or possession of game or wildlife".[1] For some unexplained reason, this citation was withdrawn and a new citation alleging the same violation was directed to Appellant.

Statute at issue: did defendant violate statute dealing with possession of wild animals?

1.   34 Pa.C.S.A. § 2307(a).

¶ 10 Appellant had become known to the Pennsylvania Game Commission by appearing to testify before the Game and Fisheries Committee of the Pennsylvania House of Representatives in September, 2001. In this testimony, the Appellant complained about the enforcement proceedings of the Pennsylvania Game Commission, and particularly complained of the fact that every year "bubba" hunters showed up in the woods near their house to drive out the deer and the hunters were guilty of various other displays of bad hunting manners. Stipulation of Facts, 8/5/03, Exhibit C. She further testified to her opinion that the Game Commission is "against any landowner who posts their property." *Id.*

¶ 11 While there is no explicit claim of retaliatory prosecution, the stipulated facts show an interesting temporal relationship between Appellant's complaints both to the Game Commission and the General Assembly and her present difficulties.

[1] ¶ 12 In any event, Appellant was convicted of the offense before a district justice and again before the common pleas court in a trial *de novo* based upon stipulated facts. She was fined $100.00 plus the costs of prosecution. While the trial court did not file an opinion, it did provide the following reasoning in support of its decision in a footnote to the order finding Appellant guilty:

*To sustain this finding, reference must be had to the PA Code Title 58 Chapter 137 in which it is provided at 137.1(a), "unless otherwise provided in this section or the Act, it is unlawful for a person to ... possess ... (9) game or wildlife taken alive from the wild or (10) game or wildlife held captive or game or wildlife held in captivity or captive bred

State agency– good example of how the state legislature gathers information through testimony. (Commonwealth of Pa. studying how to address poaching problem.)

Appellant was testifying before Pa. House of Representatives: Game and Fisheries Committee.

Relationship between state legislature & agency. (Both are rule-making bodies: legislative and executive branch.)

Convicted and fined $100. Trial court also used Pa. Code–Game Commission Regulation (executive branch source of law).

How do statute and regulation interact?

COM. v. GOSSELIN Pa. **999**
Cite as 861 A.2d 996 (Pa.Super. 2004)

in another state." Also, 137.31(b) a person violating this subchapter will be subject to the penalties provided in 2307 of the Act (relating to unlawful taking or possession of game o[r] wildlife).

Order dated 11/21/03. This timely appeal followed.[2]

¶ 13 Two issues are raised on appeal:

A. Whether, based on the exception set forth in 34 Pa.C.S.A. § 2307(c), the trial court erred in convicting [Appellant] for violating 34 Pa.C.S.A. § 2307(a)[?]

B. Whether the trial court, in convicting [Appellant] for violating 34 Pa. C.S.A. § 2307(a) improperly applied 58 Pa.Code § 137.1[?].

Appellant's Brief at 6 (emphasis deleted). The essence of Appellant's arguments is that her possession of Nutkin is permitted pursuant to the language of 34 Pa.C.S.A. section 2307(c). Appellant contends that the trial court not only failed to consider this provision, but, rather convicted her for violating a provision of the Pennsylvania Code (58 Pa.Code section 137.1) with which she was not charged.

¶ 14 Our standard of review of a trial court's adjudication entered following a *de novo* trial on a summary offense has been summarized as follows:

[An appellate court's review of a] *de novo* trial on a summary offense is limited to whether the trial court committed

2. The Commonwealth Court of Pennsylvania is conferred with jurisdiction over appeals from criminal prosecutions brought pursuant to the Game and Wildlife Code. *Commonwealth v. Neitzel*, 451 Pa.Super. 1, 678 A.2d 369, 370 n. 2 (1996) (citing *Dickerson v. Commonwealth*, 138 Pa.Cmwlth. 141, 587 A.2d 379, 380–81 (1991)). *See also* 42 Pa.C.S.A. § 762(a)(2)(ii) (providing that the Commonwealth Court has jurisdiction over criminal proceedings for violations of regulatory statutes administered by Commonwealth agencies). However, because oral argument has

an error of law and whether the findings of the trial court are supported by competent evidence. The adjudication of the trial court will not be disturbed on appeal absent a manifest abuse of discretion. An abuse of discretion exists when the trial court has rendered a judgment that is manifestly unreasonable, arbitrary, or capricious, has failed to apply the law, or was motivated by partiality, prejudice, bias, or ill will.

Commonwealth v. Parks, 768 A.2d 1168, 1171 (Pa.Super.2001) (citations and quotation marks omitted). Moreover, because the issues on appeal concern the interpretation of a statute, it is purely a question of law, over which our review is plenary. *R.M. v. Baxter*, 565 Pa. 619, 624, 777 A.2d 446, 449 (2001).

[2] ¶ 15 This case concerns the interpretation of 34 Pa.C.S.A. section 2307, under which Appellant was charged and convicted. Section 2307 provides, in relevant part, as follows:

§ 2307. Unlawful taking or possession of game or wildlife

(a) General rule.-It is unlawful for any person to aid, abet, attempt or conspire to hunt for or take or possess, use, transport or conceal any game or wildlife unlawfully taken or not properly marked or any part thereof, or to hunt for, trap, take, kill, transport, conceal,

already occurred and the parties have not challenged the Superior Court's jurisdiction, we will, in the interest of judicial economy, address the merits of the issues raised in the appeal. *Neitzel*, 678 A.2d at 370 n. 2. *See also* Pa.R.A.P. 741(a) (stating that "[t]he failure of an appellee to file an objection to the jurisdiction of an appellate court ... shall ... operate to perfect the appellate jurisdiction of such appellate court, notwithstanding any provision of law vesting jurisdiction of such appeal in another appellate court").

1000 Pa.   861 ATLANTIC REPORTER, 2d SERIES

Appellant appears to be in violation of this provision, but there's an exception.

possess or use any game or wildlife contrary to the provisions of this title.

* * *

(c) Wild Birds and wild animals taken outside Commonwealth.-Nothing in this title shall prohibit the possession, at any time, of wild birds or wild animals lawfully taken outside of this Commonwealth which are tagged and marked in accordance with the laws of the state or nation where the wild birds or wild animals were taken. It is unlawful to transport or possess wild birds or wild animals from another state or nation which have been unlawfully taken, killed or exported.

Role of the court when interpreting a statute.

34 Pa.C.S.A. § 2307(a) and (c). "The basic tenet of statutory construction requires a court to construe the words of the statute according to their plain meaning." *Grom v. Burgoon*, 448 Pa.Super. 616, 672 A.2d 823, 825 (1996) "[W]ords and phrases contained in a statute shall be construed according to rules of grammar and according to their common and approved usage." *R.M.*, 565 Pa. at 626, 777 A.2d at 451; 1 Pa.C.S.A. § 1903(a). "When the words of a statute are clear and free from ambiguity the letter of it is not to be disregarded under the pretext of pursuing its spirit." *Id.* (citing Pa.C.S.A. § 1921(b)).

¶ 16 Our review of the language of section 2307 leads us to conclude that Appellant's interpretation of the statute is consistent with the plain meaning of the text. The language of section 2307 clearly and unambiguously provides that possession of wild animals in this Commonwealth is not prohibited where: (1) the wild birds or wild animals are lawfully taken [3] outside of this Commonwealth; and, (2) the wild birds or wild animals are tagged and marked in accordance with the laws of the state or nation where the birds or animals were taken.

[3] ¶ 17 In this instance the parties have stipulated that Nutkin is a wild animal within the meaning of this section. They have further stipulated that in the state of South Carolina the taking and domestication of squirrels is legal and that there are no provisions for tagging or marking animals taken, as contemplated in section (c) of the Pennsylvania statute. Thus, because it is agreed by both parties that Nutkin is a "wild animal", and that she was "taken" outside the Commonwealth in a lawful fashion, the first element of the exception set forth in Section 2307(c) has been established. For the exception in 2307(c) to apply, then it seems that Nutkin must have been tagged and marked in accordance with the laws of the state where she was taken. We then refer to the law of South Carolina to see what the requirements of marking and tagging are. As stated above, it was stipulated that there are no such marking and tagging requirements. Hence, the lack of tagging and marking *is* in "accordance with the laws of the state ... where the ... wild animals were taken." Accordingly, we find that both elements of Section 2307(c) have been satisfied and, as such, the exception applies here.

Because Nutkin was taken in S. Carolina, where it was legal for appellant to have a squirrel, exception under 2307c allows appellant to keep

¶ 18 Nonetheless, the Commonwealth argues that this interpretation of Section 2307 is erroneous and it points to various sections of Title 58 of the Pennsylvania Code, which it claims prohibits possession of animals taken from the wild, no matter

Commonwealth's theory

Definition taken from the Code

3. The word "Take" in the context of the Game and Wildlife Code has been defined as: "[t]o harass, pursue, hunt for, shoot, wound, kill, trap, capture, possess or collect any game or wildlife, including shooting at a facsimile of game or wildlife, or attempt to harass, pursue, hunt for, shoot, wound, kill, trap, capture or collect any game or wildlife or aiding, abetting or conspiring with another person in that purpose." 34 Pa.C.S.A. § 102.

When you finish reading the text, in your own words, write a sentence that summarizes the main idea of the whole text or of each section of the text. Make sure that you name the source and the author. Include a citation that names the source if appropriate.

II. Examine How the Author Fulfills His or Her Purpose: How Does the Author Support the Point?

After you understand the author's main idea, reread the text to look for supporting details. You should read with the purpose of enhancing your understanding of the text. Try not to judge or evaluate the text at this point. Instead, try to interpret what the text says. Read actively and discerningly: Highlight the information that supports the main idea, but try not to include too many examples, specific details, or a lot of description. You should look for the most important information, not all of the supporting information. Note what sort of evidence or data is provided. Identify what kind of analogies or imagery the author uses. Mark conclusions or recommendations the author makes. Also, pay attention to the language used to hold ideas together. For example, look at thesis and topic sentences of each paragraph and at transitional phrases. Indicate any key words.

III. Write the Main Ideas and Supporting Details: How can you Objectively Paraphrase the Author's Ideas?

At this point, you should try to put the ideas in your own words. Look back at your sentence identifying the main idea and your annotations of the text. Try to paraphrase what you observe in those substantiating details. You should track the same sequence of the original text, but express the ideas in your own language in a way that allows you to synthesize these supporting details. Be objective. Capture what the author says.

Strive to capture this information in a succinct, but coherent manner. Be accurate—make sure you have not omitted any important information or added additional material. Be concise—a summary should be shorter than the original. Ideally, your summary should "stand alone," which means that a reader, including you at some point in the future, will understand the main point of the text without having to read the original text to get the point. The summary should provide an overview.

IV. Revise: Are You Accurately and Concisely Capturing the Author's Point?

Reread your summary. Check to make sure you have the right information in the right amount and that your summary is free from grammatical and typographical errors. Once you are sure you have captured the writer's ideas, you may want to evaluate the text. Make sure to clearly indicate that this evaluation is yours and not a part of the original text.

After reading the case carefully, lawyers often write a summary of the main ideas. This process, known as "briefing a case," is an analytical tool; the process and format is designed to help attorneys read critically, internalize information, and analyze opinions. Briefing has many functions: Firstly, briefing has an analytical function. It is a means of predicting what the law on a certain subject is and what the law will be—for example, how might a court apply the law to a future case? Additionally, the briefing process provides insight into value systems—judicial opinions express cultural values generally and legal cultural values in particular. Judicial opinions also illustrate individual values of judges.

Briefing also has a practical function. Briefs create a written summary of what lawyers have read. These notes can be used in the future when writing a client letter, motion, appellate brief, or, for your purposes as a law student, to answer questions about the cases in class or to prepare for exams. In other words, lawyers use case briefs to accurately recall what a case was about; case briefs provide a written record.

Finally, briefs have an educational function. Briefing will help you to learn new vocabulary and become familiar with legal culture. Writing will help you to reinforce this learning. Although law school may often seem to immerse you in the profession with little introduction to that profession, judicial opinions, and other legal texts can provide you with some background knowledge and insight to fill in any gaps in your knowledge. By carefully reading, rereading, reflecting, and discussing these cases, you can decipher a great deal about the legal system and the legal profession. Putting in the effort to read critically and brief cases you read will help you not only as a law student, but also as a legal professional. You will be able to draw upon these skills throughout your practice of law, each time you encounter an unfamiliar area of law.

Format of a Case Brief

The format of a case brief varies, but student written briefs usually include a summary for each of the following sections of a judicial opinion.

Caption: This section should include the citation of the case, including the case name, what court is deciding the case, if it is a criminal or civil matter, and an identification of the parties.

Procedural Facts, also known as the Procedural History or Procedural Posture: This section expresses the story of the case as it pertains to the legal system. It should explain what has happened so far in terms of legal action. For example, you might include information about the cause of action, about who brought the complaint, what motions have been brought, and whether there has been a trial or action by lower courts. You should also include any prior history in the appellate courts. Finally, you should include the procedural disposition in the case you are briefing.

Factual History: This section should tell the human story. It should explain the facts surrounding the dispute. Try to include relevant or dispositive facts—facts that influenced the opinion of the court. Also include any emotionally compelling facts or background facts that help to make the story clear.

Issue: This section expresses the legal issue that the court authoring the opinion had to resolve. It articulates the nature of the dispute and what needs to be answered to resolve it. The issue is usually stated as a question, and can be phrased as a direct question (Did ...? or Can ...?) or an indirect question (Whether ...?) Sometimes the court will clearly state the issue within its opinion, but often it will be implicit. The question should also reflect the procedural facts. For example, trial court and appellate court questions differ because different levels of courts have different responsibilities.

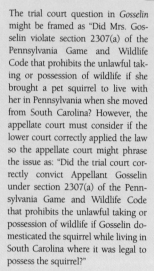

Take Note

The trial court question in *Gosselin* might be framed as "Did Mrs. Gosselin violate section 2307(a) of the Pennsylvania Game and Wildlife Code that prohibits the unlawful taking or possession of wildlife if she brought a pet squirrel to live with her in Pennsylvania when she moved from South Carolina? However, the appellate court must consider if the lower court correctly applied the law so the appellate court might phrase the issue as: "Did the trial court correctly convict Appellant Gosselin under section 2307(a) of the Pennsylvania Game and Wildlife Code that prohibits the unlawful taking or possession of wildlife if Gosselin domesticated the squirrel while living in South Carolina where it was legal to possess the squirrel?"

Holding: This section should express the court's response to the issue. It is an answer to the legal question. In this sense, it is a narrow rule of law that applies to the particular facts of the case. It should be stated as directly as possible.

Rationale: This section expresses the reasoning of the court. It should summarize why the court resolved the dispute as it did. For example, the court may have relied on precedent, the text of statutes or regulations, intent or public policy arguments, even cultural norms and beliefs. The court may have identified certain facts as particularly persuasive or dispositive. The court might also have been constrained by the procedural history of the case and the standard of review.

Make the Connection

See Chapter 12 for discussion of the scope and standard of review.

Rule of Law: This section should articulate the rule or general principle that this case represents. The rule is the law that can be applied to a future case; sometimes it is a new rule that the court articulates for the first time in the opinion; sometimes the court refines an existing rule; sometimes the court applies an existing rule and makes little change to the law except that the court had to apply the law to the unique set of facts that made up the dispute. When you try to articulate the rule—ask yourself how this case adds to the body of case law in the jurisdiction. Think about a future case: what rule might the court apply to resolve a future case with similar facts?

Below is what a brief of the *Gosselin* case might look like. You should, however, feel free to alter the brief format to meet your needs. Case briefs are personal notes and, therefore, will vary from author to author.

Caption: *Commonwealth v. Gosselin*, 861 A.2d 996 (Pa. Super. Ct. 2004)

Opinion by J. Hudock

Procedural Facts: Defendant/Appellant Barbara Gosselin was charged with violating 34 Pa. Cons. Stat. § 2307(a). She was convicted by the District Justice. She was again convicted by the Court of Common Pleas after a trial. The Court of Common Pleas found her guilty of unlawfully taking and possessing game or wildlife under 58 Pa. Code § 137.1(a), regulation of the Pennsylvania Game Commission. The Superior Court reversed and dismissed the citation.

Substantive Facts: Nutkin, a squirrel, was born in the wild, but fell out of his nest. The defendant/appellant, Ms. Gosselin, who lived in South Carolina at the time, nursed Nutkin back to health and domesticated the animal. In South Carolina, the appellant could legally have a squirrel as a pet. In 1994, the appellant, her husband, and Nutkin moved to Pennsylvania. In 2002, the appellant's husband complained about deer poaching on their property. A game officer came to investigate, but refused to pursue the matter, although the officer apparently was aware that a deer had been shot illegally on appellant's property. While at the house, the officer saw Nutkin and cited appellant under § 2307(a) after appellant refused to give Nutkin to the officer. The citation did not make reference to the Pa. Code § 137.1(a). The trial record suggests that the Game Commission already knew the appellant since she had testified in 2001 about illegal hunting before the Game and Fisheries Committee of the Pennsylvania House of Representatives.

Issue: Whether the trial court erred in convicting Appellant for taking Nutkin from the wild in South Carolina and bringing him to Pennsylvania if state regulation 58 Pa. Code § 137.1(a) makes it unlawful to possess wildlife taken from the wild in another state, but the state statute 34 Pa. Cons. Stat. § 2307 provides for an exception for wildlife taken legally in another state?

Holding: Yes, the trial court erred in convicting defendant for unlawful possession of wildlife where the plain language of the statute § 2307(a) & (c) allowed an exception for wildlife brought to Pennsylvania after having been taken legally from another state and the citation against defendant contained no reference to charges under the administrative regulation § 137.1(a).

Reasoning: Statutory construction rules require the court to construe a statute according to its plain meaning. Section 2307 is clear in allowing an exception for animals legally taken and tagged in another state. Nutkin was legally taken in South Carolina and not required to be tagged so he was lawfully maintained in South Carolina. The Appellate Court rejects the Commonwealth's view that the Game Commission Code must be considered together with the statute. The Commonwealth's reading of the regulation creates a conflict between the regulation, which is promulgated by the executive agency, and the statute, which is promulgated by the legislature. Because the function of the executive branch is to interpret the statute and not to extend the statute or go beyond the intent of the legislature, the statutory language prevails. Moreover, the appellate court notes that the regulation states that it is unlawful "unless otherwise provided in the Act." The court also notes that the citation against the defendant did not provide notice of a violation under the code so the defendant was not able to properly prepare a defense under the regulation § 137.1(a).

Food for Thought

The issue might be crafted in many other ways. Consider some of the following examples. Which do you think best captures the issue before the court?

Did the trial court err in convicting defendant under 137.1(a), a state regulation, where the statute provided an exception for animals lawfully taken outside of Pennsylvania?

Or

Whether, given defendant's citation for violating 13 Pa. Cons. Stat. § 2307(a) and the exception set forth in 13 Pa. Cons. Stat. § 2307(c), the trial court erred in applying 58 Pa. Code § 137.1 and convicting Appellant?

Or

1. Whether the trial court erred in convicting Gosselin under state law 34 Pa. Cons. Stat. § 2307(a) and accompanying regulation 58 Pa. Code § 137.1(a) that prohibits the unlawful taking or possession of wildlife if Gosselin domesticated Nutkin the squirrel lawfully in South Carolina where she lived before moving to Pennsylvania?

2. Whether the trial court erred in incorporating the regulation, 58 Pa. Code § 137.1(a) in its order if Gosselin's citation included only the statutory provision, 34 Pa. Cons. Stat. § 2307(a)?

Rule: 1. Section 2307(c) allows for possession of a wild animal in Pennsylvania if the animal was taken lawfully from another state.

2. If a statute and a regulation promulgated under that statute conflict, the statute prevails: The regulation § 137.1(a), which refers to "importation" must be

read so as not to conflict with 34 Pa. Cons. Stat. § 2307(c), which allows for possession of animals lawfully taken from outside Pennsylvania.

Briefing Exercise

Applying the principles discussed above, read and brief <u>Ingalls v. Hobbs</u>, 31 N.E. 286 (Mass. 1892). Your brief should include the following sections: caption, procedural facts, substantive facts, issue, holding, rule, rationale, concurring and dissenting opinions. You may also want to include a section for any questions or comments you have about the case. Try to keep your brief succinct, no more than one or two pages, but also try to make it an independent summary of the case. Briefs are most effective if they "stand alone" and do not require you to reread the full judicial opinion to recall the specifics of a case.

Take Note!

The briefing process we use to analyze common law decisions also works to analyze opinions of civil law courts. Consider for example how a close reading and written summary of <u>The Queen v. Immigration Appeal Tribunal et Surinder Singh</u> and <u>Knauff v. Shaughnessy</u>, the cases mentioned in Chapter 2, might reveal similarities and differences in the two cases

Food for Thought

If you would like to brief a more challenging case, you may want to read and summarize the <u>Pugh v. Holmes</u> case from Pennsylvania: 405 A.2d 897 (Pa. 1979)

Make the Connection

Briefing a case is the first step in finding and applying the law. Consider how *Ingalls v. Hobbs* might apply to a law student in Cambridge, Massachusetts who stops paying rent to his landlord when he discovers in early October that the unfurnished, basement apartment, which he moved into in August and thought was an incredible deal, does not have heat. He signed a one-year lease after looking at the apartment on August 1; he immediately moved into his new place. If the landlord sues the tenant for the unpaid rent, how do you think a court in Massachusetts would compare the factual situations? Specifically, focus on the factual differences you think will be relevant to the court in reaching a decision.

Once you have thought through your answer, write up an explanation of your reasoning by summarizing the *Ingalls* case and identifying the factual differences between *Ingalls* and the new set of facts. Your summary should include three general categories of information:

1. **An analysis of the precedent**: Summarize the relevant facts, issue, holding, and rationale from *Ingalls*, and explain the general rule that comes from this case.

2. **A comparison of the facts in the *Ingalls* case to the new set of facts**: Analogize between *Ingalls* and the new case. In other words, state precisely how *Ingalls* and our new situation are factually similar and how they differ.

3. **A critical evaluation of the law as applied to the new set of facts**: Consider how the factual similarities and differences might influence a court's decision in the new case: What do you think the court will decide in the new case? Will the landlord be able to recover the rent? Should the court change the law to yield a different result?

Summarize your answer in no more than 300 words and submit this to your professor.

CHAPTER 4

Working with Statutes

A statute is legislatively enacted law. In the United States legal system, although a common law system, much of the law you will encounter will be statutory. If a statute exists that controls the outcome of a particular dispute, the judicial branch will be bound to apply this statute. A controlling statute is mandatory authority, and the role of the judiciary is to interpret the statute in the context of the case or controversy before the court. In interpreting the statute, the judge's task is to determine the intent of the legislature and apply the statute according to this intent. The judicial branch is not permitted to rewrite a statute, even if the statute is ambiguous.

To understand how a judge will go about interpreting a statute, you will first consider the context in which statutes are enacted.[1] Article I, Section 1 of the United States Constitution vests the Congress with legislative powers. The members of Congress who implement this authority are elected officials, representing the views of their constituents. Because these views may vary widely, a statute often represents the outcome of a lengthy process of negotiation, not only as to whether a statute is needed and what it should include, but also as to the choice of language used and how the ideas conveyed in the statute should best be expressed. From the time a bill is introduced in Congress to its consideration by congressional committees, the report to the Congress, and the enactment of a statute, the language of the proposed statute may undergo a great deal of change. However, the Senate and House must resolve all their differences and agree on the language in the bill for the bill to be "enrolled." An enrolled bill is one that has been printed on parchment and certified by the appropriate members of the House and Senate, and sent to the President for approval. If approved by the President, the language in this final version is what will become the statute. When judges are confronted with the task of interpreting statutes, they will begin their analysis with the language of the statute, using the meaning of the language as a guide to legislative intent.

Your process of determining legislative intent should also begin with a careful reading of the relevant statutory language. As you read this language, consider the placement of the relevant language in the statute as a whole. Look at the

---

1.   *How Our Laws Are Made* by John V. Sullivan, <u>Parliamentarian, U.S. House of Representatives</u>, <u>http://www.gpo.gov/fdsys/pkg/CDOC-110hdoc49/pdf/CDOC-110hdoc49.pdf</u>.

table of contents if the act contains one. Pay attention to the title of the act,[2] and the titles of chapters and subsections. Then try to parse the language into its logical components. If the statute is "plain on its face," meaning that the language is unambiguous, most decision-makers and legal scholars agree that no further interpretation is required to apply the statute.

However, a statute may often require some interpretation, even statutes that are "plain on their face" may need some interpretations because language is inherently ambiguous and meaning is subject to change. Whenever you read or participate in written or oral communication, you engage in a process of interpretation, considering meaning, context, and societal norms such as rules of grammar. As a result, simply reading a statute and trying to determine whether language is "plain on its face" may require interpretation. The sort of language-based interpretation tools involved at this stage of interpretation is what is often referred to as the components of "the Plain Meaning Rule." It is the threshold analysis for statutory interpretation. This rule requires you to assume that the legislature used words, grammar, and punctuation in a standard way; that the legislature intended the ordinary meaning of the language used. Under this methodology, the text of the statute is the primary source of the legislative intent.

As you consider the plain meaning of a statutory provision, begin by reading and rereading the statutory language and all relevant parts of the statute as the whole. Then move to consider the following linguistic clues.

To read more about the plain meaning rule and statutory interpretation, see http://www.fas.org/sgp/crs/misc/97-589.pdf]

First, consider the ordinary meaning of the relevant words. Judges will often look to English language dictionaries to determine meaning of the words in the statute, or in the case of a technical language the judge will consider the word's technical meaning. If the statute contains a definition section, these definitions will usually be seen as controlling. If the highest court of a jurisdiction has interpreted language of the statute, future courts will consider that interpretation to be controlling.

Next, consider the rules of grammar and syntax. Notice the punctuation of the language. Consider whether the statute uses conjunctive ("and") or disjunctive ("or"); mandatory ("shall") or discretionary ("may") language; also consider the placement of referential and qualifying words.

---

2.   The traditional view is that titles that are above the enactment clause are not considered controlling of meaning because such title was not actually enacted into law and therefore not subject to deliberation and debate. Today, however, many lawyers and judges use titles as an aid to resolve ambiguity or confirm plain meaning, and sometimes a provision after enactment clause gives the act a specific title.

Finally, consider the Canons of Statutory Interpretation. The canons reflect presumptions about what the legislature intended or how the legislature functions. They may be very broad, including presumptions that the legislature was sane and accordingly the plain meaning should not yield an absurd result or unnecessary hardship, the legislature is presumed to avoid surplusage or redundancy, and presumptions that statutes in derogation of the common law should be strictly construed and remedial statutes should be liberally construed. The legislature is presumed to avoid repeals by implication, statutes enacted later in time should control earlier statutes, and statutes are rebuttably presumed to apply prospectively.

Take Note!

Another general or broad presumption is that statutes should be read in *pari materia* ("part of the same material"), which presumes that new legislation should be interpreted to make it consistent with existing statutes on the same subject matter. Other canons may also be linguistic based, such as *ejusdem generis* ("of the same class"), *noscitur a sociis* ("a word is known by its associates or what surrounds it"), and *expressio unius est exclussio aterius* ("the expression of one excludes the others"). Other canons that consider linguistic aspects of a statute include such presumptions as: exceptions should be narrowly construed, provisos limit what immediately preceded them, internal consistency is favored, and the specific controls the general.

If you determine through your plain meaning analysis of the statute that the meaning is clear, you should apply that meaning to resolve the dispute. If, however, you determine that the statute is ambiguous or silent, you will need to do more extensive interpretation. This sort of interpretation might be necessary because language that appears unambiguous or plain in the abstract becomes ambiguous when actually applied to a particular dispute. Further interpretation may also result because of drafting issues that create ambiguity.

If you find that you have to go beyond the "plain meaning" of a statute, you should look to external or extrinsic sources to determine the intent of the legislature. Extrinsic sources are tools that look for clues as to legislative intent outside the text of the statute. These sources include holdings by the highest court in the jurisdiction that will settle the meaning if in the same factual context or give guidance if in a different factual context. Next, you will look to interpretations by intermediate appellate courts, the interpretations of which will be binding in the absence of higher court authority. If no court interpretation exists in your jurisdiction, then you should look to court decisions in other jurisdictions for guidance; however, they will never be binding.

Other tools of interpretation can also be helpful. Many courts will look to the historical context in which the statute was enacted and to the legislative history that accompanies it. In addition, courts may use the regulations that interpret the statute to glean legislative intent.

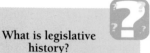

What is legislative history?

Legislative history is the path of an act or bill through the legislative process. See this interesting and useful guide published by the Law Librarians' Society of Washington DC. http://www.llsdc.org/assets/source book/fed-leg-hist.pdf.

Secondary authorities (authorities that are not law) may be used to interpret statutes. Courts may use treatises, books or law reviews to guide their interpretations, especially with a new statute that has not been litigated much or at all.

Food for Thought

Sometimes statutory interpretation will also demand that you consider international sources of law. Notice, for example, how the author of this memorandum has used the an international treaty to address the meaning of "piracy" in a U.S. statute.

All these tools will assist the court to determine the intent of the legislature and properly interpret the statute. If the legislature disagrees with the interpretation or if the statute is struck down as unconstitutional, it can amend the statute.

Discussion Question

Now read the following case, *U.S. v. Reid*. List the tools of interpretation the court uses. How does each tool contribute to the analysis or help the court reason to a conclusion?

Tell Me More

Notice how the attorney for the Prince of the Seas Cruise Line sets up the statutory analysis in the following memorandum.

206 F.Supp.2d 132
United States District Court,
D. Massachusetts.

UNITED STATES of America

v.

Richard C. REID, Defendant.

No. CR.A. 02–10013–
WGY. | June 11, 2002.

Defendant, who allegedly tried to detonate shoe bomb while traveling in airliner from Paris to Miami and was indicted for various offenses, moved to dismiss indictment count alleging violation of USA Patriot Act. The District Court, Young, J., held that: (1) Act penalized attempts to perform enumerated prohibited act, as well as performance of acts; (2) airliner was providing "mass transportation," as required under Act; and (3) airplane was not "vehicle" covered by Act.

Motion granted.

See, also, 2001 WL 1688908.

West Headnotes (3)

[1] **Carriers**
 ⚷ Offenses by Persons Dealing with Carriers
Carriers
 ⚷ Offenses
70 Carriers
70I Control and Regulation of Common Carriers
70I(A) In General
70k22 Offenses by Persons Dealing with Carriers
70 Carriers
70I Control and Regulation of Common Carriers
70I(B) Interstate and International Transportation
70k38 Offenses
70k38(1) In General
USA Patriot Act penalizes attempts to perform any enumerated prohibited acts involving mass transportation providers,

as well as performance of acts. 18 U.S.C.A. § 1993(a)(8).

[2] **Aviation**
 ⚷ Offenses
48B Aviation
48BI Control and Regulation in General
48BI(A) In General
48Bk16 Offenses
Airliner on regularly scheduled trip from Paris to Miami was providing "mass transportation" under USA Patriot Act, when passenger allegedly try to blow up aircraft through use of bomb located in his shoe, despite claim that term was limited to buses, trolleys, commuter trains and ferries carrying substantial numbers of persons. 18 U.S.C.A. § 1993(a)(1); 49 U.S.C.A. 5302(a)(7).

3 Cases that cite this headnote

[3] **Aviation**
 ⚷ Offenses
48B Aviation
48BI Control and Regulation in General
48BI(A) In General
48Bk16 Offenses
Jet airplane was not a "vehicle" under USA Patriot Act, prohibiting terroristic acts against mass transportation vehicles; general definition of term, found in Dictionary Act, did not include aircraft, and Congressional intent underlying Patriot Act was to cover means of transportation which, unlike aircraft, were not adequately covered by other statutes. 1 U.S.C.A. § 4; 18 U.S.C.A. §§ 32, 1993(a) (1); 49 U.S.C.A. 46504, 46505(b)(3).

3 Cases that cite this headnote

Attorneys and Law Firms

*133 Stephen G. Huggard, Washington, DC, for U.S. Owen S. Walker, Office of the Federal Defender, Tamar R. Birckhead, Federal Defender Office, Boston, MA, for Defendant.

Opinion

MEMORANDUM AND ORDER

YOUNG, Chief Judge.

I. Introduction

Is an airplane a "mass transportation vehicle" as that phrase is used in section 801 of the USA PATRIOT Act of 2001, Pub.L. No. 107–56, 115 Stat. 272, 374–76 (codified at 18 U.S.C. § 1993) ("section 1993"), a comprehensive anti-terrorism law enacted in the wake of September 11. That is the question raised by Richard C. Reid ("Reid"), who is accused of attempting to detonate an explosive device in his shoe while aboard an international flight from Paris to Miami that was diverted to Boston after his attempt was foiled by the flight crew and other passengers. If the answer to this question is no, as Reid suggests, then Count Nine of the indictment against him, which alleges that he attempted to "wreck, set fire to, and disable a mass transportation vehicle," in violation of section 1993, *see* Indictment at 11,[1] must be dismissed.

II. Background

The charges against Reid arise out of an incident on December 22, 2001, on American Airlines Flight 63 ("Flight 63"). According to Magistrate Judge Dein's Memorandum and Order dated December 28, 2001 [Docket No. 3] regarding probable cause and the government's motion to detain Reid, there is probable cause to believe the following facts:

Flight 63 was en route from Paris to Miami until Reid created a disturbance on board that caused the aircraft to be diverted to Boston. After one of the flight attendants smelled what she thought was a match, she observed Reid place a match in his mouth. She alerted the captain over ***134** the intercom system to what she had seen, and when she returned a few moments later, she saw Reid light another match. According to the flight attendant, Reid appeared to be trying to light the inner tongue of his sneaker, from which a wire was protruding. The attendant tried to stop Reid from lighting his sneaker, but he shoved her into the bulkhead and pushed her to the floor. She got up and ran to get water, at which point a second flight attendant tried to stop Reid. Reid bit the second

attendant on the thumb. Shortly thereafter, the first flight attendant returned and threw water in Reid's face. At this point, several passengers came to the aid of the flight attendants and restrained Reid for the duration of the flight. They also injected him with sedatives that were on board the aircraft.

Preliminary laboratory analysis has revealed that both of Reid's sneakers contained "a 'functioning improvised explosive device,' i.e., 'a homemade bomb.' " Dein Order at 4. Had the sneakers been placed against the wall of the aircraft and detonated, they might have been able to blow a hole in the fuselage, potentially causing the aircraft to crash.

III. Discussion

In relevant parts, section 1993 states: "whoever willfully wrecks, derails, sets fire to, or disables a mass transportation vehicle ... [or] attempts, threatens, or conspires to do any of the aforesaid acts, shall be fined under this title or imprisoned not more than twenty years, or both." 18 U.S.C. § 1993(a)(1), (a)(8). The phrase "mass transportation" is defined by a cross-reference to section 5302(a)(7) of Title 49 of the United States Code ("section 5302"), "except that the term shall include schoolbus, charter, and sightseeing transportation." 18 U.S.C. § 1993(c)(5). Section 5302 defines "mass transportation" as "transportation by a conveyance that provides regular and continuing general or special transportation to the public." 49 U.S.C. § 5302(a)(7). In contrast to the phrase "mass transportation," the word "vehicle" is given no explicit definition in section 1993, nor is it defined in section 5302.

Reid argues that an airplane is neither a "vehicle" nor engaged in "mass transportation," as those words are used in section 1993. The Court addresses these arguments in turn, but first it considers an argument made by Reid that section 1993 does not provide a punishment for attempt offenses.

A. Attempt Liability Under Section 1993

[1] Section 1993 enumerates a series of eight prohibited acts involving mass transportation providers. The final category punishes a person who "willfully attempts, threatens, or conspires to do any of the aforesaid acts." 18 U.S.C. § 1993(a)(8). The statute also contains a punishment provision, which states that an offender

> shall be fined under this title or imprisoned not more than twenty years, or both, if such act is committed, *or in the case of a threat or conspiracy such act would be committed,* on, against, or affecting a mass transportation provider engaged in or affecting interstate or foreign commerce, or if in the course of committing such act, that person travels or communicates across a State line in order to commit such act, or transports materials across a State line in aid of the commission of such act.

Id. § 1993(a) (emphasis added).

Reid argues that the penalty provision does not apply to attempts because it fails to mention the term "attempt," even though it does mention the words "threat" and "conspiracy," which are grouped together ***135** with attempts in subsection (a)(8). Reid also contends that the phrase "such act" in the punishment provision of section 1993 refers only to completed acts enumerated in subsections (a)(1) through (a)(7), and not to the inchoate offenses proscribed in subsection (a)(8), including attempts. This is significant, according to Reid, because it means that an attempt, rather than being punished as a committed act, could only be punished if it was mentioned, along with threats and conspiracies, as an act that could be punished if it "would be committed." Because it is not so mentioned along with threats and conspiracies, it is not subject to punishment under section 1993.

According to Reid, if "such act" is construed to apply to attempt offenses, portions of the punishment provision will be rendered superfluous. For instance, if "such act" is read to include those acts enumerated in subsection eight (the inchoate offenses), then "such act" would include threatening and conspiring.

But because threats and conspiracies are already enumerated separately following "such act" in the punishment provision, reading that phrase to comprise threats and conspiracies would make the explicit reference to those offenses gratuitous. Additionally, if "such act" embraces attempts, the requirement that "in the course of committing such act, that person travel [ ] or communicate[ ] across a State line in order to commit such act" might become meaningless, because one does not travel or communicate across state lines in order to commit an attempt, but rather to commit the crime itself. In Reid's view, reading section 1993 in this manner would offend the principle of statutory construction that courts should "disfavor interpretations of statutes that render language superfluous," *Conn. Nat'l Bank v. Germain,* 503 U.S. 249, 253, 112 S.Ct. 1146, 117 L.Ed.2d 391 (1992); *accord Atlantic Fish Spotters Ass'n v. Evans,* 206 F.Supp.2d 81, 85 (D.Mass.2002).

While it is true that courts should strive to avoid reading a statute in a way that renders some of the language within it unnecessary, courts should strive harder to avoid reading a statute in a way that renders it nonsensical. Reid's proposed construction of section 1993 would lead to an absurd result: an act that is clearly proscribed by the express language of the statute, 18 U.S.C. § 1993(a)(8), would not be *Avoiding* punishable under that statute, even though the statute *absurd results* establishes a punishment for every other act proscribed therein. The possibility that reading the statute to punish attempts would render other words within the statute gratuitous [2] does ***136** not alone compel the Court read the statute as Reid proposes, for it is well understood that "[r]edundancies across statutes are not unusual events in drafting," *Germain,* 503 U.S. at 253, 112 S.Ct. 1146. This Court is of opinion that it is more important in this case to read the statute so as to avoid an absurd result, *see United States v. X–Citement Video,* 513 U.S. 64, 68–69, 115 S.Ct. 464, 130 L.Ed.2d 372 (1994), one that would be contrary to the plain purpose of the statute, than it is to make every word of the statute meaningful. The Court therefore *Possible Scrivener's* rejects Reid's argument that Count Nine should be *Error (legislative* dismissed on the ground that section 1993 provides no *drafting mistake)* punishment for attempt crimes.

B. Is an Aircraft Engaged in "Mass Transportation"?

[2] Reid next argues that aircraft such as Flight 63 are not engaged in "mass transportation" as that phrase is used in section 1993. According to Reid, "mass transportation" "connotes buses, trolleys, subways, commuter trains, ferries—the means by which the mass of people, particularly in congested areas, get from one place to another in public conveyances," Def.'s Mot. at 4, particularly in light of the fact that the definition of "mass transportation" found in section 1993 is a cross-reference to a portion of the United States Code that addresses urban mass transit, *id.* at 4–5. The government counters that the language in section 1993 and the cross-reference defining "mass transportation" so clearly encompasses aircraft that the Court need not concern itself with the nature of the portion of the United States Code in which the cross-reference is located.

Defined within statute; Inference Across Statutes; Identical Words= Consistent Meanings; Ejusdem generis ("of the same kind")

As noted earlier, the phrase "mass transportation" is defined principally by a cross-reference to section 5302(a)(7) of Title 49 of the United States Code ("section 5302").[3] Section 5302 defines "mass transportation" as "transportation by a conveyance that provides regular and continuing general or special transportation to the public." 49 U.S.C. § 5302(a)(7). Section 1993 expands the definition supplied by section 5302, however, by adding that "the term shall include schoolbus, charter, and sightseeing transportation," 18 U.S.C. § 1993(c)(5), words that are otherwise excluded from the definition found in section 5302, *see* 49 U.S.C. § 5302(a)(7). Reading section 1993 and section 5302 in conjunction yields the following definition of "mass transportation": "transportation by a conveyance that provides regular and continuing general or special transportation to the public." The question for the Court is whether these words may be read to encompass aircraft.

Avoiding redundant and superfluous words

Ejusdem generis ("of the same kind")

Plain meaning test

*137 In answering this question, the Court "begins with the language of the statute. And where the statutory language provides a clear answer," the Court ends there as well. *Hughes Aircraft Co. v. Jacobson,* 525 U.S. 432, 438, 119 S.Ct. 755, 142 L.Ed.2d 881 (1999) (citation and internal quotation marks omitted). In determining whether the text of the statute provides a clear answer to the question presented by Reid, the Court accords each word found within the statute its ordinary or natural meaning, *e.g., Bailey v. United States,* 516 U.S. 137, 144–45, 116 S.Ct. 501, 133 L.Ed.2d 472 (1995), bearing in mind that "the meaning of a word cannot be determined in isolation, but must be drawn from the context in which it is used," *Deal v. United States,* 508 U.S. 129, 132, 113 S.Ct. 1993, 124 L.Ed.2d 44 (1993).

The Court holds that an aircraft of the type involved here engages in "mass transportation" as that phrase is defined in section 5302. Simply put, commercial aircraft transport large numbers of people every day. Certainly an aircraft of the kind that Reid boarded on December 22, 2001, provides "regular and continuing general or special transportation to the public." Flight 63 is one of a number of flights departing daily from Paris to Miami (hence it is "regular and continuing");[4] any individual who pays for a ticket and has the proper identification may board (hence it is available "to the public").

Reid attempts to dislodge the definition of "mass transportation" from this common-sense understanding of the phrase, an understanding that is buttressed by the broad language of section 5302, by pointing to the fact that section 5302 is part of a section of the United States Code, Chapter 53 of Title 49, which addresses urban mass transportation systems. Def.'s Mot. at 4–5.[5] Reid looks to the gestalt of Chapter 53, along with the titles of some of the provisions of Chapter 53, as a way to narrow the definition of "mass transportation" beyond what the words of section 5302 will allow when read in their ordinary or natural way. While context matters, it matters only insofar as it illuminates the meaning of words that are otherwise ambiguous. *See Hughes Aircraft Co.,* 525 U.S. at 438, 119 S.Ct. 755 ("[A]nalysis [of the meaning of a statute] begins with the language of the statute. And where the statutory language provides a clear answer, it ends there as well." (citation and internal quotation marks omitted)). Moreover, "[t]he title of a statute ... cannot limit the plain meaning of the text.... [I]t is of use only when it sheds light on some ambiguous word or phrase." *Penn. Dep't of Corr. v. Yeskey,* 524 U.S. 206, 212, 118 S.Ct. 1952, 141 L.Ed.2d 215 (1998) (citation and internal quotation marks omitted); *accord Carter v. United States,* 530 U.S. 255, 267, 120 S.Ct. 2159,

Plain meaning test

147 L.Ed.2d 203 (2000). Here, there is no ambiguity in the words used in section 5302 and section 1993: Flight 63 was providing regular and continuing general transportation to the public when Reid boarded it on December 22, 2001. Thus, Reid's argument that the ***138** meaning of "mass transportation" should be guided by the fact that section 5302 is found in a portion of the United States Code dealing with urban mass transportation asks this Court to draw from a broader context than is necessary to ascertain the meaning of "mass transportation." The Court is satisfied that the definition provided by section 5302 and broadened by section 1993—"transportation that provides regular and continuing general or special transportation to the public"—when read in an ordinary or natural way, encompasses aircraft of the kind at issue here.

Statutory Language -Ordinary meaning

In pari materia (statutes addressing the same subject matter generally should be read as if they were one law); Inferences across statutes

C. Is an Aircraft a "Vehicle"?

[3] Finally, Reid argues that an airplane is not a "vehicle." He points to a number of dictionaries that define the word vehicle in a way that could not be read to include aircraft. The second edition of the *Random House Dictionary of the English Language* (1987), for instance, defines vehicle as "a conveyance moving on wheels, runners, tracks, or the like, as a cart, sled, automobile, or tractor, etc." Def.'s Mot. at 3. The government responds with some dictionary definitions of its own, definitions that are broad enough to include aircraft. An example is found in the seventh edition of *Black's Law Dictionary* (1999), which defines vehicle as "any conveyance used in transporting passengers or merchandise by land, water, or air." Gov't's Opp'n at 9.

Dictionary Definition= plain meaning

It is not entirely surprising that the parties resort to a battle of dictionaries to resolve the issue, as section 1993 itself provides no definition of the word "vehicle" the way it does for the phrase "mass transportation," and the Supreme Court has on occasion resorted to dictionaries to define words that are not otherwise defined in a statute. *E.g., Toyota Motor Mfg. v. Williams,* 534 U.S. 184, 122 S.Ct. 681, 691, 151 L.Ed.2d 615 (2002); *Tyler v. Cain,* 533 U.S. 656, 662, 121 S.Ct. 2478, 150 L.Ed.2d 632 (2001). It is surprising, however, that the parties neglect to include in their litanies of definitions the definition given to the word "vehicle" by Congress.

Titles and Provisos not generally controlling, but instead used for confirmation

The Dictionary Act of the United States Code, 1 U.S.C. § 1 *et seq.,* provides general definitions for a handful of words appearing within the code, along with general rules of construction, that apply to the entire code in the absence of a more specific indication within the statute being analyzed. *See Rowland v. Cal. Men's Colony,* 506 U.S. 194, 200, 113 S.Ct. 716, 121 L.Ed.2d 656 (1993) ("[C]ourts would hardly need direction [from the Dictionary Act] where Congress had thought to include an express, specialized definition for the purpose of a particular Act; ordinary rules of statutory construction would prefer the specific definition over the Dictionary Act's general one."). Although the Dictionary Act defines but a few words appearing in the code, the word "vehicle" is one of them. It states that "[t]he word 'vehicle' includes every description of carriage or other artificial contrivance used, or capable of being used, as a means of transportation *on land*." 1 U.S.C. § 4 (emphasis added).

The Dictionary Act

In a Supreme Court case of some vintage, *McBoyle v. United States,* 283 U.S. 25, 51 S.Ct. 340, 75 L.Ed. 816 (1931), Justice Holmes wrote for the court that an individual could not be punished for stealing an airplane under a statute that prohibited stealing any "self-propelled vehicle not designed for running on rails." *Id.* at 26, 51 S.Ct. 340. In so holding, the Supreme Court observed that the definition of "vehicle" supplied by the Dictionary Act did not include an aircraft. *Id.*[6]

*139 In the seventy-one years since *McBoyle,* Congress has never amended the Dictionary Act to give the word "vehicle" a broader meaning. Congress has, however, amended the Dictionary Act recently, *e.g.,* Defense of Marriage Act, Pub.L. No. 104–199, § 3(a), 110 Stat. 2419 (1996) (creating 1 U.S.C. § 7, which defines "marriage" and "spouse"), which suggests that the Dictionary Act is not an obscure, forgotten portion of the United States Code, but instead remains vital to the process of interpreting the rest of the code.

Congressional Intent/lack of amendment

The narrow definition of the word "vehicle" set out in the Dictionary Act and clarified by the Supreme Court in *McBoyle* is consistent with the general structure of the United States Code, which distinguishes among three types of conveyances: vessels, which provide transportation on water, 1 U.S.C. § 3; vehicles, which provide transportation on land, *id*. § 4; and aircraft, which provide transportation through the air, 49 U.S.C. § 40102(a)(6). A number of statutory provisions recognize this distinction. For example, a provision of the immigration laws makes inadmissible to the United States any alien who engages in terrorist activities, defined to include "[t]he highjacking or sabotage of any conveyance (including an aircraft, vessel, or vehicle)." 8 U.S.C. § 1182(a)(3)(B)(iii)(I). A customs law provides definitions of several words, including vessel and vehicle, and in both of these definitions expressly excludes aircraft. 19 U.S.C. § 1401(a), (b). A criminal law makes it illegal to import or export a "motor vehicle ..., vessel, [or] aircraft" known to have been stolen. 18 U.S.C. § 553(a)(1). An armed forces provision authorizes the Secretary of Defense to institute a system of reporting to Congress on the readiness of the armed forces, including a measurement of "the extent to which units of the armed forces remove serviceable parts, supplies, or equipment from one vehicle, vessel, or aircraft in order to render a different vehicle, vessel, or aircraft operational." 10 U.S.C. § 117(c)(7). A conservation law states that any individual who traffics in fish, wildlife, or plants in criminal violation of the endangered species laws is subject to forfeiture of "[a]ll vessels, vehicles, aircraft, and other equipment used to aid" in the trafficking of the endangered species. 16 U.S.C. § 3374. These are but a few examples of a pattern that recurs throughout the code. *See also, e.g.,* 8 U.S.C. § 1225(d)(1); *id*. § 1324(b)(1); *id*. § 1357(a)(3); 10 U.S.C. § 2401a(b); 16 U.S.C. § 19jj-1(b); *id*. § 668b(b); *id*. § 2403(a)(8); *id*. § 2409(d)(2); 18 U.S.C. § 659; *id*. § 682(a)(6)(A)(i); *id*. § 1956(c)(4); 19 U.S.C. § 1433; *id*. § 1459(a); *id*. § 1594(a).

Precedent that used Statutory Interpretation for the same issue

Indeed, Title 18 of the code contains a separate provision making illegal the same acts proscribed in section 1993, but with respect to aircraft in particular. Section 32 of Title 18 subjects to the same punishment as section 1993 any individual who "willfully sets fire to, damages, destroys, disables, or wrecks any aircraft in the special aircraft jurisdiction of the United ***140** States," 18 U.S.C. § 32(a)(1), and any individual who "attempts or conspires" to do the same, *id*. § 32(a)(7).[7] In the Court's view, the structure of the United States Code provides compelling evidence that the word "vehicle" is used in a very particular manner

Avoid redundant and superfluous interpretation

within the code, a manner separate and distinct from the word "aircraft."[8]

U.S. Supreme Court

In the event that any doubt remains about the fact that the word "vehicle" does not comprise aircraft, the Court notes that the legislative history of the USA PATRIOT Act further supports the notion that airplanes are not within the ambit of section 1993. Senator Leahy, one of the sponsors of the bill, made the following remarks during his presentation of the bill to the Senate for final vote:

Legislative history= congressional Intent

> Just last week, a Greyhound bus crashed in Tennessee after a deranged passenger slit the driver's throat and then grabbed the steering wheel, forc[ing] the bus into oncoming traffic. Six people were killed in the crash. *Because there are currently no federal law[s] addressing terrorism of mass transportation systems, however, there may be no federal jurisdiction over such a case,* even if it were committed by suspected terrorists. Clearly, there is an urgent need for strong criminal legislation to deter attacks against mass transportation systems. Section 801 [section 1993] will fill this gap.

Consistency across legislation

*141 147 Cong. Rec. S10,551 (daily ed. Oct. 11, 2001) (statement of Sen. Leahy) (emphasis added). Senator Leahy's comments suggest that section 1993 was intended not to provide additional punishment for destruction or attempted destruction of aircraft, but rather to ensure that other modes of transportation, vulnerable to terrorist attack but believed to be outside the reach of the federal criminal laws, come within the reach of those laws. This legislation was intended to "fill in the gaps" and address modes of transportation that Congress had not already specifically protected.

Legislative Intent

There were existing federal laws addressing terrorist acts against airplanes before September 11, 2001, and Reid has been charged under these laws. As mentioned earlier, Count Seven of the indictment charges Reid with attempted destruction of an aircraft, in violation of 18 U.S.C. § 32. Indictment at 8. In addition, Count Three of the indictment charges Reid with violating 49 U.S.C. § 46505(b)(3) and (c), which makes it illegal to place or attempt to place an explosive device on board an aircraft. Indictment at 4. Counts Five and Six of the indictment allege that Reid interfered with flight crew members during the performance of the crew members' duties by assaulting or intimidating them, in violation of 49 U.S.C. § 46504. Indictment at 6–7. As the indictment against Reid illustrates, a comprehensive patchwork of laws existed prior to the enactment of the USA PATRIOT Act that address acts of terrorism against aircraft.

The government argues that the legislative history mentioned above suggests that what motivated Congress in passing section 1993 was to ensure that *acts of terrorism* against mass transportation systems, including aircraft, were criminalized. In other words, Senator Leahy's comments reflect concern that acts of terrorism generally might not be federal crimes, not that attacks against Greyhound buses, for example, were not federal crimes. The Court finds this argument unpersuasive. The government's argument does not square with the language of section 1993, particularly as it relates to section 32, which proscribes similar acts against aircraft. A comparison of these two statutes reveals that there is no difference in the two provisions in terms of the *acts* that are proscribed, except in ways that are not relevant here. Section 1993, for instance, makes it unlawful to "derail" a mass transportation vehicle, but that would appear to apply only to trains. There is no new proscription of acts of terrorism, however defined, in section 1993 that is not also found in section 32. Instead, the key distinction between section 1993 and section 32 lies in the type of conveyance that is protected by the provision.

According to the government, this form of reasoning does not advance Reid's cause, because section 1993 is necessarily duplicative no matter how it is read. The government contends that destruction of a subway train or bus is already addressed in separate statutes,[9] just as is destroying an airplane, and thus construing section 1993 to cover only buses and trains renders the statute entirely gratuitous, as it would proscribe no new conduct. The government points to the phrase "motor vehicle"—defined as "every description of

carriage or other contrivance propelled or drawn by mechanical power and used for commercial purposes on the highways in the transportation of passengers," ***142** 18 U.S.C. § 31(a)(6)—as evidence that much of what Congress sought to cover in section 1993 was already covered elsewhere. The Court agrees that this definition almost certainly encompasses buses, although it is an open question whether it covers trains, subway systems, and other forms of mass transportation.

The Court disagrees, however, that this argument *Court rebuts* compels the Court to include aircraft within the *government* definition of "vehicle." It may be true that the one form *arguments* of transportation (buses) that motivated Congress (or *based on the* at least one of its members) to pass the law in the *interpretation* first place was already covered by pre-existing law. *of vehicle based* It may also be true that the outer limits of the word *on prior statutes* "vehicle" are fuzzy and imprecise. These factors do *& precedent* not dissuade the Court from its ultimate conclusion. The clear distinction within the United States Code between vehicles and aircraft, the legislative history of section 1993 suggesting a concern with attacks on buses or similar conveyances, and the variety of pre-existing criminal laws addressing attacks against aircraft, outweigh countervailing factors and lead the Court to conclude that "vehicle," as it is used in section 1993, does not comprise aircraft.

IV. Conclusion

Reid's motion to dismiss Count Nine of the indictment against him [Docket No. 32] is ALLOWED because Reid's alleged actions are not within the scope of conduct prohibited by section 1993. While section 1993 does proscribe attempts, and the airplane that Reid allegedly attempted to destroy was engaged in "mass transportation," it is not a "vehicle" as that word is used by Congress.

It is important to note that the result the Court reaches here can have no effect at all on the sentence ultimately to be visited on Reid were he to be convicted. Even had this Court denied the motion to dismiss Count Nine and—putting *Blockburger* to one side, *see supra* note 7—were Reid convicted on this count as well, under the United States Sentencing Guidelines he cannot be made to serve one more day in prison due to this violation. *See* U.S. Sentencing Guidelines Manual §§ 3D1.2, 3D1.3(a). Nor, however, ought the government here be considered to have "overcharged" to obtain some sort of litigation advantage, e.g., piling on redundant charges just to afford the jury separate opportunities to convict. To the contrary, section 1993 is new legislation, its contours not yet fully explored. Both the defense and the government are to be commended for ably briefing and presenting this issue.

Its prompt resolution by the Court now will allow the government, should it wish, to appeal this Court's interpretation without disturbing the November 4, 2002 trial date.

SO ORDERED.

Statutory Interpretation Exercises

In each of the three statutory interpretation hypotheticals below, you will find a short explanation of the facts and legal issue, followed by the relevant statute and authority. Determine the meaning of the statutory language using a plain meaning analysis, and a more expansive analysis of the statute if warranted, to consider how the legal issue should be resolved.

Hypothetical 1:

Ms. Wright and her ten-year-old son, Marvin, rented a two-bedroom cottage in Rhinebeck, New York in March for $1500/month. The kitchen, dining room, living room, and master bedroom are located on the main floor and the attic had been converted to a second bedroom, where Marvin sleeps. The Wrights loved the cottage, until Ms. Wright began to notice stinkbugs on the windowsills in May. Although annoying to people, especially farmers, stinkbugs are harmless, but Ms. Wright found the bugs to be horrible looking and wanted them out of sight. She heard, however, that when killed, stinkbugs omit an odor that attracts more stinkbugs so she was reluctant to kill them. Because the stinkbugs had not entered her home, she did not do anything.

By June, the stinkbugs had multiplied on the windowsills, and some appeared on the ceiling in the attic. She called her landlord, Mr. Greene, to ask him if he could help with the problem. Mr. Greene noted that stinkbugs had taken over Rhinebeck and the whole Hudson River Valley region. He told Ms. Wright that he had read articles in the newspaper about the problem and had heard rumors that the standard bug killers did not kill stinkbugs, but he agreed to look into the problem. The next day, he came over to her apartment and vacuumed up the stinkbugs on the windowsills and the ceiling. This helped for a while, but in July, three times as many were back, covering the ceiling in Marvin's room. They occasionally flew noisily around the attic room, disturbing Marvin's sleep and making him uncomfortable. Ms. Wright, now angry, told Mr. Greene that she would not pay rent until he did something about the problem.

Mr. Greene, now also angry, sprayed insecticides and vacuumed up any stink-bugs that fell off the ceiling. The insecticides only made the problem worse. The stinkbugs soon covered the ceiling, turning portions of the green ceiling black from the upper armor of the stinkbugs' shells. The stinkbugs mostly stayed on the ceiling, but once Marvin woke to find three stinkbugs on his pillow. Ms. Wright withheld her July rent and threatened to withhold August rent. At the end of July, Mr. Greene hired an exterminator who sprayed toxic chemicals in Marvin's room. Marvin had to leave his room because of the smell of the chemicals, and even though the exterminator said he could safely sleep in the room, Marvin was too afraid of the bugs to return to the room. Marvin moved into his mother's room. By the time August rent was due, the stinkbugs had returned, covering more of the ceiling and the walls of the attic. Ms. Wright closed off the attic and withheld her August rent. Mr. Greene would like to recover the rent from July and August, but has he breached his duty as a landlord?

The New York Real Property Law § 235-b (McKinney 2011) states:

1. In every written or oral lease or rental agreement for residential prem-ises the landlord or lessor shall be deemed to covenant and warrant that the premises so leased or rented and all areas used in connection therewith in common with other tenants or residents are fit for human habitation and for the uses reasonably intended by the parties and that the occupants of such premises shall not be subjected to any conditions which would be dangerous, hazardous or detrimental to their life, health or safety. When any such condition has been caused by the misconduct of the tenant or lessee or persons under his direction or control, it shall not constitute a breach of such covenants and warranties.

The relevant legislative history includes the following about the law:

Governor Carey stated in his remarks upon approving the bill: "By one large step this bill moves the law of landlord and tenant into the twentieth Century." (N.Y. Legis. Ann, 1975, p. 438.)

***

In enacting section 235-b of the Real Property Law the Legislature was concerned with placing the tenant in 'legal parity' with the landlord (1975 Sen. J. 7766-7776—remarks of Sen. Barclay), not with expand-ing the tenant's rights out of proportion to those of the landlord.... The principal Senate sponsor of the warranty bill, Senator H. Douglas Barclay stated in his supporting remarks on the floor of the Senate, 'In return for rent received the landlord will warrant that the premises are habit-able. It is a very simple concept, the contractual relationship between the two parties will be changed to put the tenant in parity legally with the landlord.' (1975 Sen. J. 7776—remarks of Sen. Barclay.) Senator Barclay went on to say, 'We are treating a lease or rental agreement for residential premises as a contract. The full range of remedies in contract law could be considered by the court. These include damages, specific performance and recission. The most frequently applied measure of damages is likely to be the decrease in rental value caused by the breach. Such abatement of rents have been applied by those courts in the state which now recognize the implied warranty.' (1975 Sen. J. 7771—remarks of Sen. Barclay.)

***

Senator Barclay stated 'The use of the word 'misconduct' is a word that the courts must interpret. We've avoided the word 'negligence' because this is a contractual matter rather than a question of tort law.' (1975 Sen. J. 7774—remarks of Sen. Barclay; emphasis added.)

Segal v. Justice Ct. Mut. Hous. Coop, 108 Misc. 2d 1074 (N.Y. Civ. Ct. 1981).

The New York statute codified the common law rule in *Tonetti v. Penati*, 48 A.D.2d 25 (N.Y. App. Div. 1975): "By a parity of reasoning, a warranty of habitability and fitness for the purpose intended (unless specifically excluded) should be implied from the very nature of a rental for residential purposes.... we relegate to the limbo of history the orthodox view of *caveat lessee* and hold that, unless expressly excepted, there is an implied warranty of habitability when a landlord leases premises for residential use."

A. Look at the New York Real Property Law § 235-b (1) and divide the subsection into components. Using only a plain language interpretation of the Act, determine whether the landlord, Mr. Greene, has breached the implied warranty of habitability.

B. Next, consider your review of the *Park West Management* and *Solow* cases in your understanding of the statute. How do these cases change your analysis?

   Park W. Mgmt. Corp. v. Mitchell, 47 N.Y.2d 316, 325 (N.Y. 1979).
   Solow v. Wellner, 86 N.Y.2d 582, 588 (N.Y. 1995).

C. Now assume this case occurred in Pennsylvania. How would this case be resolved under *Pugh v. Holmes*, 405 A.2d 897 (Pa. 1979)?

Hypothetical 2:

ABC Importers, Inc. ("ABC") imports golf sets for children. ABC imports this item from a country with which the United States maintains "Normal Trade Relations." The golf set consists of a nylon carrying bag, two plastic regulation-size golf balls, and three metal golf clubs with Puppy designs. The nylon bag is twelve inches high and has an opening large enough to hold three golf clubs and a side zipper pocket to hold the balls. The three golf clubs are representative of a full golf set, and each is seventeen inches long. The clubs include: one driver, one iron, and one putter. ABC sells only a right-handed set and imports these items for sale to retail toy stores.

The United States Customs Service (Customs) is charged with classifying imported items under the Harmonized Tariff Schedule of the United States (HTSUS) for purposes of assessing the tariff rate. Customs classified ABC's New Puppy Putters Golf Club Set under Chapter 95 of the HTSUS, heading 9506 "[a]rticles and equipment for ... outdoor games ...," subheading 9506.31.00 "[g]olf clubs and other equipment; parts and accessories thereof: golf clubs complete" which are taxed at 4.4% *ad valorem*. Harmonized Tariff Schedule of the United States, Ch. 95, § 9506, 19 U.S.C. § 1202 (2003). ABC argues that the correct classification of this item under Chapter 95, heading 9503 "[o]ther toys; reduced-size ("scale") models ..." under which the New Puppy Putters Golf Club Set would be imported duty free. Harmonized Tariff Schedule of the United States, Ch. 95, § 9503, 19 U.S.C. § 1202 (2003).

Are ABC Importers, Inc. likely to be successful in their appeal to the U.S. Customs Service, arguing that the Puppy Putters should be imported duty free? Consider the following authority to address this question:

1. The statute: The Harmonized Tariff Schedule of the United States, <u>HTSUS</u>

2. Relevant case law:
   a. <u>*Schulstad USA, Inc. v. United States*, 240 F. Supp. 2d 1335 (CIT 2002)</u>;
   b. <u>*R. Dakin & Co. v. United States*, 752 F. Supp. 483 (CIT 1990)</u>.

3. Dictionary definitions:
   • **Golf:** game played on a large open-air course, in which a small hard ball is struck with a club into a series of small holes in the ground, the object being to use the fewest possible strokes to complete the course.
   http://oxforddictionaries.com/us/definition/american_english/golf?q=golf

- **Model:** a three-dimensional representation of a person or thing or of a proposed structure, typically on a smaller scale than the original: a model of St. Paul's Cathedral [as modifier]:a model airplane. http://oxforddictionaries.com/us/definition/american_english/model?q=model
- **Toy:** an object for a child to play with, typically a model or miniature replica of something. http://oxforddictionaries.com/us/definition/american_english/toy

and

4. Trade association rules: The United States Golf Association, http://www.usga.org/Rule-Books/Rules-of-Golf/Appendix-II/

Hypothetical 3:

Alex Hamilton and Aaron Burr are neighbors. They do not get along. Alex purchased a Labrador Retriever puppy last year, which is now 75 lbs. and approaching adulthood. Aaron dislikes dogs, particularly large ones, though his wife owns a small dog. On the morning of June 1, 2012, Alex was planting flowers in her front yard. She had her dog, Franz, sleeping two feet away. He was not restrained by a leash and her yard is not fenced. Aaron Burr returned home a short time later, parking his car along the edge of Alex's yard. His house borders Alex's yard opposite the side on which she is planting. Upon Burr's arrival, Franz woke up and began barking. He advanced halfway across Alex's yard, he stopped in the middle and began to jump around barking in Aaron's direction. Aaron was frightened by this and felt that the dog was lunging in his direction. He knew that nothing prevented the dog from leaving its yard. Alex Hamilton loudly commanded the dog to sit down and then walked over to it and led it by the collar into her house. Burr expressed the opinion that Hamilton needed to control her dog and promptly called the police. The police charged Hamilton with violating "The Leash Law," 3 P.S. section 459-305 (a)1 and (a)2, which states:

§ 459-305. Confinement and housing of dogs not part of a kennel

(a) CONFINEMENT AND CONTROL.—It shall be unlawful for the owner or keeper of any dog to fail to keep at all times the dog in any of the following manners:

(1) confined within the premises of the owner;
(2) firmly secured by means of a collar and chain or other device so that it cannot stray beyond the premises on which it is secured; or
(3) under the reasonable control of some person, or when engaged in lawful hunting, exhibition, performance events or field training.

FYI

Confined: (of a space) restricted in area or volume; cramped.

Control: the power to influence or direct people's behavior or the course of event; the ability to manage a machine, vehicle, or other moving object.

Premises: a house or building, together with its land and outbuildings, occupied by a business or considered in an official context.

A. Consider the hypothetical based on the statute alone—the statute does not define "confined," "premises," or "reasonable control." How would you defend Hamilton based on the text of this section of the dog law, using only the tools of plain meaning? Identify the essential facts that a defense would hinge upon.

B. How does *Miller v. Hurst*, 448 A.2d 614 (Pa. Super. Ct. 1982) and its introduction of the legislative intent of the dog law influence your thinking? Does your defense change if the definition of "premises" in *Commonwealth v. Glumac*, 717 A.2d 572 (Pa. Super. Ct. 1998) is considered? Does this make additional information from the hypothetical relevant? Notice that the language of the dog law has changed since these cases were decided. What does the more recent case, *Commonwealth v. Raban*, 31 A.3d 699 (Pa. Super. Ct. 2011) add to your understanding of the law?"

C. What might happen if the dog's head had crossed the owner's property line? What if it had crossed the line but was on a secured chain with too much slack, allowing its head to cross the property line? What if the facts remained the same as the hypothetical except Hamilton was not present at all, and her dog just stood in her yard barking?

The above diagram depicts the position of Hamilton and her dog (H) and Burr (B).

CHAPTER 5

Understanding and Using Legal Rules

Learning to brief a case is an important skill for new law students. But what do lawyers do with these discrete components of a judicial opinion? After successfully identifying the procedural posture, the court's reasoning, the determinative facts, and the rule of law from an individual case, lawyers will use these judicial opinions to identify the rule of law governing a particular subject area and will use this rule to address legal problems. This chapter will focus on learning to use legal rules.

Using Case Precedent

Once you have identified the parts of a judicial opinion and are able to articulate the rule of law, you are ready to use the rule to predict a legal outcome or to argue that the court should decide in favor of your client. Applying the rule from one case to a new situation requires that you pay careful attention to the facts in the precedent case as well as the facts of the new dispute. Facts in a common law legal system are extremely important. The facts are what change from one case to another, and we expect lawyers, and then judges, to analogize and distinguish precedent when a case presents a new set of facts. This is the way the law changes, precedent case by precedent case.

For example, consider *Kohr v. Weber*, in which the Pennsylvania Supreme Court upheld injunctive relief and affirmed an award of monetary damages for neighbors who sued for unreasonable interference with the enjoyment of residential property. The unreasonable interference in that case was caused by the noise, lights, and dust resulting from a drag racing strip on property adjacent to plaintiffs' residences.

Start by reading and briefing the case. As you read, note how the Court supports its decision by relying on precedent deciding the same legal principle but on different facts. Then, using *Kohr* as precedent, consider the following hypothetical.

Exercise: Applying Precedent From a Single Case to New Facts

Your clients, Joe and Cynthia Robinson, live in a largely rural area near Hershey, Pennsylvania. They bought their house on two acres about a year ago. They quickly realized that their nearest neighbor, Kevin Matthews, was a musician. Matthews had lived in the house for about four years, and soon thereafter he began holding jam sessions with other musicians. The crowds have grown to the point where Matthews is now holding regular performances every Friday and Saturday night, year-round. Several hundred people usually show up, and Matthews charges admission.

Joe and Cynthia have complained to Matthews about the noise, but he is not sympathetic. He has told them he moved to the country so there would be room to play music with his friends. He also insists that he can make as much noise on his property as he likes, and points out that he only has musical events two nights a week. But the electric guitars and fiddles, keyboards, and drums are so loud that his neighbors can't carry on conversations inside their home and have trouble sleeping. There are loud crowds spilling all over the property, singing and dancing. The music is amplified inside and out, with some speakers hung from trees around the property.

> **Food for Thought**
>
> Using *Kohr* as precedent, what advice would you give Joe and Cynthia Robinson? What is the legal rule in *Kohr*? How does the Court apply it to the facts of that case? What is the Court's rationale? How are the facts in *Kohr* similar to your client's facts? How do they differ? Do you predict that they would have a successful claim against Kevin Matthews under Pennsylvania law?

Matthews has room to park that many cars, but neighbors notice the traffic and the honking horns until three or four a.m. He has erected tall, very bright lights so that visitors can see where to park, and can easily find their way to the house. The parking and lights are on the part of Matthews' property nearest Joe and Cynthia's house.

Using Case Precedent: Rule Synthesis

In their written opinions, judges often do not spell out the rules for application of different laws in neat lists of necessary elements. This is why a successful lawyer must be able to synthesize this broad and lengthy language into short and specific points that should be established before a court can grant the relief sought. However, when looking for the law, a lawyer will not usually read only one case and its decision. Most likely, there will be multiple cases, from different levels of court authority and different jurisdictions. Synthesizing a legal rule from a series of precedent cases allows you to draw a composite rule and give a more complete picture of how the courts have applied precedent. This composite rule is then applied to new facts. Rule synthesis is a core lawyering skill.

Although you may not realize it, you already have much experience applying synthesized precedent to fact in order to predict an outcome.

For example, you have a friend coming from out of town to visit you for the weekend, and you are trying to decide whether he will enjoy a hike in the mountains. Your first step is to think about other activities you have done together. On a recent trip your friend enjoyed the long bicycle ride you took through the countryside. On another visit, you both enjoyed a morning spent kayaking on the river. On the other hand, he did not enjoy an afternoon at an art museum. Nor did he enjoy going to the symphony; he fidgeted in his seat and kept glancing at his watch when he thought you were not watching.

Now ask yourself: what do the activities he enjoyed have in common? Your friend likes participating in outdoor sports. Ask yourself the same question about the activities he did not enjoy. He does not like more sedentary, indoor, cultural activities. Based on this past experience, you can predict that he is likely to be enthusiastic about a hike in the mountains.

What have you done? You have made each part fit together. You have synthesized information from a series of past experiences and identified a combined rule. Then you have applied all you know from past experiences to a new set of facts—a mountain hike—to predict an outcome and make a decision. You have synthesized a rule from precedent.

Follow a similar approach when synthesizing a legal rule from a series of cases. Begin by reading and briefing each case. Then consider how the cases fit together, and decide whether the cases are addressing similar issues. If so, decide if the court is applying the same legal rule or whether the court develops a new rule over time. Break the rule into its elements, and consider what each case tells us about the rule. Decide whether the courts have been consistent in their application of this rule or in their results. If there are inconsistencies, try to understand them according to the date of the decision, hierarchy of the court, facts of the case, or some other reason.

Rule Synthesis in the Legal Context

As a lawyer, you will need to assimilate and synthesize large amounts of information into just a few words. Therefore, you may find visual comparisons helpful. For example, a synthesis chart can help an attorney transform several court opinions into a single list of necessary elements. This is done by stating all of the relevant information in one place and considering it together as a whole instead of as separate court opinions. Here are some examples.

In Chapter 3, you used <u>Ingalls v. Hobbs, 31 N.E. 286 (Mass. 1892)</u> to evaluate the following set of facts: A law student in Cambridge, Massachusetts stops paying rent to his landlord when he discovers in early October that the unfurnished, basement apartment, which he moved into in August and thought was an incredible deal, does not have heat. He signed a one-year lease after looking at the apartment on August 1 and he immediately moved into his new place.

However, a court will rarely rule on the basis of one case alone, but will synthesize several cases in order to reach a decision. In considering this example, the court might consider <u>Boston Hous. Auth. v. Hemingway, 293 N.E.2d 831, 842 (Mass. 1973)</u> and <u>Lynch v. James, 692 N.E.2d 81 (Mass. App. Ct. 1998)</u> in addition to the *Ingalls* case. To help analyze the problem and to keep the information organized, a lawyer might use the following sorts of synthesis charts.

A chart might be organized around each case you have briefed:

	Ingalls—Mass. Supreme Ct. 1892	Hemingway—Mass. Supreme Ct. 1973	Lynch—Mass. Appellate Ct. 1998
Facts	Tenant rented furnished vacation home. House was infested with bugs.	Housing code violation issued; tenants withheld rent after making repeated demands to landlord to fix defects. Defects made apartments uninhabitable. Housing code allowed tenant to withhold rent if tenant gives landlord written notice. Tenant did not give written notice.	Tenant's child fell from a third-floor window and sustained serious and permanent injuries. The tenant alleged that the landlord breached the implied warranty of habitability by not installing window stops.
Issue/ Holding	Whether there was an implied agreement on the part of the landlord that the house was in a proper condition for the immediate use as a dwelling house? (Yes, because house was furnished.)	Whether the tenant needs to comply with the housing code and alert the landlord that they are withholding rent? (No, the tenant's payment of rent is dependent upon the landlord maintaining habitable premises.)	Whether the landlord breached the implied warranty of habitability by not installing window stops? (No, the landlord did not breach his duty because although dangerous, the lack of window stops did not make the premise uninhabitable.)

	Ingalls—Mass. Supreme Ct. 1892	Hemingway—Mass. Supreme Ct. 1973	Lynch—Mass. Appellate Ct. 1998
Rule	A furnished apartment rented for a short period of time implies an agreement or warranty that the premise is fit for habitation.	The landlord has an implied duty to maintain habitable premises: Implied Warranty of Habitability (IWH). A breach of this duty constitutes a total or partial defense to the landlord's claim for rent. The tenant's claim for damages should based on this breach should be limited to the time the premises are uninhabitable after the landlord has notice of the defects.	The condition in question must be vital to the use of the premise.

Or the chart could be organized according to the elements of the rule and the factors courts have considered, which will quickly show what each case adds:

Rule	Ingalls	Hemingway	Lynch
There is an Implied Warranty of Habitability (IWH) that premises are fit for human occupation	Creates a limited exception to caveat emptor—IWH for a short term lease	Extends the rule to all residential leases.	Not within IWH
Factors courts consider:			
Seriousness	Bug infestation	Extensive code violations	Window stops
Length of time defect persists	Vacation home	Extended period	Not clear
Notice	Yes	Yes	Yes
Ability to make habitable in a reasonable time	No	No	N/A
Result of abnormal conduct or use by tenant	No	No	No-but no guarantee that a tenant would use window stops even if available (not within landlord's control)

Food for Thought

On the basis of these three cases, if the landlord sues the tenant for the unpaid rent how do you think a court in Massachusetts would decide? Do you think the landlord's suit will be successful?

Practicing Rule Synthesis: Take Me Out to the Ball Game

RULE SYNTHESIS EXERCISE:
Take Me Out to the Ball Game

Directions: Predict from past situations when the owners of sports facilities have a duty to protect patrons who are injured by activities within the facilities. After reading each scenario, choose the best statement of the outcome in that case. Then, synthesize the general rule for owners of sports facilities that is simply stated, readily applied, and consistent with all of the prior outcomes. After you have synthesized the rule, you should be ready to predict the outcome in new situations involving injuries in sports facilities by applying your rule.

1. At a hockey game, a patron was injured after being struck by a hockey puck unintentionally shot by a player into the stands. At the time of injury, plaintiff was seated, and the game was in progress. The court held that the stadium owner was not liable for the harm.

   a. A sports facility had no duty to protect patrons injured by any flying objects within the stadium.

   b. A sports facility had no duty to protect patrons injured by a risk common and expected in the sport.

2. A woman had finished her downhill ski run and was traveling away from the base of a ski slope when another skier struck her. The court held that the facility owner was not liable.

   a. A sports facility owner had no duty to protect patrons injured on the property of the facility.

   b. A sports facility owner had no duty to protect patrons injured while sufficiently engaged in the common activities of the facility.

3. At a baseball game, Ms. Jones was struck in the head by a baseball hit during batting practice. At the time of her injury, she was located in the stadium's enclosed second-level concourse, which contained several large openings through which patrons could view the game. The game had not yet begun, and Ms. Jones was standing with her back to the field when she was hit. The court held that the owner was liable.

    a. <u>A sports facility owner had a duty to protect patrons from risks not inherent to attending an event in that facility.</u>

    b. <u>A sports facility owner had a duty to protect patrons who are injured while they are buying refreshments.</u>

4. At a football game, Mr. Magoo was tackled by an unruly mob of fans clamoring for a football. Mr. Magoo stood up from his assigned seat to catch a football that had just been kicked into the stands. Mr. Magoo caught the ball, but was injured when a group of fans attacked him in order to obtain the souvenir. The fans causing his injury were not located near their assigned seats, and the stadium was aware of the fans' behavior but did nothing to prevent it. The court held that the stadium owners were liable.

    a. <u>A sports facility owner had a duty to protect patrons who are injured by risks that are not common, frequent or expected</u>.

    b. <u>A sports facility owner had a duty to protect patrons who are injured by other fans</u>.

Click here to check your answer.

Synthesize all prior rules into one rule that can be applied to all future potential situations. Write your rule.

Apply the new rule to predict whether the "no duty rule" would apply to the following situations:

1. A fan in his seat during a Marauders game (a professional baseball team) is hit by a little leaguer's grand slam from a nearby recreational ballpark unaffiliated with the Marauders.

    <u>Duty/No Duty</u>

2. An employee launches a rolled-up t-shirt into the stands and a man dives with his arm extended in an attempt to catch the shirt in his glove. Instead, the man whacked the woman next to him in the face with his gloved fist. She received a broken nose.

    <u>Duty/No Duty</u>

3. An exasperated ballpark vendor chucked a full beer can at a man who had been heckling him. The man hit suffered a broken nose.

    Duty/No Duty

4. Buck Wyld was tailgating with his fraternity in a parking lot owned by the ballpark on which only people with tickets to the game on that day may park. Buck and his friends continued tailgating long after the game had started, in the hopes of catching a fly ball. While Buck was doing a keg stand, a fourth-inning batter hit a grand slam out of the park. The ball hit Buck on his left inner elbow, causing him to collapse out of the keg stand onto his head.

    Duty/No Duty

    ————————

Understanding Legal Authority

In the example concerning the law student whose apartment was without heat, would the Massachusetts court be required to follow every case or statute decided on this landlord-tenant topic? As you research a legal issue, whether to address a client's concern, predict an outcome, or to prepare a persuasive argument, you may find many different sources of law. It can be difficult to decide what to use and what significance to give these sources. Additionally, you may encounter materials that discuss the law, but don't actually have the force of law. An understanding of the hierarchy of legal authority will tell you that some authority has greater weight than others. This section examines how lawyers decide what information or "authority" to use.

Hierarchy of Authority

Where there is a conflict between two legal sources, consider these general principles as to the order, or weight, of primary legal authority:

*   A constitution will prevail over a statute if the statute conflicts with the constitution.
*   A constitution or statute will prevail over common law if the common law is in conflict.
*   A constitution or statute will supersede a regulation or court rule if the regulation or rule is in conflict with the constitution or statute.
*   A more recent statutory enactment will prevail over an older statute.
*   Case law interpreting a constitution or statute will prevail over inconsistent administrative regulations or cases dealing with common law.
*   Decisions of the highest appellate court are mandatory authority and bind those of the intermediate appellate court and the trial court.

- Decisions of the trial courts in any jurisdiction, state or federal, decide the dispute between the parties but are not binding on other courts. (They may be used as persuasive authority.)
- These principles on the hierarchy of authority and the weight of that authority apply to state and federal courts.
- A decision from United States Supreme Court is binding mandatory authority on all federal courts.
- A decision by the Supreme Court will bind state courts only on issues of federal law.
- A decision from a panel of one of the federal appellate courts, such as the Court of Appeals for the Ninth Circuit, is binding only on other appellate courts and the federal district courts in that circuit.

Primary vs. Secondary Authority

In legal research, there are two types of authority: "Primary" authority and "secondary" authority. Primary authority is the law. It includes state and federal constitutions, statutes, regulations promulgated by administrative agencies, court rules, and case law.

Secondary authority is writing about the law, but it is not law. It includes Restatements, treatises, law reviews, or scholarly articles. Secondary authority will often help you to locate primary authority. It can also help you to understand a particular legal theory or unfamiliar area of law. Attorneys and judges typically cite secondary authority if the area of law is undeveloped and little primary authority exists on the topic.

Practice Pointer

Digests, *American Law Reports*, legal encyclopedias, and legal dictionaries are not authority, but are good background reading. They are not written by legal scholars. Restatements are secondary authority. However, if the highest court in a jurisdiction adopts a section of a Restatement, as frequently occurs, it becomes primary authority for that jurisdiction.

Mandatory v. Persuasive Authority

Primary authority is either "mandatory," which must be followed in a particular jurisdiction, or "persuasive," which does not have to be followed in that jurisdiction. Secondary authority may only be persuasive.

Mandatory, primary authority includes constitutions, statutes, case law, court rules, and regulations from the governing jurisdiction. A court must apply mandatory, primary authority when resolving a dispute in that jurisdiction.

What is mandatory, primary authority in one jurisdiction is only persuasive primary authority in a different jurisdiction. Persuasive authority includes constitutions, statutes, case law, court rules, and regulations from another jurisdiction.

For example, in a landlord-tenant case involving an apartment in Boston, Massachusetts, Massachusetts law would control the outcome of the case. Therefore, mandatory primary authority in such a case would come from Massachusetts. Because Massachusetts does not have a statute on point, the controlling law is Massachusetts common law. Decisions of a state's highest court are binding on the lower courts in that state. To address the issue, you must first consider the decisions of the Massachusetts Supreme Court, the Commonwealth's highest court, taking note of the year of the decision. If an earlier case from the Massachusetts Supreme Court is inconsistent with a more recent case from that court, the more recent case will control the outcome. Look next to state intermediate appellate court decisions, which are binding on the lower trial courts but not on the Massachusetts Supreme Court.

If that same apartment were located in New York and the landlord had filed a claim in New York, then New York law would be mandatory authority and Massachusetts law persuasive. Your research would reveal that a statute addressing the implied warranty of habitability would control this issue. This enacted law would prevail over inconsistent New York common law. However, appellate decisions by the state's highest court, applying the statute and directly on point, would also be mandatory authority for the New York courts to follow. Similar decisions by the intermediate appellate court would have less weight, but would still control decisions of the lower courts. Statutes are often written broadly, with the expectation that the courts will decide how a provision applies to specific facts.

> **Make the Connection**
>
> In the earlier part of this chapter, you considered three cases: *Ingalls*, *Hemingway*, and *Lynch*. How would you rank these cases in terms of their hierarchy and weight of authority?

Food for Thought

Now consider *Doe v. New Bedford Housing Authority, 630 N.E.2d 248 (Mass 1994)*. What is the weight of this authority? What does this case add to your understanding of the Implied Warranty of Habitability in Massachusetts? How might you place it into a synthesis chart?

What rule emerges from this series of cases? Based on your understanding of the law of the Implied Warranty of Habitability, do you predict the law student in Cambridge, Massachusetts will be obligated to pay his rent?

Types and Weight of Authority in the Civil Law

The use of legal authority is quite different in civil law legal systems. The common law changes case by case, as courts interpret and apply it to new facts. In civil law jurisdictions, however, lawyers and judges apply legislation, or legal codes, as written. Any interpretation is done by legal scholars, not the courts. Articles by authoritative scholars are regarded as stronger legal authority than a judicial decision applying the statute in a particular instance would be. Judges and lawyers rely on such scholarly commentary to help them decide whether a statutory provision applies.[1]

Using the Hierarchy of Authority in a Legal Memorandum

An understanding of the hierarchy of authority will strengthen your legal analysis and writing. Consider the following example, which presents a contract dispute between a Belgian gourmet natural foods restaurant owner and a Pennsylvania farm selling "All Natural Artisanal Corn Tortillas." The restaurant owner and the farm entered into a contract for 20 cases of the tortillas. The restaurant owner believed that "all natural" would exclude "genetically modified food," but the parties never actually discussed the term. When the restaurant owner learned that the tortillas contained corn genetically modified for pest resistance, he wanted to sue for breach of contract in federal district court. The contract included a choice of law provision for disputes to be settled under Pennsylvania law.

---

1.   For an interesting discussion of this issue, *see* Vivian Curran, *Romantic Common Law, Enlightened Civil Law: Legal Uniformity and the Homogenization of the European Union,* 7 COLUM. J. EUR. L. 63 (2001).

The attorney for the restaurant owner identified the following sources:

International Org. Master, Mates and Pilots of Am., Local No. 2 v. International Org. Masters, Mates and Pilots of Am., Inc., 439 A.2d 621 (Pa. 1981)

Mellon Bank, N.A. v. Aetna Bus. Credit, Inc., 619 F.2d 1001 (3d Cir. 1980)

Bohler-Uddeholm Am., Inc. v. Ellwood Group, Inc., 247 F.3d 79 (3d Cir. 2001)

Steuart v. McChesney, 444 A.2d 659 (Pa. 1982)

THE AMERICAN HERITAGE DICTIONARY (2d ed. 1982) (defining "all natural")

Kripp v. Kripp, 849 A.2d 1159 (Pa. 2004)

A European *Union* Directive defining a "genetically modified organism," Council Directive 18/2001, art. 2(2), 2001 O.J. (L 106) (EC) and Council Directive 1829/2003, arts. 13(1)(a) & (1)(c), 2003 O.J. (L 268) (EC)

Practice Pointer

Notice how an attorney used these sources in Sample Memorandum (Chapter 6), discussing the use of extrinsic evidence to determine the intent of the parties. As you read this memo, consider the sources the writer uses, and the role each plays in the analysis.

First, consider the list of sources. What law controls the outcome of this dispute? Which sources are mandatory authority? Which are persuasive? Is any secondary authority included in the list of sources?

Putting It All Together

Try the following assignment: The plaintiffs are the Nolan family, a mother and a daughter, who claim they were injured on their international flight from Germany to New York. The Nolans, passengers on your client's aircraft, have sued your client, Augsburg Airways, under the Montreal Convention (formerly the Warsaw Convention) for the injuries to their health caused by the tainted sprouts in their onboard meal. The suit has been brought in a District Court for New York. Please explore whether the airline is liable for the Nolans' injuries by analyzing whether they can state a claim under Article 17 of the Montreal Convention. Please address all four elements under Article 17. Do not explore remedies or third party liability in this memo.

Click on the links to reveal the process:

☑ **Step 1**: Identify Relevant Statutory Law

☑ **Step 2**: Identify Relevant Case Law

☑ **Step 3**: Find Additional Relevant Case Law

☑ **Step 4**: Create a Synthesis Chart and Populate the Chart

Once a lawyer has completed the case law research and is certain that there are no other applicable cases, it is time to start filling in the Synthesis Chart.

Using the case summaries in Step 2, decide what you would put in each section. When you are finished, you can click on each case name to see what is included in this chart.

Saks	Price	Gezzi	Curley	McCaskey	Kwon	Girard	Husain
Accident (unexpected & unusual external event)							
On Board							
Caused							
Physical Harm							
Notes							
Authoritative							
Not Authoritative							

Courts are only bound by precedent from a higher court in their jurisdiction. A Court's own precedent is generally binding, but the Court has freedom to overrule it in any subsequent case. For this assignment the Nolans are bringing their case in New York district court. *Price* is a case from the Southern District of New York, therefore, the Court may find it authoritative or just overrule it. The case is dealing primarily with the element of "accident," clarifying that the event must have had a "relation to the aircraft's operation" in order to be an accident. This would be worth noting except for the fact that the case was not published. Unpublished cases are generally not authoritative on a court. Therefore, *Price* would not make any change to the elements from *Saks*. This entry into the synthesis chart will look like this:

The next case in the list is <u>*Gezzi*</u>. *Gezzi* provides an example for what is considered an external event for accident purposes. It also adds the requirement from *Price* that the accident must result from the aircraft's normal operations or during plaintiff's process of embarking or disembarking. However, the case comes from a circuit court in California, therefore, it is not authoritative for plaintiffs' case. Even though it is a higher court than a district one, it is not in the circuit of the New York court. An attorney may use it as persuasive authority if the facts he is arguing are similar enough, but the court in New York will not be bound by that decision. → <u>View Chart</u>

<u>*Curley*</u> is another case from the Southern District of New York that clarifies the meaning of "accident" from *Saks*. The Court states that an accident must deal with the "operations" of or "embarking or disembarking" from the aircraft. This would be a useful case for the Nolans, because serving food is arguably a part of the regular operations of an international flight. Therefore, plaintiffs' case would satisfy this element. *Curley* would be authoritative in this case, because it is from the jurisdiction of New York and was decided after *Saks*. However, since it is from the lowest court it can be easily overruled. → <u>View Chart</u>

<u>*McCaskey*</u> is a case that spells out the elements from *Saks* and also clarifies that the Montreal Convention provides the exclusive remedy for injuries caused during international air travel. *McCaskey* is a case from the lowest court in Texas; therefore, it is not binding on a New York court. This case can be used as a persuasive authority or as a way to show the elements from *Saks* clearly listed. → <u>View Chart</u>

<u>*Kwon*</u> clarifies that a carrier can claim the defense of reasonable conduct. Under that argument, a carrier is not liable for accidents if all reasonable measures have been taken to avoid it. *Kwon* could provide Augsburg Airways, in this case, with a clear defense to use against the Nolans' claim, because all reasonable measures had been taken in avoiding using tainted food on board. However, this case was decided in the lowest court of California and will not be binding on the New York court. This does not mean that the Nolans can simply ignore it, because the New York court is free to adopt this defense if it agrees with it. Plaintiffs should construct a good argument for why this decision should not be adopted by the New York court. → <u>View Chart</u>

<u>*Girard*</u> further clarifies the *Saks* and *Curley* requirements that an accident must be a part of the aircraft's normal and usual operations and not the wholly internal reaction of the plaintiff. Since the court found an accident in *Girard* it is a useful case for the Nolans to analogize with. It would be authoritative, because, like *Curley*, it is from a district court in New York. However, like *Price*, this case is unpublished, so a court will likely not give it much weight. → <u>View Chart</u>

In *Husain*, the U.S. Supreme Court finally decided another case under the Montreal Convention. There, the Court confirmed the requirements from *Saks* and *Curley* that the accident must be an unexpected and unusual external event to the plaintiffs and a part of the aircraft's ordinary operations. The plaintiffs in our assignment may be able to argue that serving food contaminated with E coli and having the flight attendant not warn the passengers is analogous to not changing the seats for the plaintiff in *Husain*. This case would be as authoritative as it gets, because it was decided by the U.S. Supreme Court with no cases afterward.
→ View Chart

☑ **Step 5**: View the Completed Synthesis Chart

☑ **Step 6**: Articulate the Rule

What If There Is No Precedent on Your Legal Issue?

If there is no precedent on point, and, no mandatory authority covers your legal question, then, you have a "gap" in the law. You must look to persuasive authority from other jurisdictions that have considered the same legal problem to fill the gap.

For example, if an appeal is in the Court of Appeals for the Sixth Circuit and there is no precedent on point, decisions by other federal courts of appeals may be persuasive. The same principle applies in state law: a deciding court may consider decisions from other states or federal courts applying similar legal rules on similar facts.

FYI

Sometimes a gap in the law is the result of a case of first impression in your jurisdiction.

FYI

When the Supreme Court of Illinois was faced with deciding whether an implied warranty of habitability applied to leases of residential real estate where no housing code had been enacted, there was no Illinois precedent on point. *Glasoe v. Trinkle*, 479 N.E.2d 915, 919 (Ill. 1985). However, the Pennsylvania Supreme Court had decided the same issue, and the Illinois court agreed with that reasoning. The Illinois court explained:

"In <u>*Pugh v. Holmes*, 405 A.2d 897, 906 (Pa. 1979),</u> the Supreme Court of Pennsylvania noted that there was no statewide housing code in that State and that many municipalities had not enacted local housing regulations. The court refused to hold that a breach of the implied warranty is dependent upon the proof of violations of housing codes. The court pointed out that the existence of housing code violations is only one of several evidentiary considerations that entered into the materiality of the breach, citing <u>*Bos. Hous. Auth. v. Hemingway* (1973), 363 Mass. 184, 293 N.E.2d 831,</u> <u>*Foisy v. Wyman* (1973), 83 Wash. 2d 22, 515 P.2d 160,</u> <u>*King v. Moorehead* (Mo. App. 1973), 495 S.W.2d 65,</u> and <u>*Mease v. Fox* (Iowa 1972), 200 N.W.2d 791.</u> Thus, we hold, as the Pennsylvania court held, that the absence of a statewide housing or building code in Illinois and the absence of such a code in St. Joseph does not preclude the application of the implied warranty of habitability to the property in question."

As this excerpt shows, the Illinois Supreme Court relied on a Pennsylvania Supreme Court case as persuasive authority to fill a gap in Illinois state law. Similarly, the Pennsylvania court reached its decision after considering and being persuaded by decisions from the appellate courts in Massachusetts, Washington, Missouri, and Iowa. Identifying the specific gap you must fill with persuasive authority from other jurisdictions is essential for readers who will rely on your analysis. Explaining what is left open in the legal rules in your jurisdiction will guide your research. It will also explain to the reader why you are not using mandatory legal authority.

——————————

Challenge Exercise: Using Cases to Fill a Gap in the Law

Our client, Argyle Manufacturing, wants to sue the Republic of Kotor for breach of contract. Under the contract, Argyle would construct, deliver and install 10 oilrigs for a price of $180 million. Argyle has constructed the oilrigs and is ready to install them, but Kotor has cancelled the agreement.

Suit could be properly filed in the U.S. District Court for the District of Delaware. However, we are concerned that Kotor will be immune from suit in the U.S. courts under the Foreign Sovereign Immunities Act ("FSIA").

Under the FSIA, a foreign state has immunity from suit unless an exception to immunity applies. You have been asked to research the narrow question of whether Kotor's act of cancelling the contract is a "commercial activity" under the FSIA. If so, then the suit will go forward. If not, then the Republic of Kotor has immunity and cannot be sued in the U.S. courts.

Delaware is in the Third Circuit, a jurisdiction which has not decided this question. Your research has led you to the following cases, which all apply the commercial activities exception to sovereign immunity. Assume that each of these case summaries is an accurate statement of the current law.

Republic of Argentina v. Weltover, 504 U.S. 607 (1992)

Bond holders brought a breach of contract action against the Republic of Argentina and its central bank arising out of Argentina's unilateral extension of the time for payment on the bonds issued as part of a currency stabilization plan. Argentina defaulted on its payment agreement, and Weltover suffered financial loss.

Argentina asserted sovereign immunity under the FSIA, which provides "[T]he commercial character of an activity shall be determined by reference to the nature of the act, rather than by reference to its purpose." 28 U.S.C. § 1603(d).

The Supreme Court held that an activity of a sovereign is commercial if it is the type of action by which a private party engages in trade and traffic and commerce. Issuing bonds was analogous to a private commercial transaction, because the bonds were negotiable and could be traded on the open market. Argentina's purpose, to stabilize its currency, was irrelevant. Only the nature of the transaction was important, and this was a transaction that a private party could carry out. Argentina did not have sovereign immunity and could be sued in the U.S. courts.

Texas Trading v. Federal Republic of Nigeria, 647 F.2d 300 (2d Cir. 1981)

"When a foreign government acts, not as a regulator of a market, but in the manner of a private player within it, the foreign sovereign's acts are commercial within the meaning of the FSIA." The court analyzed 28 U.S.C. § 1603(d) and concluded that Nigeria's breach of a contract for the sale of cement was a commercial activity because it was the sort of contract a private party could enter into. Thus Nigeria did not have sovereign immunity and could be sued in the U.S. courts.

MOL, Inc. v. People's Republic of Bangladesh, 736 F.2d 1326 (9th Cir. 1984)

Bangladesh revoked a license granted to MOL to capture and export rhesus monkeys. The court held that this was a license designed to regulate the country's national resources, and that revoking it was thus an act that only a sovereign could undertake. Under 28 U.S.C. § 1603(d), this was not commercial activity and the company could not sue Bangladesh in the U.S. courts.

S & Davis Int'l, Inc. v. Republic of Yemen, 218 F.3d 1292 (11th Cir. 2000)

The court held that the Government of Yemen engaged in commercial activity under the FSIA when it entered into a contract to purchase grain from an American corporation because the contract was "just a contract and ... not based upon regulatory reasons." Thus Yemen could be sued for breach of that contract in the U.S. courts.

Beg v. Islamic Republic of Pakistan, 353 F.3d 1323 (11th Cir. 2003)

Beg sued the Islamic Republic of Pakistan for allegedly expropriating his property without compensation. Beg alleged that he owned eleven and one-half acres in the Punjab region of Pakistan valued at $10 million, which were expropriated from him by the Pakistani government. The property was then used for military housing or otherwise transferred to members of the military.

The court emphasized that "the touchstone for determining if a foreign government's act is commercial is whether the *nature* of the act is public or private." The court concluded that the Pakistani government's actions involved the power of eminent domain and, therefore, were not commercial because eminent domain is a sovereign act. The *nature* of the foreign government's act was public and not commercial. Pakistan was immune from suit under the FSIA.

Now that you are familiar with the state of the law, ask yourself these questions:

Are you in state court or federal court?

What jurisdiction controls your legal question? Is there any mandatory authority?

Does mandatory authority decide your issue? Is there a gap in the law? Why or why not?

Now that you have identified the gap in the law that must be filled by persuasive authority from other federal courts of appeals, review your case summaries and construct a synthesis chart. The following chart organizes the relevant cases around the elements of the legal test. For each case applying the FSIA, you'll see the important categories of information: the specific activity that was the basis of the claim, whether the nature of the act

Food for Thought

You are in federal court, and your jurisdiction is the Court of Appeals for the Third Circuit. *Republic of Argentina v. Weltover*, a United States Supreme Court case, is mandatory authority. In *Weltover*, the Supreme Court sets out the rule, but does not apply it to facts like ours. *Weltover* tells us that courts must focus on the nature of the activity, and ask whether the transaction is one that a private party could perform. However, we must look to other jurisdictions to see whether Kotor's breach of its contract to purchase oilrigs is likely to be considered commercial activity under the FSIA or not.

was public or private, whether the court found the act was commercial activity or not, and whether there was sovereign immunity under the FSIA.

Case	Act	Nature:Public/ Private	C/Activity
Republic of Argentina v. Weltover, Inc., 504 U.S. 607 (1992).	Issuing bonds	Private party could issue bonds	Yes, no SI
Texas Trading v. Federal Republic of Nigeria, 647 F.2d 300, 304 (2d Cir. 1981).	Nigeria's breach of a contract for the sale of cement	Private party could enter into this contract	Yes, no SI
MOL, Inc., v. People's Republic of Bangladesh, 736 F.2d 1326 (9th Cir. 1984).	Bangladesh revoked a license granted to MOL to capture and export rhesus monkeys	Public; only a sovereign can control natural resources	Not CA, so SI

Case	Act	Nature:Public/ Private	C/Activity
S & Davis Int'l, Inc. v. Republic of Yemen, 218 F.3d 1292 (11th Cir. 2000).	Breach of contract to purchase grain from an American corporation	Private; "just a contract and … not based upon regulatory reasons."	CA, so no SI
Beg v. Islamic Republic of Pakistan, 353 F.3d 1323 (11th Cir. 2003).	Allegedly expropriating property without compensation	Public; eminent domain is a sovereign power	Not CA, so SI
Our case?	Breach of contract for sale of oil rigs	Similar to *Davis & Texas Trading*; private party could enter this contract for the sale of goods	Likely CA, so no SI

Looking at these cases you can predict that the Court of Appeals for the Third Circuit will decide that Kotor's breach of contract for the sale of oil rigs to Argyle Manufacturing is a commercial activity under the FSIA. This is in accordance with decisions of the other courts that have applied the commercial activity exception to similar facts. Courts have held that a contract for goods, whether the purchase of grain or cement, is an act that a private party could enter into and qualifies as a commercial activity. By analyzing what other courts of appeals have done, you are able to fill the gap in the law of the Third Circuit.

In this chapter, you have learned about types of legal authority. You have also applied a rule, synthesized a rule from multiple authorities, and learned to evaluate the strength of legal authority. Now, you will use these skills to draft an objective memorandum.

————

CHAPTER 6

Legal Memoranda

I. Analyzing the Text

In this chapter, you will learn how to draft a legal memorandum. To begin this process, study the two legal memoranda below. As you read these documents, consider who wrote each document and why? Also, consider the problem the author addressed and the solution he or she proposed. Try to summarize the main idea expressed in each memorandum in one sentence. Next, re-examine the organization of the documents and the language the authors used to express his or her ideas. Finally, consider your reaction to each memorandum: do you think it is effective? Why or why not?

> **FYI**
>
> When using sample texts as a model for your own writing, you may find it helpful to consider the following questions:
> - Audience: For whom was this text written? (Consider what definitions, rewording, and examples the writer used.)
> - Purpose: Why is the writer writing this text, and how does it influence the writing style?
> - Organization: How is the text arranged? (Is it a familiar pattern: general-specific; problem-solution; cause-effect, chronological?)
> - Style: What language does the writer use? (Formal/informal? First person? Active/Passive verbs? Verb tense? Outside sources?)
> - Flow: How does the writer connect one idea to another, one paragraph to another, or one sentence to another?

MEMORANDUM (Sample 1)[1]

To: Supervising Attorney
From: Junior Associate
Date: September 12
Re: Aggravated Assault Case

Issue

Can the court infer that Mrs. Bennett attempted to cause serious bodily harm to Mr. Darcy from Mrs. Bennett's throwing of a hammer at Mr. Darcy's head, and thus, charge Mrs. Bennett with aggravated assault under 18 Pa. Cons. Stat. § 2702(a)(1) (2008)?

Brief Answer

The court will be likely to uphold a charge of aggravated assault against Mrs. Bennett, because the act of aiming her attack at the victim's head indicates her intent to harm, and the weapon-like nature of the implement that she used suggests that she intended serious bodily injury.

Facts

Mr. Darcy moved into Pittsburgh's Bellevue neighborhood in January of 2009, with his wife and Lulu his dog. Mr. Darcy's backyard adjoined Mrs. Bennett's, with thirty feet between the houses and a short hedge separating the two backyards. Mrs. Bennett, the assailant in this case, is a sixty-two year old, 124-pound active and very fit woman. Within a month, Mr. Darcy began to have trouble with Mrs. Bennett. By March, she had filed five complaints with the police about Lulu. Mrs. Bennett also filed two police reports in July about the backyard parties that the Darcy's began hosting in May, complaining about the noise level and the garbage that she found in her yard after the parties.

The event surrounding our client's cause of action occurred on August 14, 2009, at about 7:00 p.m. While Mr. and Mrs. Darcy were hosting a backyard party. Mrs. Bennett was using a hammer on her back porch. Mrs. Bennett noticed some garbage from the party in her yard, and she approached Mr. Darcy. Mr. Darcy asked what she wanted, to which Mrs. Bennett replied by gesturing angrily to the garbage with her hammer, demanding that he clean it up. A shouting match ensued during which both parties insulted and swore at each other. Mrs. Bennett returned to her porch, still yelling insults. Mr. Darcy stated that neither party had threatened the other, that he had not acted threateningly, and that he had remained in his yard.

---

1.   Parties' names were taken from Pride and Prejudice by Jane Austen, with apologies to Miss Austen.

At approximately 7:05 p.m., Mr. Darcy called Mrs. Bennett "an impossible neighbor." Mrs. Bennett, extremely infuriated by Mr. Darcy's words, threw the hammer that was still in her hand at Mr. Darcy, missing his left ear by only an inch. Mrs. Bennett immediately sat down, seeming shocked at her behavior. Mr. Darcy heard Mrs. Bennett tell police about this shock, as well as her belief that Mr. Darcy was too far away to be hit by the hammer.

Discussion

The court will find Mrs. Bennett guilty of aggravated assault because she aimed and threw a hammer at Mr. Darcy's head. A person is guilty of aggravated assault where no serious bodily injury occurs, if he or she "attempts to cause serious bodily injury to another ...." 18 Pa. Cons. Stat. § 2702(a)(1) (2008). A person has attempted to cause serious bodily injury if "with intent to commit a specific crime, he [or she] does any act which constituted as substantial step toward the commission of that crime." 18 Pa. Cons. Stat § 901 (2009). In other words, a person acts with intent when "it is his conscious object to engage in conduct of that nature or to cause such a result." 180 Pa. Cons. Stat § 302 (2009).

A defendant commits an attempt in terms of aggravated assault when, with the conscious object to cause serious bodily injury, the defendant acts in a manner that constitutes a substantial step toward inflicting such injury. *Commonwealth v. Rosado*, 684 A.2d 605, 608 (Pa. Super. Ct. 1996). For example, in *Rosado*, the defendant fired shots into the second story lit window where the victims slept. *Id.* at 606. Similarly, in *Commonwealth v. Lopez*, Lopez fired eight shots into the front door of his ex-girlfriend's residence. 654 A.2d 1150, 1152 (Pa. Super. Ct. 1995). Although neither defendant injured anyone, the court held in both cases that the defendants "attempted to cause another person to suffered serious injuries." *Id.* at 1155; *Rosado*, 684 A.2d at 609.

For purposes of this memorandum, we will assume that throwing a hammer would satisfy the "substantial step" aspect of an attempt if Mrs. Bennett had the requisite intent. Thus, the two elements in dispute are (I) whether there was intent to cause harm and (II) whether the harm intended was "serious bodily injury."

I. Intent to Cause Harm: Circumstantial Evidence of Mrs. Bennett's Intent to Cause Serious Bodily Harm

Mrs. Bennett demonstrated the intent to cause serious bodily harm when she threw a hammer with sufficient precision and force to narrowly miss her neighbor's head. To constitute an attempt, the defendant must act with intent, that is, with the "conscious object to engage in conduct of that nature or to cause such a result." *Commonwealth v. Matthews*, 870 A.2d 924, 929 (Pa. Super. Ct. 2005). Intent is a subjective element and is therefore difficult to establish. *Id.* The court thus allows the Commonwealth to prove intent "by direct or circumstantial evidence" and to infer it "from acts or conduct or from the attendant circumstances." *Id.*

The court has inferred intent from a variety of circumstances. In the cases of *Lopez* and *Rosado*, the court established the defendants' intent with the acts such as firing a deadly weapon. In *Lopez*, the defendant's acts of firing into a residence that he believed to be occupied constituted a major factor in the court's ultimate finding of his intent to harm. 654 A.2d at 1155. Likewise, in *Rosado*, the court inferred intent to harm from the defendant's act of shooting into a building at only lit windows. Since Rosado shot into a residence with lit windows, the fact finder could infer that the defendant knew the residence to be inhabited and "intended to cause serious bodily injury upon both victims, which would be a natural and probably consequence of [the] defendant's act of shooting at the victims' bedroom windows." 684 A.2d at 609.

In this case, as in *Rosado* and *Lopez*, Mrs. Bennett directed her projectile toward the location of the victim. Mrs. Bennett's act of throwing the hammer at Mr. Darcy suggests her intent to harm him. The fact finder can infer that Mrs. Bennett intended the "natural and probably consequence" of throwing a hammer at Mr. Darcy's head, which would cause harm to Mr. Darcy.

Mrs. Bennett's defense may attempt to distinguish her case from those of *Rosado* and *Lopez*, arguing that Mrs. Bennett could not have intended the consequences of throwing a hammer to the same degree that the defendants in *Rosado* and *Lopez* intended the consequences of shooting a gun. The distance and instrument suggests recklessness, but not intent. Additionally, they may liken Mrs. Bennett's actions to cases involving defendants who delivered a single blow to the head with their fist. *Commonwealth v. Alexander*, 383 A.2d 887, 888 (Pa. 1978); *Commonwealth v. Roche*, 783 A.2d 766, 767 (Pa. Super. Ct. 2001). The court vacated the charges of aggravated assault in *Alexander* and *Roche* because the State failed to establish the defendants' specific intent to commit serious bodily injury. The court did, however, find a specific intent to harm. The difference between harm and serious bodily injury in these cases will be addressed in the following section.

II. Causation of Serious Bodily Injury: Mrs. Bennett Intended to Inflict Serious Bodily Injury

Mrs. Bennett risked causing permanent injury to Mr. Darcy by throwing the hammer at Darcy's head. Serious bodily injury is "bodily injury which creates a substantial risk of death or which causes serious, permanent disfigurement, or protracted loss or impairment of the function of any bodily member or organ." 18 Pa. Cons. Stat. § 2301 (2008). Where there is no actual serious bodily injury, the court infers a person's intent to inflict such harm from the circumstances surrounding the attack, especially the use or lack of weapons. *Matthews*, 870 A.2d at 933. A deadly weapon is "any firearm ... or any other device or instrumentality which, in the manner in which it is used or intended to be used, is calculated to produce death or serious bodily injury." *Id.*

The court often finds the requisite intent to inflict serious bodily injury when the defendant uses a weapon for his or her attack. The court upheld a charge of aggravated assault in *Matthews*, where the defendant held his victim at gunpoint, threatened his victim, and released him only when a third party intervened. 870 A.2d at 933. The court in *Rosado* states that discharging a weapon into an occupied structure is enough to demonstrate intent for aggravated assault. 684 A.2d at 610.

The statements of courts in cases where the defendant attacks with his or her fist show the importance of the use of weapons for inferring the defendant's intent. The court in *Alexander* vacated the charge of aggravated assault, because it lacked circumstantial evidence such as the aggressor's greater size, the intervention of a third party, the use of a weapon or "implement," or statements indicating intent. 383 A.2d at 889. The court in *Roche* also vacated the charge of aggravated assault stating, "[m]oreover, and importantly, Appellant did not possess or use a weapon or other instrumentality of harm at any time before or during this attack." 783 A.2d at 771.

Mrs. Bennett's uses of any "implement" to aid her attack plays a major role in establishing the level of harm she intended. While a claw hammer is not a firearm, it could be considered an "implement" aiding an attack, or an "instrumentality of harm." Mrs. Bennett's choice to use such an instrument in her attack distinguishes her act from the "one punch" cases *Alexander* and *Roche*. Mrs. Bennett did not attempt to deliver one blow with her fist. Rather, she threw a claw hammer, an instrument that could have caused much greater injury to Mr. Darcy. One can infer, as the courts probably will, that the "natural and proximate" result of throwing a claw hammer at a victim's head is the causation of serious bodily injury to the victim.

The lack of any of the other circumstances that the courts use to determine the intent of the defendant could seem problematic. The defense could point to Mrs. Bennett's failure to follow through with her attack despite ample opportunity, and the lack of specific threats directed at Mr. Darcy. However, the *Matthews* court overturned the *Mayo* court by stating specifically that the Commonwealth can establish a defendant's intent to commit serious bodily injury, even if the defendant failed to take advantage of opportunity to continue the attack and inflict such injury. *Matthews*, 870 A.2d at 932. Further, in cases in which a defendant used a weapon, the lack of threats directed at the victim did not affect the court's ability to infer the defendant's intent.

Conclusion

The court will probably uphold a charge of aggravated assault against Mrs. Bennett because she consciously directed her attack at Mr. Darcy's head, indicating her intent to harm, and she used an implement or "instrumentality of harm," suggesting her intent to inflict serious bodily injury.

Respectfully Submitted,

Signature of Junior Associate

Junior Associate

Practice Pointer

Consider how the focus of a memo might change as the client changes. The author of Memorandum (Sample 2), who represents Mrs. Bennett, gives greater consideration to Bennett's perspective. However, as Bennett's attorney, the author must still consider the arguments Mr. Darcy's attorney might raise in order to prepare a proper defense for Mrs. Bennett. Read Sample 2, and consider how well these authors were able to anticipate the other side's analysis.

MEMORANDUM (Sample 2)

To: Senior Associate
From: Junior Associate #2
Date: October 1
Re: Bennett Aggravated Assault

Issue

Did Mrs. Bennett possess the intent sufficient to establish a prima facie case of aggravated assault under 18 Pa. Cons. Stat. § 2702 where she threw a hammer at Mr. Darcy, where Darcy did not suffer injury, and where Bennett claims she did not wish to harm Darcy?

Brief Answer

Probably not; Bennett possessed the intent to commit aggravated assault if it were her conscious object to throw the hammer at Darcy or to seriously injure Darcy. Bennett admits that she did not intend to cause harm. Bennett did not make any statements before, during, or after the attack indicting intent to injure. Bennett neither anticipated nor intended using the hammer as a weapon. Bennett did not escalate or continue the attack after throwing the hammer. This direct and circumstantial evidence does not prove the element of intent beyond a reasonable doubt.

Facts

Mrs. Bennett is a sixty-two year old Pittsburgh resident who has lived in the same house in Bellevue for thirty-four years. Eight months ago, the Darcy family moved to a house with a back yard adjacent to Bennett's. Since that time, Bennett has encountered numerous problems with the Darcys. The Darcy's dog defecates in Bennett's yard, and the dog's barking often wakes Bennett up early in the morning. Moreover, the Darcys host loud parties several times each month. The parties often keep Bennett awake until 4 AM. The attendees at these parties leave their empty beer cans and trash in Bennett's yard. Bennett has confronted the Darcys numerous times to address these concerns. Bennett also called the police twice in July and once in August to address her noise and trash concerns. Despite these police interventions, the Darcys continue to host weekend parties, and the attendees continue to use Bennett's yard as a dumpster.

On the night of August 14th, the Darcys were hosting one of their frequent gatherings. Around 7 PM that evening, Bennett was working on a home improvement project on her back porch. The porch is fifteen feet from the boundary between Bennett's yard and the Darcy's yard and thirty feet from the Darcy's porch. By that time, Bennett's yard was already littered with trash. Bennett walked to the Darcy's backyard to speak to the Darcys about the trash on her property. When Bennett arrived at the Darcy's yard, the Darcys immediately began yelling in an abusive and obscene manner. Bennett denied the accusations made by the Darcys, but she did not verbally or physically threaten the Darcys. Convinced that the Darcys would not be receptive to her concerns, Bennett turned around and began walking back towards her porch. As Bennett walked away, the Darcys continued to hurl insults. Bennett abruptly and spontaneously turned around and threw the hammer she had been using for her porch project at Mr. Darcy. The hammer flew by Darcy's head, missing Darcy's left ear by an inch. Darcy sustained no physical injury. At the time of the incident, Bennett was still in the Darcy's yard. Bennett cannot recall her distance relative to Darcy at the time Bennett threw the hammer.

After the incident, Bennett returned to her porch and sat in a state of shock. The time between the initial confrontation and the alleged assault was five minutes. Mr. Darcy called the police who arrived shortly thereafter and arrested Bennett. Darcy and Bennett did not engage in any further interaction after the incident. Bennett claims that she did not take the hammer to the Darcy's yard with the intention of using it as a weapon. She further claims that she had no intention of harming Darcy. Bennett is older, smaller, and frailer than Darcy. Bennett characterizes her actions as the result of an instinctive and spontaneous fit of emotion.

Discussion

The court will not find Mrs. Bennett guilty of aggravated assault because she lacked the necessary intent. A person is guilty of aggravated assault if s/he "attempts to cause serious bodily injury to another or causes such injury intentionally, knowingly, or recklessly under circumstances manifesting an extreme indifference to human life." 18 Pa. Cons. Stat. § 2702(a)(1) (2008). Serious bodily injury is defined as "bodily injury, which creates a substantial risk of death or which causes serious, permanent disfigurement, or protracted loss or impairment of the function of any bodily member or organ." 18 Pa. Cons. Stat. § 901 (2009).

I. Intent to Inflict Serious Bodily Injury

Mrs. Bennett did not possess the intent to inflict serious bodily injury upon Darcy. "A person acts intentionally with respect to a material element of an offense when, if the element involves the nature of his conduct or a result thereof, it is his conscious object to engage in conduct of that nature or to cause such a result." 18 Cons. Stat. § 302(b)(1)(I) (2009). Intent can be proven by direct or circumstantial evidence; intent may be inferred from the defendant's conduct or words or from the attendant circumstances. *Commonwealth v. Matthews*, 870 A.2d 924, 929 (Pa. Super. Ct. 2005). In *Matthews*, the defendant detained the victim by placing a revolver against the victim's throat, repeatedly threatened to kill the victim, and continued to point the revolver at the victim until the defendant fled the scene when a third party arrived. *Id.* at 926-933. The Court ruled that the defendant's use of a weapon to detain the victim, coupled with his repeated threats to kill the victim, constituted sufficient evidence for an inference of intent to commit aggravated assault. *Id.* at 931.

In *Commonwealth v. Alexander*, the Court applied a similar totality of the circumstances test in holding that a single, closed-fist punch to the head that did not result in serious bodily injury was insufficient to support a conviction of aggravated assault. 383 A.2d 887 (Pa. 1978). In *Alexander*, the defendant walked up to any unsuspecting victim on a street corner, delivered a single blow to the victim's face (resulting in a minor nose injury), and then walked away. *Id.* at 887. The only evidence of the defendant's intent was his own testimony that he did not intend to seriously injure the victim. *Id.* The defendant made no statement before, during or after the attack, which indicated an intent to cause harm. *Id.* He did not continue or escalate his attack after delivering the lone blow. *Id.* Accordingly, the Court held that the circumstantial evidence did not sufficiently prove that the defendant intended to inflict serious injury. *Id.*

In *Commonwealth v. Rosado*, the Court upheld a conviction of aggravated assault where the defendant fired bullets into the lit rooms of a person's home in the belief that the structure was not actually used as a residence. 684 A.2d 605, 609 (Pa. Super. Ct. 1996). Mr. Rosado's use of a weapon distinguishes *Rosado* from *Alexander*. The defendant, hired by an enemy of the victim, used a semi-automatic firearm to shoot at the windows of the lighted rooms in the victim's property. *Id.* at 608. Although the incident did not result in any injuries, the Court held that the possibility that the bullets might injure a person in the home constituted sufficient evidence supporting an inference of intent. *Id.* at 609.

In this case, Bennett's claim that she did not intend to harm Darcy is the only direct evidence of intent. As in *Alexander*, the circumstances surrounding the incident do not support a finding that Bennett possessed the intent to inflict serious bodily injury. Bennett is significantly older and smaller than Darcy. Bennett did not continue or escalate her attack upon Darcy after she threw the hammer. Bennett made no statement before, during, or after the attack that indicated any intent to harm Darcy. After the incident, Bennett walked back to her porch and sat there until the police arrived. Similar contextual considerations supported the Court's finding in Alexander that the defendant did not intend to inflict serious injury.

The prosecution will probably argue that, similar to *Matthews* and *Rosado*, Bennett's intent to cause harm may be inferred from her use of a weapon that has a high probability of inflicting serious injury. Unlike the firearms used as weapons in *Matthews* and *Rosado*, the primary purpose of a hammer is not to injure, destroy, or damage. Unlike Mr. Rosado, Bennett did not take the hammer to the victim's property in anticipation of using it as a weapon. She did not deliberate over using the hammer as a weapon before throwing it. Unlike Mr. Matthews, Bennett did not use the hammer as a source of intimidation and apprehension. Moreover, Bennett made no threat to kill Darcy with the hammer. Finally, Bennett did not require a third-party to intervene before ending the attack. Based on the holdings in *Rosado* and *Matthews*, Mrs. Bennett's actions do not warrant a conviction of aggravated assault.

Conclusion

Bennett likely did not harbor the intent to commit aggravated assault under 18 Pa. Cons. Stat. § 2702. Bennett did not verbally or physically respond to Darcy in a manner indicating intent to inflict injury. Bennett did not take the hammer to the Darcy's yard in anticipation of using the hammer as a weapon. She did not deliberate over using the hammer as a weapon before hurling the hammer. Bennett did not continue to attack Darcy after throwing the hammer. In short, it was not Bennett's conscious object to throw the hammer or to inflict injury, and the attendant circumstances do not support an inference of intent.

Respectfully Submitted,

Signature of Junior Associate

Junior Associate

Exercise: Summarizing a Memorandum

Read and summarize one of the two sample memoranda above. Although memos are research papers and often are a type of problem-solution paper, note the typical organizational structure of the legal memo contains a header, an issue statement/question presented, a brief answer, a factual summary, a discussion section, a conclusion, and a closing signature. In your summary paper, please summarize the problem and proposed solution discussed in the memo. Include a summary of any potential counter-arguments addressed in the memo. Finally, complete your summary with your critical analysis of this memo; this analysis should capture your thoughts, ideas, reactions, or questions about the memo. This is an important section; devote an ample amount of space to this evaluation. The summary should be **no more than 300 words**. Please include a word count at the bottom of your summary.

Take Note

As you review this sample memo, practice the summarizing skills below. This exercise will help you look closely at the structure and text of the document and will help you to learn from actual documents and think critically about the form of the document as well as the content.

Practicing Your Summarizing Skills

Step 1: Find "The Point":

Goal: Understand the writer's purpose

Survey the document. Examine the title, any headings, illustrations, or any information about the author that may help you focus your reading.

Consider subheadings. When reading, think about how to divide the text into subheadings or consider the subheadings already established by the writer.

Identify the organization. Think about the type or organizational structure of the text to help you identify the important information. (Consider, for example, if the text follows a typical form of legal writing such as a judicial opinion, legal memorandum, appellate brief, problem-solution law review article.)

Summarize the main point(s). After you're finished reading, write down a one sentence summary of the main point of the whole, or of each section, in your own words.

Step 2: Find the Key Details that Support "The Point":

Goal: Select more important information and delete less important material

Identify and underline important information. Once you clearly understand the writer's main point (or purpose) for writing, read the memo again. This time, underline the most important information supporting the point: this may include topic or thesis sentences, findings, conclusions and recommendations. Often, these should be words or phrases rather than complete sentences.

- In addition, underline key transitional elements that show how parts are connected.

- Omit specific details, examples, description, and unnecessary explanations.

Step 3: Write, Revise, and Edit to Ensure Accuracy, Completeness, Readability and Conciseness:

Writing Stage: Begin with the main idea and proceed to cover the major supporting points in the same sequence as the original text

- **Paraphrase and synthesize the main points.** Start with a sentence naming the source (*i.e.*, the author or case name or the fact that you are reviewing a particular document) and stating the text's main idea. Then write your summary, using the most important information and striving for overall coherence through appropriate transitions.

- **Be objective when summarizing the author's point.** Do **not** insert your own opinions or thoughts; instead summarize what the writer has to say about the subject. But keep in mind that reading is a matter of interpretation. Read with a purpose to enhance your understanding of the text. Take an active role in reading and develop for yourself an understanding of what the text means. Be sure to state that you are summarizing someone else's work.

Revision Stage: Include all important ideas.

- **Check for accuracy.**
    - Have you omitted anything important or added ideas?
    - Does your summary read smoothly with all parts clearly related?
    - Can your audience understand the main point of the text by reading your summary? (Can it "stand alone"?)
- **Strive to be concise.** A summary should generally be no more than one-third the length of the original. If your summary is too long, cut out words rather than ideas. Then look for non-essential information and delete it. Refer to PLAIN ENGLISH FOR LAWYERS by Richard Wydick or STYLE: LESSONS IN CLARITY AND GRACE by Joseph M. Williams for more specific instructions on simplifying language.

Editing Stage: Correct grammar, spelling, and punctuation errors, looking particularly for those errors common in your writing.

Step 4: Using a Summary As Part of a Critical Analysis:

When summarizing a source as part of a critical analysis, as you will do for this second paper, make sure that your evaluation of the author's work or of the source is well substantiated. In other words, provide support for your opinion. Give examples of features you found to be particularly strong or weak.

———————

II. Drafting a Legal Memorandum

Legal memoranda are written summaries of research results. They often explore potential solutions to a problem and, therefore, have elements in common with other types of problem-solution papers with which you may already be familiar. However, legal memoranda adhere to a particular organizational structure that might be unfamiliar to you. This structure usually includes the following sections or categories of information: 1) a header; 2) an issue statement, sometimes referred to as the question presented; 3) a brief answer; 4) a factual summary; 5) a discussion section; 6) a conclusion or recommendation; and 7) a closing and signature. Although lawyers may vary the order or label the categories in slightly different ways depending on the circumstances, most attorneys will recognize these categories and using these in your memorandum will make it easier for a legally trained reader to follow your document. The following section will consider these categories in greater depth; you will also examine what comprises an effective memorandum, and how you might go about writing a memorandum.

A. Effective Legal Memoranda

A legal memorandum should present an objective analysis of your research findings including the relevant law, legal problem, and the particular facts of your client's case. Memoranda are often predictive in that they consider the likelihood of success and the potential outcomes should a case advance to trial. In this respect, memoranda are strategic planning documents. However, while a memorandum may deal with strategy or anticipate advocacy on behalf of a client, a good memorandum will also openly acknowledge the shortcomings of a client's case and recommend ways of addressing those shortcomings as well as identifying ways to exploit the strengths of the case. In other words, a memorandum should be "objective" in the sense that it should consider both the strengths and weaknesses of a client's case and of a possible course of action. It should be a "balanced" assessment of the situation and how to address it, rather than an argument on behalf of your client. You should not persuade your reader that your client should "win." You should only persuade your reader that you have thoroughly researched the issue and have accurately evaluated the situation.

Take Note

Keep in Mind These Features of an Effective Memo. The Memo:

1. Objectively evaluates the strengths and weakness of a client's claims and defenses.
2. Presents a balanced analysis of the dispute.
3. Anticipates advocacy on behalf of the client.
4. Discusses potential outcomes or solutions.
5. Recommends means of overcoming the weaknesses in the client's case.
6. Identifies ways to exploit the strengths of the client's case.

B. Preparing to Write the Memorandum

To write a memorandum, consider the following general points:

1. Who Is the Audience?

Memoranda are "in house" documents that are written to the lawyers involved with a legal issue or case. Typically, the audience will be an employer or supervisor or an attorney who assigned the research. Legal memoranda are almost always written for legally trained readers and are not usually read by a layperson. There may also be a secondary audience, for example a lawyer who uses the memo in the future or another law firm. The legal audience will often be very busy and very skeptical so they will want to read quickly and will have to be convinced of the accuracy of your work. Therefore, you should organize carefully, use plain English,[2] and substantiate your ideas.

2. What Is the Purpose?

A memorandum provides a written explanation of research results and recommends a course of action based on the drafter's analysis of these results. It provides information so that decision-makers can evaluate or select a course of action. Most immediately, the person who requested that you do the research, a supervising attorney, for example, will read the memo. Additionally, by capturing your results in writing, the memorandum becomes a permanent record. The research can then be used in the future as the basis of a client letter or to write a brief to a court. Attorneys encountering similar issues may also use the memo. Many law firms will maintain memoranda to serve as models or templates.

Make the Connection

The skills you practiced in section I of this chapter can be applied to work with law firm models or templates as well as law school samples.

Even when your supervising attorney has not specifically requested that you put your research in writing, you may also want to write a memorandum just as a way to organize your ideas.

The memorandum articulates research results. Usually the author of the memorandum is researching potential solutions to a legal problem. The author should strive to be objective or "neutral" in his or her research, analysis, and writing of the memorandum. The memorandum should predict the likely outcome of a legal dispute should the problem be resolved through a trial. Memoranda are planning documents and often discuss strategy, whether pre-litigation, trial, or settlement strategy.

The memorandum should be a balanced analysis of the dispute. To achieve this balance, the author will need to consider the situation from multiple perspectives and present these perspectives. In other words, the author should consider both the strengths and weaknesses of the client's case. Particularly when the memorandum is used in developing a problem solving strategy, the goal of the memorandum is to anticipate consequences of certain courses of action and to eliminate surprises or unexpected turns of events to the extent possible. In this sense, the memorandum should present an honest assessment of the case. The author must be careful not to fool him or herself, the boss, or the judge by biasing the results of the research in favor of his or her client.

---

2.   *See* RICHARD WYDICK, PLAIN ENGLISH FOR LAWYERS.

3. What About the Style?

Legal memoranda also share some common features of style. These stylistic features concern the way the document is written in terms of organization of the overall document, placement of paragraphs, construction of sentences, and choice of words. The legal community is busy; readers may be very interested or not interested at all in the case, but they will want to read the memo quickly so they are looking for a style that promotes effi-

Major Themes

A memo provides:

Written explanation;

Research results;

Predictions;

Balanced analysis of the dispute;

Honest assessment of the case.

ciency. Many law firms have a set style or format they require for memos. This is to promote efficiency. Readers will know where to find information within the document. The author may, therefore, be limited creatively in terms of the form of the memo, but creativity will emerge in the content and legal analysis and in the author's ability to pose a solution to a problem.

Readers may not be experts on the topic, but will likely be legally trained. Readers will probably be skeptical or critical. The author should write in anticipation of this critical analysis, providing clear evidence for his or her conclusions. The reasoning structure within the memorandum is representative of the way lawyers have been trained to reason from legal authority. The author of the memorandum should offer proof that the analysis is accurate. The readers may have given the author the research assignment so they did not have to do the research. As a result, the author should not assume too much knowledge on the part of the readers—they may not know details of the particular law so details and concrete examples illustrating the law will be very helpful.

Take Note!

Do not assume too much knowledge on the part of your reader. Your reader is probably legally trained, but will not be as familiar with the issue as you are. You likely received this assignment so that your reader did not have to do the research and synthesis. In the process of writing the memorandum, you have probably become an expert on the topic.

A good memorandum should "stand alone," meaning that readers should not need to do independent research to either test the veracity of the research or to understand the content of the memo. The document should contain everything a reader needs to understand the writer's conclusions. The author must show his or her reasoning and explain it in sufficient detail. The author must be careful not to assume too much knowledge.

The reader will probably be legally trained, but will probably not be as familiar with the issue as the author of the memorandum.

Also, as you write, keep in mind some general traits about audiences:

Their attention span will vary—it will be greatest in the beginning and at the conclusion of a text. Documents with features such as a brief answer, headings, subheadings, and strong thesis sentences help keep the reader focused. Put the most important points first so the reader can find these points quickly. Make sure the style you use to write your memorandum reflects an understanding of audiences generally and your particular audience.

What's That?

A thesis sentence is a sentence within a paragraph that expresses the main idea of the paragraph. In legal writing, it ideally appears within the first one or two sentences of the paragraph. The sentences that follow should tend to support or "prove" this main idea or assertion. In this sense, a thesis sentence differs from a topic sentence that expresses the main idea of a paragraph in a more neutral manner.

Make the Connection

Consider how the memorandum sample 3 at the end of this section uses thesis and topic sentences to guide the reader. Presented below are the 18 thesis/topic sentences from her discussion section. Notice how much information you can gain just by reading these sentences:

1. The court will find the term "all natural" to be latently ambiguous and will interpret the ambiguity to exclude genetically modified corn.
2. To determine the outcome of the claim, the court must first decide if the contract is ambiguous.
3. In *Kripp*, a couple going through a divorce proceeding executed a property settlement agreement, in which it stated alimony to the wife was to stop upon her "cohabitation."
4. In *Bohler*, the Third Circuit affirmed the part of the trial court's decision that found ambiguous a joint venture agreement between a PA corporation, Ellwood, and a foreign corporation.
5. Like the term "cohabitation," "all natural" seems clear; however, when placed in context, they have various meanings.
6. Like *Uddeholm*, D'Ancanto offers a reasonable alternative to the terms of the contract.
7. The defense will be likely to argue that the contract is not ambiguous.
8. Even if the court accepts Summers' and Grey's argument that the contract is unambiguous based on the plain meaning rule, D'Ancanto could still possibly argue interpretation for Cyclops Farms would be absurd and unreasonable.

9. Secondly, the defense might argue that, like in *Mellon*, even if the contract is deemed ambiguous, the alternative interpretation presented is unreasonable.

10. Because the term "all natural" is latently ambiguous and susceptible to more than one reasonable interpretation that does not contradict the writing, the court is free to consult extrinsic evidence to resolve the ambiguity and ascertain the parties' intent.

11. In *Local No. 2*, the local union sued the national union when the national union failed to fund the pension plan as required under a consent decree.

12. Unlike the agreement in *Local No. 2*, the contract in this case is a standardized order form, so it will not give the court much insight as to the parties' intention.

13. In *Kripp*, the parties' status as lay people within their own situation was important to the court's interpretation of extrinsic evidence.

14. After arriving at Cyclops Farms, Summers and Grey took D'Ancanto on a tour of their entire operation, including their corn section and did not mention, even in passing, they used genetically modified corn.

15. Although Pennsylvania law does apply, reference to European Union Directives will help clarify D'Ancanto's understanding of the term and his conduct in this situation.

16. If D'Ancanto had tried to purchase the tortillas in the EU, because of their strict genetic modification labeling requirements, he would have known immediately if the product had any ingredient that had been genetically modified.

17. As the extrinsic evidence implies, before and during the sale D'Ancanto had no indication or clue that Summers and Grey would use "all natural" to include genetically modified corn....

18. The defense could also use cases like *Bohler* and *Kripp* to argue that D'Ancanto's status as a merchant makes him more susceptible to reasonable knowledge that genetically modified corn would be included in the meaning.

The document is highly readable and can be skimmed quickly largely because of these strong thesis and topic sentences.

MEMORANDUM (Sample 3)

To: Supervising Attorney
From: Promising Young Attorney
Date: xx/xx/xxxx
Re: GMOs

Issue

Will Jean Marie D'Ancanto be able to prove a breach of contract claim based on latent ambiguity against Scott Summers and Jean Grey of Cyclops Farms in Lancaster for the sale of all natural corn tortillas that included genetically modified corn?

Brief Answer

D'Ancanto will be able to prove breach of contract. The portion of the agreement at issue is the definition of "all natural." The court will conclude that an examination of the sales agreement does not resolve the ambiguity nor does it give any insight into the parties' intention. By showing through extrinsic evidence that the term has more than one reasonable interpretation, which does not contradict the writing, the court will find a latent ambiguity in the contract. The court will then determine from the extrinsic evidence that Summers and Grey had reason to know of D'Ancanto's meaning of the term and thus breached the contract because "all natural" excludes genetically modified foods.

Facts[3]

While passing through the United States Jean Marie D'Ancanto, a Belgian gourmet natural foods restaurant owner, stopped in Lancaster to visit old college friends. These friends, Scott Summers and Jean Grey, own Cyclops Farms. They grow corn, make, and sell "All Natural Artisanal Corn Tortillas." D'Ancanto, impressed with their operation, told them about an international whole food-cooking contest he had been invited to compete in as the Belgian representative. The group discussed using the tortillas in his entry dish. Summers and Grey were aware that the competition was "all natural," but they never specifically discussed genetically modified food. D'Ancanto then took a sample case of tortillas back to Belgium to work on his entry dish. After testing the tortillas with his recipes, D'Ancanto ordered 20 cases. The order form indicated only quantity, price, and a choice of law provision for disputes to be settled under Pennsylvania law. D'Ancanto received and paid for the tortillas. For the competition, D'Ancanto needed a list of ingredients of all items used. He emailed Summers and Grey requesting a list. They then faxed a list of ingredients that showed the corn was

---

3.   The names in this memorandum are based on the X-MEN comic book series by Marvel Comics.

genetically modified for pest resistance. Because of the genetic modification of the corn, D'Ancanto could not use the tortillas in the competition.

He called Summers and Grey, told them the problem and asked for a refund. They refused, stating they had fulfilled the contract. D'Ancanto had to find a farm in Spain that could substitute non-genetically modified tortillas. Because of the short notice, they cost him over twice as much as the Cyclops Farms tortillas. D'Ancanto feels the tortillas lost him the competition and hurt his reputation. In Europe, all natural would never have included a genetically modified food. He would like to sue in federal district court for his losses.

Discussion

The court will find the term "all natural" to be latently ambiguous and will interpret the ambiguity to exclude genetically modified corn. Under Pennsylvania contract law the court must ascertain the objective mutual intent of the parties. *Kripp v. Kripp*, 849 A.2d 1159, 1163 (Pa. 2004). In the case of a written contract, that intent is located in the writing. *Id.* When the terms of a contract are clear and unambiguous, the intent of the parties is to be found only from the document. *Id.* However, when a latent ambiguity exists, parol evidence is admissible to explain, clarify or resolve it. *Id.* A contract will be found ambiguous if it is reasonably susceptible to different constructions and is capable of being understood in more than one sense. *Bohler-Uddeholm Am., Inc. v. Ellwood Group, Inc.*, 247 F.3d 79, 93 (3d Cir. 2001).

I. Ambiguity

To determine the outcome of the claim, the court must first decide if the contract is ambiguous. The court will find in this case the contract between Cyclops Farms and D'Ancanto latently ambiguous. In order to aid the judge in determining a latent ambiguity, the court will only admit certain forms of extrinsic evidence that will support a reasonable alternative meaning. *Id.* at 94. The ambiguity inquiry must be about the parties' words rather than their subjective expectations. *Id.* at 96. If the alternative definition is not reasonable under the circumstances, there is no latent ambiguity and the court resolves the dispute as a matter of law. *Id.*

In *Kripp*, a couple going through a divorce proceeding executed a property settlement agreement, in which it stated alimony to the wife was to stop upon her "cohabitation." *Kripp v. Kripp*, 849 A.2d 1159 (Pa. 2004). The parties themselves, neither being lawyers, hand wrote the cohabitation term on the actual typed document. *Id.* at 1162. When the wife began living with a woman, the husband ceased alimony payments. *Id.* at 1160. The agreement did not specify to which gender "cohabitation" referred. *Id.* at 1162. The Pennsylvania Supreme

Court stated the trial court was correct in admitting parol evidence to ascertain the parties' intended definition of "cohabitation" because the word was susceptible to different constructions, or ambiguous. *Id.* at 1164. "Cohabitation" was not defined in the document, no other language in the document clarified the term, and the dictionary gave several reasonable definitions. *Id.*

In *Bohler*, the Third Circuit affirmed the part of the trial court's decision that found ambiguous a joint venture agreement between a PA corporation, Ellwood, and a foreign corporation, Bohler-Uddeholm. *Bohler-Uddeholm Am., Inc. v. Ellwood Group, Inc.*, 247 F.3d 79, 86 (3d Cir. 2001). According to the court, Uddeholm offered a reasonable alternative interpretation of the terms in question that did not contradict the other terms or make the interpretation absurd. *Id.* at 94. Its interpretation merely narrowed the disputed terms, and thus was permissible. *Id.* at 100. The court went on to note that Uddeholm presented other extrinsic evidence that suggested it had clearly communicated its understanding of the ambiguous term. *Id.* at 99. The court stated that it is a principle of contract interpretation that when a party knew or had reason to know of the other parties' interpretation of terms of a contract, the first party should be bound by that interpretation. *Id.*

Like the term "cohabitation," "all natural," seems clear; however, when placed in context, they have various meanings. *Kripp v. Kripp*, 849 A.2d 1159, 1162 (Pa. 2004). In neither case is the term defined within the contract, nor does any other language within the document help clarify. *Id.* at 1164. "Cohabitation" was defined in the divorce code, but the court found that section of the Code does not have to apply in private agreements. *Id.* at 1162. In this case, neither Pennsylvania nor U.S. Codes help define whether "all natural" includes or excludes genetically modified food. The court in *Kripp* allowed several dictionary definitions into evidence to help explore the question of ambiguity. *Id.* The court held that "cohabit" has several meanings that did not necessarily limit the definition to a living arrangement between a man and a woman. *Id.* "All natural" as well is defined and used in a number of different ways. In the *American Heritage Dictionary*, "natural" is defined as, "Not acquired, inherent; Free from affectation or artificiality; Not altered, treated, or disguised"; while "natural food" is defined as, "food that contains no additives, as preservatives or artificial coloring or flavoring." The *American Heritage Dictionary* (2d ed. 1982). Even with the definition, "all natural" could reasonably apply to either genetically modified foods or non-genetically modified foods. Thus the court will find, as did the *Kripp* court, the term is ambiguous because it is susceptible to several reasonable constructions. *Kripp v. Kripp*, 849 A.2d 1159, 1165 (Pa. 2004).

Like *Uddeholm*, D'Ancanto offers a reasonable alternative to the terms of the contract. *Bohler-Uddeholm Am.*, 247 F.3d 79, 100 (3d Cir. 2001). The court accepts Uddeholm's proffered meaning of the term because it was reasonable in that it would not have rewritten the contract, only refined its meaning. *Id.* "All natural" by excluding genetically modified foods, would only sharpen its meaning within the contract, serving an explanatory function. It would not contradict nor add any terms to the agreement. *Id.* By showing that the definition of "all natural" is reasonably susceptible to alternate meanings that do not contradict the writings, the court will find that the term is latently ambiguous.

The defense will be likely to argue that the contract is not ambiguous. To claim that the contract is unambiguous, the defense will try to analogize the facts of this case to cases like *Stewart* where the court determined no ambiguity existed. *Stewart v. McChesney*, 444 A.2d 659, 662 (Pa. 1982). In *Stewart*, the contract was clear and because the parties had specified the original word, they intended that word. *Id.* The defense will attempt to show that in this case the language of the contract is clear because "all natural" has a plain and fixed meaning, which includes genetically modified foods. Since the parties used that term, they should be held to that term. *Id. Kripp* is an example of an argument that is just the opposite. A word, even if it has a usual meaning, can become ambiguous when placed in context. *Kripp*, 849 A.2d at 1163.

Even if the court accepts Summers and Grey's argument that the contract is unambiguous based on the plain meaning rule, D'Ancanto could still possibly argue interpretation for Cyclops Farms would be absurd and unreasonable. *Bohler-Uddeholm Am., Inc.*, 247 F.3d at 96. It would make no sense for D'Ancanto to buy 20 cases of tortillas knowing he could not use them. The court would then have to construe the term in his favor to make the only sensible interpretation. *Id.* at 96.

Secondly, the defense might argue that, as in *Mellon*, even if the contract is deemed ambiguous, the alternative interpretation presented is unreasonable. *Mellon Bank, N.A. v. Aetna Bus. Credit, Inc.*, 619 F.2d 1001, 1013 (3d Cir. 1980). Summers and Grey would say that excluding genetically modified corn is unreasonable because it contradicts or distorts the meaning of the contract, like the term "insolvent" offered by Mellon. *Id.* Unlike in *Mellon*, D'Ancanto's meaning of "all natural" does not challenge the other terms of the agreement. *Id.* Including or excluding genetic modification would merely refine the definition. Once all of this evidence is presented, the court will then decide that "all natural" is latently ambiguous within the agreement.

II. Interpretation of Extrinsic Evidence

Because the term "all natural" is latently ambiguous and susceptible to more than one reasonable interpretation that does not contradict the writing, the court is free to consult extrinsic evidence to resolve the ambiguity and ascertain the parties' intent. Because the court will probably interpret the meaning of "all natural" to exclude genetically modified foods, Cyclops Farms will be in breach of the contract. In order to ascertain the intention of the parties, the court may consider the surrounding circumstances, the situation of the parties, the objects they apparently have in view, and the nature of the subject-matter agreement. *International Org. Master, Mates and Pilots of Am., Local No. 2 v. International Org. Masters, Mates and Pilots of Am., Inc.*, 439 A.2d 621, 624 (Pa. 1981) [hereinafter *Local No. 2*].

In *Local No. 2*, the local union sued the national union when the national union failed to fund the pension plan as required under a consent decree. *Id.* The court held that the consent decree was ambiguous and to ascertain the parties' intention, the court looked at the decree itself as well as other indicia of the parties' circumstances. *Id.* at 624. It examined other relevant documents, including a pension plan booklet with definitions, and correspondence prior to execution of the decree by means of testimony and letters. *Id.* Besides this extrinsic evidence, the court reasoned that it would have been absurd to expect the local union to accept anything less than an equal pension. *Id.* at 626.

Unlike the agreement in *Local No. 2*, the contract in this case is a standardized order form, so it will not give the court much insight as to the parties' intention. *Id.* at 624. No other provisions, booklets, or codes exist that can help define "all natural." *Id.* Because the contract itself does not aid in interpretation or completely clarify the ambiguity, the court will turn to extrinsic evidence outside the document. *Id.* In this case, the only relevant written documents prior to the execution of the agreement are emails sent during the negotiation of sale. The emails show that D'Ancanto was still planning on using the tortillas for the cooking competition, and thus still believed the tortillas to be "all natural," as in not genetically modified, at the time of sale. As in *Local No. 2* and in *Bohler*, it would be absurd to think that if D'Ancanto had known the meaning Summers and Grey had attached to "all natural," he would not have bought the tortillas at all. He would not have been able to use them in the competition or in his restaurant.

In *Kripp*, the parties' status as lay people within their own situation was important to the court's interpretation of extrinsic evidence. *Kripp v. Kripp*, 849 A.2d 1159, 1162 (Pa. 2004). "Cohabitation" did have a common usage, but the factual situation was shown to have helped form the parties' understanding of the word, which was entirely specific to the parties' unique situation. *Id.* In this case, the same is true with respect to "all natural." The term was not handwritten in the contract, but each party's status as merchants, their cultural backgrounds, and their conduct within the specific factual situation, formed the parties' understanding of "all natural." The surrounding circumstances, as in *Kripp* and *Bohler*, will be important to the court for its conclusion of what the parties had reason to know and reasonably expect. Like Uddeholm in the *Bohler* case, D'Ancanto can probably provide, through the forms of extrinsic evidence discussed above, that

Cyclops Farms knew or had reason to know of his definition of "all natural" and that therefore that definition should control the contract. *Bohler-Uddeholm Am., Inc.*, 247 F.3d 79, 96 (3d Cir. 2001).

After arriving at Cyclops Farms, Summers and Grey took D'Ancanto on a tour of their entire operation, including their corn section, and did not mention, even in passing, they used genetically modified corn. They then allowed D'Ancanto to take a sample home. Still Summers and Grey did not give any indication that the tortillas were made from genetically modified corn and neither did the package because it did not include a list of ingredients. While it is true that Summers and Grey have never sold a product in the EU, D'Ancanto could argue that they, as merchants, should be aware of the requirements and regulations of a country to which they wish to export their products. When D'Ancanto contacted Summers about purchasing the tortillas, it is clear he still had no indication or else he would never have purchased them.

Although Pennsylvania law does apply, reference to European Union Directives will help clarify D'Ancanto's understanding of the term and his conduct in this situation. For instance, a main argument for the defense might be that since D'Ancanto knew he needed the tortillas for a competition that expressly prohibited genetically modified foods, he should have just asked about the ingredients; however, by using the term "all natural" he did perceive himself to be asking that question. In the EU "genetically modified organism means an organism, with the exception of human beings, in which the genetic material has been altered in a way that does not occur naturally by mating and/or natural recombination." Council Directive 18/2001, art. 2(2), 2001 O.J. (L 106) (EC).

If D'Ancanto had tried to purchase the tortillas in the EU, because of their strict genetic modification labeling requirements, he would have known immediately if the product had any ingredient that had been genetically modified. Council Directive 1829/2003, art. 13(l)(a), 2003 O.J. (L 268) (EC). Even if there had been no ingredients list, the package would have had "genetically modified" or "produced from genetically modified" somewhere on the label. Council Directive 1829/2003, art. 13(l)(c), 2003 O.J. (L 268) (EC).

As the extrinsic evidence implies, before and during the sale D'Ancanto had no indication or clue that Summers and Grey would use "all natural" to include genetically modified corn; however, because of the discussion about the competition occurring in the EU and because the tortillas were going to be exported to the EU, Summers and Grey as responsible merchants did have reason to know or reason to expect that the "all natural" contracted for would exclude genetically modified foods. Because there is not much of a written agreement or negotiations, the parties' status as merchants from different countries and their conduct are the best indication of their intentions. *International Master, Mates and Pilots of Am., Local No. 2 v. International Org. Masters, Mates and Pilots of Am., Inc.*, 439 A.2d 621, 624 (Pa. 1981).

The defense could also use cases like *Bohler* and *Kripp* to argue that D'Ancanto's status as a merchant makes him more susceptible to reasonable knowledge that genetically modified corn would be included in the meaning. *Kripp v. Kripp*, 849 A.2d 1159, 1162 (Pa. 2004). He is a natural whole foods restaurant owner and must buy non-genetically modified foods on a regular basis for his restaurant. Although, he has never purchased a product from the United States, he should have checked into their food laws before purchasing. While this argument is persuasive, D'Ancanto's argument will probably be more persuasive because Summers and Grey had an opportunity to mention their product's genetic modification in face to face interactions, emails, while touring the property with D'Ancanto, or by putting an ingredients list on the package. They chose not to do so. By examining the contract and its surrounding circumstances, the court will probably conclude Summers and Grey reasonably knew or should have known that the meaning of "all natural" excluded genetically modified corn.

Conclusion

This issue in this case is over the term "all natural." D'Ancanto alleges that his construction of "all natural," excluding genetically modified corn, properly reflects the intent of the parties and is required for a rational interpretation of contract. Cyclops Farms, on the other hand, alleges "all natural" does include genetically modified corn and their construction properly reflects the intent of the parties. The agreement in this case is a standardized order form, so its examination will not give the court much insight as to the parties' intentions. By showing through extrinsic evidence that the term has more than one reasonable interpretation, which does not contradict the writing, the court will find a latent ambiguity in the contract. To resolve the ambiguity, the court will examine evidence relating to the circumstances surrounding the transaction, like the actual document, prior negotiations, the status and the conduct of the parties. From this evidence, the court will then determine that Summers and Grey had reason to know or at least reason to expect D'Ancanto's meaning of the term and thus breached the contract because "all natural" excludes genetically modified corn.

Respectfully Submitted,

Attorney's signature

Promising Junior Associate

C. Selecting the Format for Your Memorandum

Although the form, or arrangement, of memoranda will vary according to your audience, legal memoranda usually contain the following sections: Heading, Question Presented, Brief Answer, Facts, Discussion, Conclusion, Closing and Signature. Make sure your memo contains these sections and use headings to clearly identify the question presented, brief answer, facts, discussion, and conclusion.

1. Heading: The heading orients the reader and provides information about the intended audience and the author. It typically includes a "To, From, and Date" line, and information about the subject as indicated by "re" ("in the matter of").

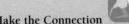

Make the Connection

Notice how the three sample memoranda in this chapter use headings and subheadings to organize information and to guide the reader.

2. Question Presented: (also referred to as the "Issue"). Identify the question you have been asked to answer so that your reader can confirm your understanding of the question; the question will remind the reader of the question you were asked to analyze. Lawyers working on other cases or future cases can determine the relevance of your memo to those cases by looking at the question presented. The question should be tailored to your particular perspective, but should also be objective. Remember that you are not trying to persuade a decision-maker that your client should win. You are evaluating your client's case at this stage in the process.

Food for Thought

Memoranda may have a single question presented or issue or multiple questions presented or issues. The samples use a single question in the issue section, but the discussion section addresses several issues that make up the single question. The decision to use multiple questions or to discuss multiple issues or a single issue will depend on the controlling law and how it is defined by the common law or statute.

The question may state a legal question (When can a person recover for emotional distress?) or be applied to a particular set of facts (Can Mrs. Hope recover for emotional distress if she heard the accident that injured her son but was not in immediate danger herself?).

Make the Connection

Notice how the author in sample memorandum 1 identifies the controlling rule and raises some of the significant facts in the issue statement: "Can the Court infer that Mrs. Bennett attempted to cause seriously bodily harm to Mr. Darcy from Mrs. Bennett's throwing of a hammer at Mr. Darcy's head...?" The author identifies "intent" as a legal issue in the case and then focuses the reader on the item Mrs. Bennett threw, a hammer, and the direction in which she threw it, at Mr. Darcy's head. These are the aspects of the facts that the author believes are fundamental to the analysis of intent. Now look at how the author in sample memorandum 2 focuses on the fact that Bennett threw a hammer, the lack of injury, and Bennett's claim that she did not intend to harm Darcy.

Food for Thought

Look at the issue in sample memorandum 3: "Will Jean Marie D'Ancanto be able to prove a breach of contract claim based on latent ambiguity against Scott Summers and Jean Grey of Cyclops Farms in Lancaster for the sale of all natural corn tortillas that included genetically modified corn?" How might the attorney for Summers and Grey have drafted the issue?

Keeping in mind that an effective question presented in a memo should be objective, which question do you prefer: 1. "Will Scott Summers and Jean Grey, owners of Cyclops Farms, be able to present a successful defense to a breach of contract claim based on latent ambiguity brought by D'Ancanto of Rogue Restaurant, where D'Ancanto ordered 'All Natural Artisanal Corn Tortillas,' and received tortillas that were genetically modified?" or 2. "Will Summers and Grey, owners of Cyclops Farms successfully defend a breach of contract claim by D'Ancanto of Rogue Restaurant if D'Ancanto is a seasoned merchant and the owners of the farm had no reason to know that "all natural" in Europe excludes genetically modified foods?"

3. Brief Answer: This is your prediction, your solution to the problem, or the answer to the question presented—be as direct or certain as you can be: say "yes" or "no" in answer to the question presented. Summarize what will happen and why. Indicate determinative facts and rules and why you predict the result to be this way. Also use the brief answer to define the scope of your memo. Provide the bottom line for a busy reader. Often the brief answer can be phrased in a way that does not require citation to legal authority. The brief answer should provide the reader with the controlling law and an understanding of how that law applies to the facts of the client's case. The length of the answer will vary according to the length of the memorandum. In a five-page memo, the answer will probably be no more than a paragraph.

Take Note!

A complete question presented and brief answer, when read together, provide the reader with a summary or abstract of a memo's contents. In a short memo, this means that a busy reader can get a quick understanding without having to turn a page.

4. Facts: This section answers "who, what, when, where, and why." It provides a record for the future and explains to readers upon what information your answer is based. Your readers may be unfamiliar with the facts. For example, you may acquire the facts from a client interview in which your reader did not take part. Your reader may have no prior knowledge of the case, but is reading it to gain such knowledge. In such a situation, your fact section may need to be longer and more detailed than if the reader knows the facts.

Alternatively, readers may be extremely familiar with the facts before reading your memo and, in this case, the fact section will serve to clarify the scope of your analysis and provide a written record of the story. If the reader is familiar with the facts, the fact section ensures that you understand the facts in the same way your reader understands them. The section may also refresh the reader's memory. The fact section may also help readers realize that a fact is missing. Keep in mind that, even where your primary audience is very familiar with the facts, there may be other readers who don't know the facts so they will learn of the facts for the first time by reading your memo. Include sufficient background if your memo is likely to go to a secondary audience.

In writing your fact section, make sure to include favorable and unfavorable facts, determinative facts (facts relevant to question presented and background facts needed to provide context for these legally significant facts), and emotionally significant facts. Tell a story—typically chronological but the story could also be arranged topically. Identify your client and describe the problem and desired goals of the client. Include the procedural history: Explain what has been done in the case so far.

5. Discussion: The discussion section is the body of the paper or the analysis section. In this section, readers expect to find an analysis of the law and the facts and the author's conclusion as to how the law will apply to resolve the question presented. In this section, you must prove the credibility of your conclusions by analyzing both the law and the facts. The discussion should: 1) tell the reader what law applies to the situation; 2) cite the appropriate law; and 3) explain this law in detail. Where the question involves a client, the memorandum should apply the law to the client's case to evaluate and to predict the outcome of the case should the case go to court.

Begin the discussion section by explaining the legal standard upon which your answer is based. In other words, begin with a statement of the general rule or controlling law that applies to the situation. This should be the opening paragraph of your discussion section.

Once you have introduced the controlling law in full, this law is often best understood by breaking the explanation of the law into smaller units, analyzing the law through its elements or subparts. By breaking the law into smaller parts and using legal authority and precedent to explain the meaning of each part, you and your reader will develop a better understanding of the law and how the law is likely to apply to your particular case. In this sense, writing a memorandum is an effective analytical tool for the author: It is a way to process the information uncovered in the research phase; it provides an opportunity to reflect on what you have found and to consider the implications of these findings.

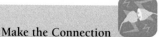

Make the Connection

Notice that in the sample memos 1 & 2, the controlling law is based on a statute and the cases interpreting that statute. In sample memo 3, the controlling law is based on common law.

After you have decided on the parts of the law you will discuss, your discussion section should explain or define the law and the particular legal vocabulary for the reader. The legal language used to state a rule of law has precise meaning, which could be very different from the way the same words are used outside the law. Additionally, legal language often takes on new or additional meanings as it is applied to new contexts. It is critical that your reader understands the meaning of this language. You should define the relevant language for your reader using formal definitions, if available, and extended definitions. An extended definition might include an example of how the language was used in a past case.

Make the Connection

Notice how the author of sample memo 3 uses an extended definition to define "ambiguity" in a contract. She also uses an extended definition to explain the term "all natural" and the meaning the court will likely attribute to this term.

How much explanation you provide your reader will depend on how important particular principles, concepts or words are in resolving a dispute or solving a problem and will depend on how much conflict you anticipate surrounding

CHAPTER 6 *Legal Memoranda* 101

the meaning of a principle, concept or word or about a particular issue. For example, if you think that the meaning of a particular element of a rule will be hotly contested, challenged, or questioned by the opposing side in a potential lawsuit, you should devote a significant amount of space to illustrating how the court has defined a term in the past. Describe the meaning of the legal language to your reader using the facts, holding, and rule from a past case so that the reader will understand exactly what the words meant in that context. You must cite to the legal authority so that your reader will know exactly where this information appears and the strength of the authority. This explanation including the citation to legal authority will enable your reader to understand how your current case compares to the precedent.

After explaining the meaning of the language and providing examples of how an element or particular part of the rule has been applied in the past, you should apply the law to your client's facts if you have been asked to consider a client's situation. This is often referred to as reasoning by analogy, which is a common reasoning technique in legal analysis. This type of reasoning requires that you compare and explain why your new case is or is not like the precedent. To do this, you might draw analogies to or distinctions with the authority and discuss how the specific facts of your case tend to support your conclusions. This analysis of your client's case should be balanced; in other words, you should discuss the strengths and weaknesses of the case. Include a counter-analysis that discusses how the other side might approach the case and openly acknowledge potential problems with your approach.

As you complete your discussion section, review carefully and be prepared to revise and redraft to make the document as easy to read as possible. Remember that the people reading your memo are probably legally trained. They are likely to be skeptical and may probe your analysis to see if it is sound. Using more detail may not cut off this sort of critical-analysis by your reader, but it will increase the likelihood that your reader fully understands your analysis. Additionally, using subheadings will help you to

Make the Connection

Notice how the authors in our three sample memos use different styles in their subheadings. Some authors use their conclusion or prediction as subheadings so that the subheadings read like thesis sentences. Other authors will use more general topic statements or even questions as subheadings.

Notice that the discussion section in the sample memos are organized according IRAC ("Issue," "Rule," "Analysis/Application," and "Conclusion") as discussed in Chapter 7 on Predictive Analysis. Keep in mind that IRAC is an organizational tool, but it is also a model of the way lawyers are taught to think through problems so it works as an analytical tool as well.

categorize and set off the analysis of the law. Headings and subheadings indicate the issues involved or the elements of the rule, and can be used to focus and guide readers through your discussion. Headings and subheadings will also enable your reader to skim and locate information quickly.

6. Conclusion. In your conclusion you want to sum up your analysis and provide the reader with the highlights of your analysis. Try not to repeat your brief answer, but make sure to match the brief answer. You may also include suggestions on how to overcome any weaknesses or areas for future research, and you may want to recommend a certain approach.

7. Closing & Signature. A common closing is: "Respectfully submitted" followed by your signature.

———————

III.   Memorandum Drafting Exercise

You have received the following information from your supervising attorney:

In March, Miss Havisham moved into a two-floor apartment located in the Back Bay section of Boston, Massachusetts with her daughter, Estella. Miss Havisham slept in the master bedroom on the first floor, and Estella slept in the attic on the second floor. In May, Miss Havisham noticed stinkbugs outside on her windowsills, but did not mention their existence to her landlord, Mr. Wemmick, as they had not entered into her apartment. However, in June, Miss Havisham noticed that some of the stinkbugs had shown up on the ceilings of the attic where Estella slept. She informed Mr. Wemmick, who immediately vacuumed up the stinkbugs. However, a few days later, the stinkbugs returned in greater numbers. Miss Havisham immediately reported their return to her landlord, and threatened to withhold July's rent if Mr. Wemmick did not fix the problem. Subsequently, Mr. Wemmick sprayed insecticides and vacuumed up any stinkbugs, but did not succeed in remedying the problem. When her room became infested with large numbers of stinkbugs, Estella began to experience heightened levels of distress. Miss Havisham withheld July's rent, and threatened to withhold August's rent if Mr. Wemmick failed to fix the problem immediately.

Mr. Wemmick hired a professional exterminator, who sprayed toxic chemicals into Estella's room. As a result of the toxic chemicals, Estella has to sleep with her mother on the first floor, and now, also experiences nightmares and fears bugs. Unfortunately, the stinkbugs have returned and multiplied. Miss Havisham closed off the attic, and withheld August's rent.[4]

Now consider, on the basis of these facts, whether the landlord breached the Implied Warranty of Habitability as expressed by Massachusetts law. You should then draft a memorandum predicting the outcome of this dispute should the dispute go to trial. Your memorandum should fully discuss the controlling law and the strengths and weaknesses of your client's case following the format discussed above. To complete this analysis, use the following cases as your authority: *McAllister v. Boston Hous. Auth.*, 708 N.E.2d 95 (Mass. 1999); *Doe v. New Bedford Hous. Auth.*, 630 N.E.2d 248, 253-54 (Mass. 1994); *Boston Hous. Auth. v. Hemingway*, 293 N.E.2d 831, 842 (Mass. 1973); *Jablonski v. Casey*, 835 N.E.2d 615, 618 (Mass.App. Ct. 2005); *Feldman v. Jasinski*, No. 09-ADMS-10018, 2011 Mass. App. Div. 243 (Mass. App. Div. 2009); *Lynch v. James*, 692 N.E.2d 81 (Mass. App. Ct. 1998); and *Ingalls v. Hobbs*, 31 N.E. 286 (Mass. 1892).

---

4.   The names in this hypothetical are derived from GREAT EXPECTATIONS by Charles Dickens.

CHAPTER 7

Predictive Legal Analysis

When you are drafting a predictive document, such as a memorandum, the discussion section must explain the process and authorities you used to arrive at your prediction. All legal readers will expect this analysis and expect you to present it in a particular way. The analysis must also give the reader a clear and usable explanation of your legal thinking. The reader should be able to use your analysis and fully understand the law and your suggested solution to the legal question without consulting other texts. This may seem like a daunting task now, but you will learn to master it.

This text will use IRAC as the format you will use for your analysis. While you may also hear other acronyms from your professors, all refer to the structure of legal analysis, and all are essentially the same. The IRAC acronym stands for Issue, Rule, Analysis and Conclusion. While you will use this format to structure your analysis, do not include as titles any part of the acronym. It is the unwritten architecture for your analysis. If you have several parts to your analysis, you will repeat the IRAC format for each section. This chapter will explore each of these ideas and explain how to incorporate them into your legal writing.

Issue

When stating the issue in a predictive document, you are really giving your answer to the legal question you have been asked. Typically, you may not know this until you have completed your analysis. Usually, this answer takes one or two sentences to complete. It includes some reference to the facts of the case, and your predicted answer to the legal question you have been asked. Here are a few examples:

Dorothy Gale has a cause of action in negligence against her neighbor, Ms. Gulch, for the harm Dorothy received when Ms. Gulch's dog bit Dorothy's arm.[1]

---

1.   With apologies to L. Frank Baum, The Wizard of Oz (1900).

A court is unlikely to find that Three Flags' employees falsely imprisoned the riders in the Demon Death House.

Billy Presley will be able to prove publicity given to private facts against Teddy Logan who wrote about Billy's private life in a song and performed it publically.

The issue statement will tell your reader what legal conclusion you will be proving in your analysis, and will give some essential facts of the case.

Rule

The rule has two parts: the abstract rule and the concrete examples of the rule. In the rule, you are educating your reader about the law. You are defining the law for the reader as you discerned it from your reading of the cases and/or statutes. In a way, you are providing something similar to a dictionary definition for your reader. First, you will give the abstract meaning of the rule that will apply in every case. This rule will always be followed by a citation to a case or statute or both. Then, you will put the rule in the context of the cases that the court has decided, just as a dictionary will put a word in context or in a sentence. You should give several examples of the concrete rule in cases, as factual differences will make a court decide cases in different ways. The discussion of the cases should also have citation to the cases and the pinpoint cites to the pages on which the material is found.

Here Are Some Examples of the Abstract Rule:

A dog owner's liability for the vicious acts of his or her dog is based on the "owner's knowledge of his dog's viciousness and his [or her] failure to take proper steps to prevent that viciousness from displaying itself." *Andrews v. Smith*, 188 A. 146, 148 (Pa. 1936).

To establish intent to falsely detain, the plaintiff must first show that the actor intended to confine the plaintiff within fixed boundaries. *Caswell v. BJ's Wholesale Co.*, 5 F. Supp. 2d 312, 315 (E.D. Pa. 1998).

The abstract rule need not conform to any length requirements. It should be as long as necessary to explain the abstract legal principle to the reader. However, usually you will be able to do this in a few sentences or a paragraph.

Here Are Examples of the Concrete Rule or Putting the Rule in the Context of the Cases.

In *Andrews*, a German Shepherd bit the victim on his leg, drawing blood. *Andrews*, 188 A.2d at 148. The court found no evidence that the owners had any previous knowledge that the dog was vicious, as it had never demonstrated any vicious conduct in the past. *Id.* Absent such knowledge, the owners were not liable for the injuries sustained by the victim. *Id.*

In *Caswell*, the plaintiff went to the store to pick up her developed photos and was informed that there was a problem with the content of her photos. *Caswell*, 5 F. Supp. 2d at 315. The plaintiff was taken to a back room in the store and informed that the police would arrive shortly. *Id.* The plaintiff left the room by walking around the manager who was standing in front of an open door. *Id.* The court held there was no false imprisonment because the plaintiff could prove no threat of force or any attempt to force her to stay within the fixed boundaries of the room. *Id.*

As you can see, the concrete rule puts the words of the abstract rule into a real-world factual situation and also explains how the court held in each case. In order for your reader to fully understand the law you will use in your analysis, you must first explain both the nature of the rule and how it has been used previously by the courts. If you can complete these steps of your analysis well, your reader can fully rely on your written document to understand the applicable law, without doing further research. This is enormously helpful to a busy reader who may not be fully familiar with the legal principles at issue in the case.

Analysis

When you have finished explaining the law that supports your conclusion, you are ready to show your reader your legal reasoning. It is in the analysis section that you demonstrate and explain your reasoning and prove to your reader that you are addressing the question of law properly in light of existing statutes and precedent. Your analysis must be objective. Therefore, you must objectively explain your reasoning for your issue conclusion, and you must objectively explain the reasoning that may oppose your result.

In order to analyze your legal issue, you must examine the facts of your case as they relate to the facts of the precedent cases. The more your facts resemble the facts in precedent, the more likely the court is to reach the same result as in the precedent case. However, even small factual differences between your case and precedent may make a difference in the

What's That?

Terms important to analogical reasoning:

Analogy—In logic, meaning identity or similarity of proportion. Where there is no precedent in point, in cases on the same subject, lawyers have recourse to cases on a different subject-matter, but governed by the same general principle. This is reasoning by analogy.

Distinguish—To point out an essential difference; to prove a case cited as applicable, inapplicable.

legal outcome. This analysis of comparing facts is called analogical reasoning, and is the basis of common law reasoning.

Therefore, as you begin to analyze, you should specifically compare the facts of your case to the facts in the precedent cases. You should analyze in this way, issue by issue, rather than listing cases and comparing them to your case. Think about the issues that you must resolve and the facts that were important in the cases for each issue. Then discuss your case and how its facts compare to relevant facts from precedent. Explain why the similarities or differences in the cases might lead the court to a particular conclusion.

Here Is an Example:

Like the plaintiff in *Caswell*, the plaintiff does not have evidence of confinement. Here, the guards were standing in the doorway, but the plaintiff could have simply walked around them as did the plaintiff in *Caswell*. The security guards did not threaten the patrons and only told them not to leave until they found the missing key to the door. A court would probably determine that the guards' words and actions gave no indication that they would forcefully prevent the plaintiff from leaving the premises. Without a physical or verbal threat, there could be no confinement.

In doing this kind of analysis, you will use inductive reasoning. In other words, you will be using factual specifics and their comparisons to reach a general legal principle or legal conclusion.

In addition to providing the analysis that supports your conclusion, every objective and predictive memo must also include a **counter analysis** of the opposing legal perspective. This analysis will proceed in the same way by comparing your case to the specifics of the precedent cases, but will demonstrate how the court could reach a different conclusion by

Make the Connection

The opposing type of reasoning is called deductive reasoning. Here, one reasons from general principles to reach a specific individualized conclusion.

For More Information

To understand more about inductive and deductive reasoning, read Ruggero Aldisert, LOGIC FOR LAWYERS 45-115 (2001).

viewing the facts or legal precedents slightly differently. You may also rebut the analysis, if possible.

For Example:

The plaintiff could argue that *Caswell* does not apply and there was intent to confine because the guards stood in the doorway. He considered them to be a physical threat to him, and he inferred intent to confine. However, in *Caswell*, the store security employees stood blocking the doorway, and the court did not hold that there was intent to confine. Those charged with confining must pose an actual threat. Here, as in *Caswell*, the plaintiff could have just walked around the security guard.

Conclusion

The last part of your analysis is the conclusion. This is a sentence that reminds the reader of your issue prediction.

For Example:

The plaintiff is unable to prove intent to confine him within fixed boundaries, and therefore cannot prove the first element of false imprisonment.

Using IRAC

You should use the IRAC format for each analysis you include in your writing. Therefore, if you address several elements of a legal claim, you will analyze each element using the IRAC format. Some analyses will need more explanation than others, but all will follow the same basic form.

Make the Connection

Before beginning to draft your memorandum assignment, refer to the sample memoranda in Chapter 6 to review the discussion section of each memo to see the use of IRAC to structure each analysis.

Exercise

Answer the following questions based on these paragraphs to test your understanding of the IRAC analytical format.

(1) Dorothy Gale will be able to prove that Ms. Gulch owed her a common law duty of care. (2) A dog owner's liability for vicious acts of his or her dog is based on the owner's knowledge of the dog's vicious propensities and the failure to take proper steps to prevent that viciousness from harming other human beings. (3) *Andrews v. Smith*, 188 A. 146, 148 (Pa. 1936); *Snyder v. Milton Auto Parts, Inc.*, 428 A.2d 186, 187 (Pa. Super. Ct. 1981). (4) In *Snyder*, a boy suffered injuries to his neck, hand and armpit when a dog belonging to the owner of a nearby scrap yard attacked him. (5) *Snyder*, 428 A.2d at 187. (6) The court held that the owner knew of the dog's vicious propensities because he had seen the dog baring its teeth and lunging at people. *Id.* (7) In addition, the owner used the dog to protect his property against trespass and theft; therefore he had a duty to protect others against the dog.

(8) Dorothy's circumstances were similar to those in *Snyder*. (9) Here, as in *Snyder*, Toto had been known to bare his teeth and snarl at strangers, and had even done so at Dorothy. (10) In addition, Ms. Gulch also used Toto as a source of protection, and knew of his vicious propensities. Therefore, the court should hold that Ms. Gulch owed a duty to protect Dorothy from Toto.

(11) Ms. Gulch could distinguish Toto from the dog in *Snyder*. (12) She could claim that she had no knowledge of Toto's vicious propensities as he was a well-trained dog and not trained as a guard dog. Further, Toto had never harmed anyone. (13) The court would not be convinced by these arguments because liability will attach if the dog owner knew or should have known that the animal was capable of harm. *Id.* at 188. (14) Thus, the court will hold that Ms. Gulch owed Dorothy a duty to protect.

Sentence (1) is:

    a.   The abstract rule

    b.   The issue prediction

    c.   The analysis of your case applying the precedent case

    d.   The counter-analysis

Sentence (2) is:

    a.   The abstract rule

    b.   The counter-analysis

    c.   The conclusion

    d.   The concrete rule

Sentences (4-6) are:

    a.   The conclusion

    b.   The abstract rule

    c.   The concrete rule

    d.   The facts of your case

Sentence (9) is:

    a.   The counter-analysis

    b.   The concrete rule

    c.   The application of precedent to your case

    d.   The conclusion

The writer's primary purpose in these three paragraphs is:

    a.   To demonstrate that there are other cases similar to Dorothy's

    b.   To show that Toto is a vicious dog

    c.   To predict that a court would hold that Ms. Gulch would probably have a duty to protect others against Toto

    d.   To show that Ms. Gulch should pay for Dorothy's injuries

Fill in the blanks.

Which sentence demonstrates the holding in the precedent case?

_____

Which sentence shows the authorities on which the writer relies?

_____

Which sentence explains the counter-analysis?

_____

Which sentence gives the conclusion?

_____

CHAPTER 8

Gathering Facts

Attorneys in the common law system carefully read and analyze the facts of a case. Attorneys learn to distinguish the important or "determinative" facts by examining the relevant rules of law governing a dispute and by reading judicial opinions and identifying the facts that judges find important. The existence or non-existence of a fact can change the outcome of a case or the decision as to whether to bring a case.

As a lawyer, you will have the responsibility of determining the relevant facts of a case and establishing the accuracy of those facts. You must learn how to gather facts through client interviews, through informal and formal investigation or "discovery," or through the review of the record. You must "prove" facts. The law is concerned with what is provable, not simply what happened. Therefore, your responsibility in relation to the facts will include not only determining the truth-value of the facts, but you will also have to find the evidence that tends to prove or disprove a given fact.[1]

In this chapter, you will explore how lawyers collect facts by first examining how the law defines facts. You will then look at how lawyers determine the facts of a case, and finally how they use the facts in predictive writing.

What is a fact?

In the non-legal context, people think of a fact as synonym for a truth, certainty, reality or an actuality. In the legal realm, for a fact to be considered a reality or actuality, it must be established or proven to be true or accurate.

Facts make up the client's story and the opposing side's story. In a lawsuit, parties plead certain facts, but these facts are not necessarily "truth." Rather, they are a claim to the truth, a claim to what has occurred. That claim, however, must

---

1.   According to Richard Neumann, a fact is an "Objective, discoverable truth or an allegation upon which a party has met a given burden (burden of production or burden of proof)." RICHARD K. NEUMANN, LEGAL REASONING AND LEGAL WRITING (2005).

be proven. Sometimes, the stories the parties tell are the same. Sometimes, the facts differ in non-meaningful ways. Sometimes, the facts differ in meaningful ways and will become the subject of a lawsuit. In other words, the truth-value of a fact in a legal dispute is something that often must be decided in court by the "finder of fact."

Often, the lawyers will agree to agree on a fact or "stipulate to" a fact. In a lawsuit, parties may agree on the facts by admitting to the facts as stated in a complaint when the party answers that complaint.

Make the Connection

Recall that when there are issues of fact in a case, these issues are resolved by the jury, if there is a jury. If there is no jury, the judge will determine the facts.

If the parties cannot agree on the facts, the facts will be determined at trial. The decision as to what facts must be presented at trial depends on the issues in the case and the law governing these issues. Identifying what facts are important to the case begins by identifying the law—whether statutory or common law—and examining precedent to see what facts were relevant in cases involving similar issues. You must compare the facts in the new case to the prior cases to decide what matters or what is "relevant." A relevant fact is one that tends to prove an element of the rule or a part of a law. It might also include emotionally compelling occurrences or background facts that influenced the decision maker.

Recall the case of *Kohr v. Weber*, 166 A.2d 871 (Pa. 1960) that you examined in Chapter 5. The controlling rule in *Kohr* required that the plaintiffs prove, among other things, that the noise was unreasonable. Prior cases held that noise rises to the level of a nuisance, if it is "so great at certain times and under certain circumstances .... it is not only disagreeable, but it also wears upon the nervous system, and produces that feeling which we call 'tired.'" *Id.* at 874. The plaintiffs' attorney brought forward a witness to testify "that the noise 'is so intense if two people, facing each other, are talking, they just stop talking or you don't hear what the other fellow is saying, you might as well stop.'" *Id.* Notice that the court did not actually go to the drag-racing strip to hear the noise. The court made the decision as to the facts of the case from the evidence the lawyer presented through witness testimony. The court believed this testimony and found this noise level to be a fact from which it could infer that the noise was unreasonable. The court also considered the nature of the animals and the fact that chinchillas are "sensitive," "extremely nervous in the presence of violent sound," and when nervous, they chew at their fur, which ruins their fur for pelting and is an "unbreakable" habit. *Id.* at 872. This information, likely established at trial by the testimony of an expert, was important to the court in *Kohr* because the plaintiffs had 1,100 chinchillas, and, according to the plaintiffs, many of these animals were chewing their fur because of the noise from drag racing at a nearby racetrack.

The court next had to determine if the noise caused the chinchillas "abnormal behavior." The plaintiffs "averred" that their chinchillas were suffering because of the noise from the racetrack. *Kohr*, 166 A.2d at 872. This means that the plaintiffs asserted this as a fact in their complaint. However, the defendants pled contrary facts. They disagreed that the races were causing the harm and pointed to the fact that "the neighborhood involved was a noisy one even before the drag racing began." *Id.* at 875. Although the court agreed that there was noise before the drag racing moved to the neighborhood, the trial court still had to determine if that fact alone disproved plaintiffs' claim that the drag racing caused the animals to chew their fur. To determine this, the judge looked at the timing of the chinchillas' behavior: The plaintiffs built their ranch with full knowledge of the noise from an airport and a highway. The chinchillas did not exhibit unusual behavior initially; the chinchillas only began chewing their fur some time later, after the drag racing began. The court also considered the defendant's testimony that the plaintiffs had complained early on to defendant about the noise and the chinchillas' conduct. The defendant also reported that, at the plaintiffs' request, he had actually gone to the ranch to see the chewed fur during the first racing season.

After hearing all the evidence, the court found the plaintiffs' story to be the correct version. The court believed that the noises were extraordinary and did cause the chinchillas fur chewing. On appeal, the plaintiffs' story became the facts of the case. The appellate court, without collecting evidence on its own, reviewed the record and held that it "support[ed] the Chancellor's finding that the abnormal behavior of the Kohr chinchillas was directly attributable to the extraordinary noises produced by the drag-racing ...." *Id.* at 875.

An attorney will pay attention to the facts that a court, like the court in *Kohr*, finds relevant because these offer guidance as to what a future court will find relevant. Based on the court's reasoning in a past case, an attorney can predict what facts will matter in a future case. A knowledge of what was relevant in past cases will also help an attorney to formulate questions to ask a potential client. For example, if a potential client came to you about a nuisance claim, based on *Kohr*, you would want to find out, among other things, about the extent of "disagreeable circumstances" and the timing of the events.

Determining the Facts of a Case

An attorney has many ways to collect the facts of the case. The means available to determine the facts will depend on how far a dispute has advanced in the trial process. Initially, an attorney will gather facts through informal processes, which are governed by the rules of professional responsibility, but are not governed by court rules or rules of civil procedure. For example, some attorneys may begin with a very cursory interview by phone or may have a paralegal or office assistant complete an intake form to decide whether a potential claim should be pursued. If an attorney believes that he or she may be able to offer help, the attorney will likely conduct a client interview. If a claim is filed in a civil matter, the process of formal investigation will begin. This process is known as "<u>discovery</u>."

Client interviews serve many purposes in addition to gathering the client's view of the facts. Interviews also help you to determine whether you and this person will form an attorney-client relationship, give you an opportunity to understand your client's goals, and allow you to address any anxiety a client might have and to problem-solve. You want to conduct the interview in a manner that enhances communication so that you can collect all the information you need to research the problem thoroughly and advise your client correctly, while at the same time allowing you to bond with your client.

Take Note

Discovery is a pre-trial investigation that is carried out by the parties. During the discovery phase, a party may question the other parties and, in some cases, witnesses. Discovery is governed by court rules such as the rules of civil or criminal procedure. Common forms of discovery include: 1) Interrogatories, which are written questions that a party must answer under penalty of perjury; 2) Depositions, which provide parties to a lawsuit the chance to question other parties or witnesses under oath while a court reporter creates a transcript; 3) Document production requests, through which parties can force other parties to produce physical evidence; and 4) Requests by one party that another party admit the truth of certain facts.

Practice Pointer

As you conduct the client interview, keep the following stages of the interview process in mind:

- **Pre-Interview.** Prepare carefully. Get as much information as you can prior to the interview. Ask the potential client for a brief summary of his or her problem so that you can do preliminary research if possible. Encourage the potential client to bring any relevant documents to the interview.

  Consider the objectives of the interview. Anticipate what this person wants: a solution to a problem; information; acknowledgment of some emotional issue. Try to establish if the person is anxious or fearful. Decide what help this person needs and if you are the appropriate person to offer the help. If you decide to help this person, consider the nature and scope of the attorney-client relationship and your short and long-term goals.

- **Opening the Interview.** Try to connect with the person and show empathy for his or her concerns. Typically, the interview will begin with small talk or informal conversation focused on this individual. Select a location where he or she will be comfortable. Use body language to indicate that you are actively listening, making regular eye contact and nodding your head to signal that you are following the conversation.

  In the early stages of your interview, you should ask if this person has seen another attorney about this matter. You will also need to determine if there are any conflicts of interest. If there are other parties involved, you will also need to determine if they have legal representation.

  You should mention your fees early on in the meeting. Explain the general fee structure and explain that you can give a more accurate estimate of the costs when you have gathered more information. To encourage open communication, be sure to ask the person directly if he or she has any questions or concerns about your fees. As you discuss fees, you need to convey that you will both do everything you can to meet his or her needs, while at the same time working to keep the costs down if fees are an issue.

- **Gathering Information.** Start the information gathering stage by letting the person talk. The small talk at the beginning of your interview may help you to identify why the client has come to see you. To get the conversation going, you might want to rephrase what the person has told you to make sure you understand his or her point of view. You might say something like, "So, if I understand, you are here because ...." If your interviewee is reluctant to talk, try to ask open-ended questions rather than yes-no questions to see if you can get the person to be more forthcoming.

  After you have determined why the person has come to see you, try to collect as much information as you can, again using open-ended questions to gather the potential facts. Say, for example, "Can you tell me more about ...?" or "What happened next?" Keep your questions broad. You want to learn about the person, not just the legal problem.

  Be patient and allow the person to take his or her time. If this means allowing for some silence, then be patient. Avoid jumping in too quickly with questions. If you focus the interview too early on, you risk losing important details and may have an incomplete view of the issues involved.

  Treat the person's concerns with the same import that you treat the legally relevant facts. If you brush aside this individual's concerns, you may send the message that you really do not care. You may also miss the opportunity to learn about certain aspects of this person's personality that will be useful to know when preparing a strategy.

Testing the Veracity of the Information. When you have an overview of the facts, try to refine the information to get more detail and to test the accuracy of the person's information. One way to do this is to put the events into chronological order. As you try to order the information, you may find gaps that you need to fill, either by asking more questions or by investigating the situation. At this stage, you want to probe a bit and understand the "who, what, when, where, and why" of the circumstances.

If your interviewee seems to be too heavily focused on something you regard as tangential, instead of ignoring this information, acknowledge it. Say that you will come back to that or that you'd like to hear more about this, but that first you would like to get more information about the initial topic. Once you have that information, be sure to go back to your client's point.

When you feel satisfied that you have collected as many details as you can, gently probe the counter-analysis. At this stage, you want to identify what information you can actually verify and what information your interviewee may not actually possess. In other words, you want to test to see if you have verifiable facts. You need to be somewhat skeptical so that you can make sure you get an accurate view of the situation. The person you interview may be giving you a biased version of the story so you need to try to identify the individual's assumptions and beliefs if you can. To do this, ask the person to explain certain statements in more detail. If the person is drawing conclusions, ask him or her to explain how he or she reached that conclusion. Imagine the circumstances from this person's perspective. If there is another party involved, imagine what version that side might tell.

• **Reviewing the Information.** Before completing the interview, make sure to summarize your understanding of the information. Make sure to identify what remedy the individual desires. Consider the situation and the ramifications of potential solutions available to this individual before offering advice. Depending on what your interviewee wants, you may need to help him or her to prioritize goals. You may want to explore some possible courses of action and to consider the legal and non-legal consequences of each action. Evaluate these options practically in terms of both financial and social costs for this individual.

• **Closing the Interview.** Tell the individual what the process will be. Outline the course of action you will take, and tell him or her what immediate steps you will take and what the long-term plan will be.

Do not rush to a definitive answer. Often you will need some time to investigate so you may only be able to give a plan. Be realistic about what you can provide. Try not to promise certain results if the situation does not lend itself to such certainty. You will need to verify facts and research the legal issue so be sure to give yourself time to complete those tasks.

If you decide to establish an attorney-client relationship, consider giving the individual some assignment so that he or she will feel involved in the process. The assignment could be to collect necessary documents or to find further information. Be sure the client knows how to reach you and leaves your office with a clear understanding of what the next steps will be.

- **Following Up.** Be sure to keep you client informed as to where you are in the process. Answer any correspondence from this person in a timely fashion.

Role Play

In pairs, practice your client interview skills using the underlined following client script about a landlord-tenant issue. One of you should act as the client and one of you should act as the attorney. The client should click on the link for "Client Facts." Read the script several times, trying to commit to memory as much of the information as possible. Prepare to be interviewed by your classmate-attorney. Try to get in role, answering questions as though you were actually a client with a landlord-tenant issue. The attorney should be prepared to interview the client. The attorney should try to gather as much information as possible. Try not to leave any of the determinative facts undeveloped, but at the same time try to attend to your client's emotional needs. At the end of the interview, the client should provide the attorney with feedback: Explain any information the attorney failed to recover and indicate whether the attorney showed the appropriate level of empathy. For example, indicate whether your attorney:

- greeted you appropriately;

- created a comfortable environment for you to talk;

- maintained a professional but friendly attitude;

- explained the purpose of the interview;

- listened actively, encouraged you to speak;

- allowed you to say everything you wanted to say;

- elicited key information that you might not have otherwise volunteered; and

- made sure you understood what the next steps in the process would be.

Tell Me More

If you'd like to switch roles, <u>here is another client script</u> to try. The law for these facts is discussed in <u>Sample Memorandum #3</u> in the chapter on memoranda writing.

Client Interviews Across Cultures

Interviewing styles vary across cultures. An awareness of these differences will help you to put your clients at ease and make them more incline to share information with you no matter what their background. The following clips will expose you to some of the different styles throughout the world. As you watch each clip, notice how the attorney-interviewer conducts the interview. Is there anything surprising about the style? How does it compare to the U.S. style discussed above?

United States

This interview is an example of the style of many U.S. attorneys. As you watch this clip, notice whether it follows the stages of an interview discussed in the previous section. What do you like about the attorney's style? What might you have done differently?

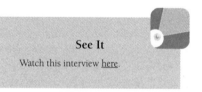

See It

Watch this interview <u>here</u>.

China

The attorney in this interview spends relatively little time engaging in small talk with her interviewee. There is no time devoted to "breaking the ice." Instead the attorney begins the interview by handing the interviewee her business card, making a short introduction, and then she begins to ask what remedies the interviewee seeks. Notice the way in which the attorney presents her business card with two hands, and notice also how the interviewee accepts the card in the same manner, holding it in two hands, reading it, and rather than immediately putting it away, she places it on the table next to her. This is an important ritual in many parts of Asia and is more formal than the exchange of business cards in the United States. The attorney spends a considerable amount of time listening and asks very few ques-

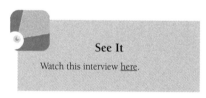

See It

Watch this interview <u>here</u>.

tions. The questions that she asks later in the interview focus particularly on the landlord's response to the tenant's complaints and whether the landlord has, in the tenant's opinion, tried to be responsive. The attorney closes the interview by giving the tenant a questionnaire to complete and told the interviewee that the firm would be in touch.

Jordan

In this interview, the attorney opens the interview with a chat. He offers the interviewee coffee, engages in light conversation, and then gently turns the conversation to ask why the interviewee has come to the law

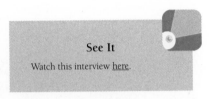

See It

Watch this interview here.

office. The small talk is an important part of the interview. An attorney from the iddle East will often begin an interview with questions about the interviewee's life, marital status, family members, and friends. The attorney might focus on relationships to determine if he or she might share any relationships in common with the interviewee. For example, the attorney might try to identify if he knows anyone in the interviewee's family and if so, will ask about the health and activities of those family members. In other words, the "icebreaking" is more extensive than the typical "icebreaking" session in the United States that tends to focus on less personal questions. In this interview, as the tenant describes the circumstances, the attorney is interactive and frequently asks questions to clarify and to elicit more information. The attorney closes the interview by giving the interviewee his business card and asking him to contact him if he has any questions.

Kenya

The attorney opens this interview with a short self-introduction and some information about his practice area and then begins to ask the interviewee about his problem. He listens to the tenant's story and then asks questions to clarify

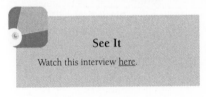

See It

Watch this interview here.

parts of the story. The attorney asks several questions related to the chronology of the events. The attorney explains to the tenant why he is asking certain questions and offers simple explanations as to the law that applies to the situation. He attempts to engage the tenant in the problem solving by presenting possible courses of actions and getting input from the tenant. He also spends time discussing his fee structure and seems to anticipate some bargaining over the fee. He appears somewhat surprised that the attorney agreed to the initial suggestion. The attorney closes the interview with small talk, a review of what they covered. Notice as you watch this clip how the reputation of the firm and the attorney and the firm's value system comes up several times in the interview.

Make the Connection
Interviewing a Legal Professional

As a law student, you can use client interview skills to learn more about the legal profession. For example, you can use your interview skills to carry out an informational interview with a lawyer whose work is potentially of interest to you or is in an area about which you would like to know more. You may want to approach someone you know already or request an informational interview with someone you have not met. The interview may take many forms, but the goal is to expose you to the variety of roles that lawyers play in the profession and society. By engaging in this interview, you will gain a better appreciation of the practical and intellectual aspects of different professional roles.

To preserve the results of your interview, you may want to write up the highlights in a short summary. Your summary should synthesize the answers to your interview questions; you may focus on the information you found to be the most interesting or "the highlights" of your interview. You may want to address the following four areas in your summary:

1. **Explain whom you interviewed and why you selected this person.**

2. **Identify this person's practice area. For example, does this person practice in one of the following areas or in a more non-traditional area? Explain your answer.**

   Commercial litigation   International law

   Family law   Public interest law

   State/federal agency   Personal injury litigation

   In-house work   Environmental

   Criminal/ defense and prosecution   Health law

   ADR   IP/technology law

   Employment law   Estates and trusts

3. **Describe the nature of most of his or her work, using the following questions as a guide. There are many other questions you might want to add, but be sure to keep track of the questions you ask and the responses you elicit so that you can access the information in the future.**

   Who are your clients? Is that mix typical for someone in this practice area?

   What proportion of time do you spend meeting with people, reading, drafting documents, doing research, negotiating, engaging in discovery, etc.?

   Do you work alone or with other people? (What is a typical week like?)

   With whom do you work most closely? Your clients? Other attorneys? Allied staff (e.g., paralegals, clerks)? Professionals in other disciplines?

What is most interesting about the work? Satisfying? Challenging? Frustrating?

What do you like least about the work?

What kinds of ethical challenges do you confront in the work?

How do you draw upon the concepts or skills learned in Law School?

If law students want to work in this field, in what areas of law should they consider taking classes?

Are there particular skills used regularly that students should try to begin developing?

What kinds of opportunities will junior attorneys have in this field in coming years?

What is a common career path for someone in this field? What was your career path?

Are there lifestyle features (sane vs. impossible hours; predictability; flexibility; heavy or no travel; etc.) that characterize this work?

4. **Evaluate whether this type of work is of interest to you: do you think you would like to do this kind of work? Why or why not?**

Using the Facts in the Predictive Memo

In a predictive memorandum, the facts are presented neutrally in a fact section and appear again in the application section of the discussion. The focus in the memorandum is on the evidence or circumstances that, if proven, would tend to prove or disprove the legal rule at issue. Often the available information does not directly prove a rule, but will lead to an inference that, if believed, satisfies the rule.

Consider an attorney evaluating whether his or her client, a security firm operating on the high seas, perpetrated an illegal act of violence within the meaning of a piracy statute. This attorney might determine through statutory interpretation and research of the existing case law that the violence used must exhibit an intent to do serious physical harm that amounts to

Tell Me More

Lawyers don't always have direct evidence so they build "inferences" or make assumptions and generalizations about the facts that exist. But there might be several inferences from a given fact and how strong an inference is will depend on the generalizations upon which an inference or assumption is based. This is why lawyers use facts to explain their conclusions: The Application section of IRAC functions as a way to show readers upon what assumptions lawyers base their conclusion and to test the strength of these assumptions. For example, a prosecutor might try to infer guilt from the fact that a suspect in a high crime area fled when a police car approached. The defense attorney might argue that other assumptions, such as a fear of police officers and racial bias might be equally valid inferences.

deadly force or a disregard for human life. The client, the alleged pirates, may not have expressly stated such an intent. The alleged victims may not have heard anything threatening, but if the attorney determines that it is a verifiable fact that his client boarded a cruise ship without permission and that the defendants were carrying AK-47s and grenades, than these facts will tend to prove the necessary intent. If, however, the client never boarded the ship, but instead fired Long Range Accoustic Devices (LRADs) at those on deck, the inference of intent to do serious physical harm will be weaker.

In drafting a memorandum, the attorney will have to explain the inferences he or she is making about the fact that the defendant used LRADs as did the author of the memorandum in Chapter 6. Notice how that author discusses the inferences surrounding the fact that the client used LRADs: "LRAD devices are simply not capable of the same type of damage as AK-47s and grenades. While assault rifles and grenades can cause seriously bodily harm and death at their worst, LRADs trigger annoyance, nausea, dizziness and possibly permanent hearing loss, which is not a likely consequence. Thus these devices are in completely different weapon classes."

The author also considers the reasonableness of other inferences that could be made about the use of LRADs: "Plaintiff could argue that [because] the Bloodwater employees' use of the LRADs caused distress and pain to the passengers onboard the cruise line, the LRAD is a non-lethal weapon, and thus it could be seen as an "illegal act of violence." Also, there is no indication that the plaintiffs threatened the Bloodwater employees, and thus the employees may not have been using the LRAD as a communication device to ward off an attack." Ultimately, the author concludes that the first inference is stronger: "The LRAD, however, is usually considered to be a non-lethal weapon, while assault rifles and grenades are inherently violent. Even if the LRAD could arguably be called a weapon, it is not even in the same class as other vehement weapons."

Practice Pointer

In practice, lawyers will often construct a proof chart or a fact investigation plan to determine what facts they have and how they intend to prove those facts. The chart format can help lawyers to identify missing information or to see gaps in their logic. A proof chart for the pirate case above might look something like this:

Element	Facts that tend to prove or disprove the element	Source	Discovery Plan that attorney will use to verify the fact
An illegal act of violence	Security firm fired LRAD toward crew of cruise ship; did not attempt to board ship	Client interview; the LRAD	Research about LRADs; Send interrogatory to other side to identify their version of the situation; depose opposing side.
Private Ends			

In this chapter, you explored the way lawyers identify relevant facts, gather facts, and use facts in objective writing, such as a legal memorandum. You can also use facts persuasively, as you will see in the chapters on advocacy. Whether attorneys are using the facts in objective or persuasive writing, the identification and collection process is the same: You must identify the controlling rule of laws, analyze what facts were considered relevant in past cases, and identify what facts are provable in your current case. Then, based on similarity of the facts in your case to those in the precedent cases, you begin the process of predicting the legal outcome to your client's dispute.

CHAPTER 9

Revising and Editing

Revising and editing written work aids both writers and readers: 1) It enables writers to analyze and test that their reasoning is sound; 2) It also ensures that the work is readable. For many law students, legal writing is their first experience with professional communication and its emphasis on writing for a reader. Producing a draft that is written with a reader in mind may take multiple drafts. So while completing a first draft of your memorandum or brief is a major accomplishment, you are not yet finished. You will probably need several additional drafts before your work is well-organized, well-reasoned, and polished.

You want to submit the strongest possible memo or brief to other attorneys or to a court. This means you must reconsider each component of your work to assure yourself that it is logical, clear, concise, and error-free. Your goal is two-fold. You aspire to a professional document, one that other lawyers would understand because it is in a standard format and because the writing is clear and easy to follow. You also want a document on which judges and lawyers would not hesitate to rely because you have supported your legal conclusions with a well-structured analysis of the applicable legal rules and the cases that illustrate how these rules apply.

As you revise and edit, remember that every legal document is written with a specific audience in mind. The audience affects both word choice and the overall tone of the written work. You will probably select different words to explain a legal outcome when writing for a client who is a lawyer or sophisticated business-person than you would in a letter to a client less versed in law and legal language. Similarly, more formal and respectful language is appropriate in a document being submitted to a court, while a memorandum written to a colleague might be more informal. When working through the exercises in this chapter, keep the audience for your document in mind to assure that the tone is appropriate and consistent. And whoever the audience may be, remember that you are writing as a professional.

Lawyers do much of their writing under time pressure, and must learn to build in time to revise and edit before submitting their work to other lawyers or filing it with the court. Revising, editing, and proofreading are separate steps, and the best writers realize that these should be done during separate readings of the text because they focus on different elements. This chapter will introduce you to several helpful techniques for revising, editing, and proofreading the discrete components of your document. Specifically, it will provide you with a systematic approach to revising and editing your own work and the work of others. The chapter begins first with large-scale organization. It next examines the small-scale structure of your document, focusing particularly on paragraphs. Finally, the chapter considers the detailed level of individual sentences, citations, and word choice.

———————

Reviewing the Overall Structure of Your Work

Once you have a complete draft of your document, you should review it to check the large-scale structure of your work. Begin by checking to see that you have included all the necessary sections of a memo or a brief. For example, a memo typically includes a heading, question presented, brief answer, fact section, discussion section, a conclusion and a closing signature. Check your work to see that you have all the categories and if they are placed in the appropriate order. Additionally, in legal writing, most often checking for large scale organization means checking to ensure that you have used the IRAC structure discussed in Chapter 7. Following IRAC will help you to produce a logically sound document. It will also help you to produce a document that is ordered in a way that legally trained readers expect. Looking closely at whether you are using IRAC can also help you to deepen your analysis. If you see, for instance, that you have not explained the rule in both abstract and concrete terms, you may find that it is because your understanding of the law is incomplete. Therefore, you may need to do more research or read the law again to improve your writing. In other words, evaluating your use of IRAC can help you to examine the completeness and accuracy of your work. Using IRAC in this way will also help you to deepen your legal expertise in a particular area of law or on a topic.

Before examining the large-scale organization of your own document, look at the passage below from a student memo. The IRAC structure from one section of this memorandum is scrambled. Try to put it in the correct order by identifying the I, R, A, and C of IRAC.

Discussion

I. The Red Ryders[1] probably did not owe a duty of care to Mr. Farcus

The Plaintiff will make two arguments against viewing the wave as an activity inherent to baseball: first, like the actions of the displaced fans in *Telega*, the fans' behavior at the Red Ryders game was not expected; and second, because of his lack of knowledge of baseball, Mr. Farcus could not appreciate which activities were common to the game. However, the actions of the *Telega* fans scrambling for a ball cannot be accurately compared to stadium-wide fan cheering. Whereas the *Telega* fans acted unpredictably, and illegally, when assaulting a patron, the fans at the Red Ryders game acted within the constraints of the wave, performing the cheer in its typical and expected manner. Also, the Pennsylvania Superior Court held that a plaintiff, though having never attended a baseball game prior to her injury, was held to have assumed a risk of unknown conditions, and to have possessed general knowledge relating to sporting events. *Schentzel v. Phila. Nat'l League Club*, 96 A.2d 181, 186 (Pa. Super. Ct. 1953). Mr. Farcus is intelligent, spoke with stadium attendants on the subject of baseball, and witnessed fans performing the wave as it moved towards his section, all of which demonstrates his awareness of the game's activities.

The Pennsylvania Superior Court applied the "no-duty" rule to a case in which a patron at a hockey game was injured after being struck by a hockey puck unintentionally shot by a player into the stands. *Petrongola v. Comcast-Spectacor, L.P.*, 789 A.2d 204, 206 (Pa. Super. Ct. 2001), *appeal denied*, 803 A.2d 736 (Pa. 2002). The court stated that at the time of injury, plaintiff was seated, and the game was in progress. *Petrongola*, 789 A.2d at 211. The court held that being struck by a puck while watching a hockey game was a risk common and expected in the sport, and an occurrence well known to fans. *Id.* The court upheld a decision finding the stadium owner not liable for the harm. *Id.* at 215.

Red Ryder, the defendant in this case, will not be found negligent. The elements required to prove a negligence claim are: "that the defendant owed a duty of care to the plaintiff, the defendant breached that duty, the breach resulted in injury to the plaintiff, and the plaintiff suffered an actual loss or damage." *Martin*, 711 A.2d at 461. Where the defendant is the owner of a sports facility, Pennsylvania law holds that the owner does not owe a duty of care to protect patrons from risks inherent to the activity. *Jones*, 394 A.2d at 551.

---

1.   The names used in this exercised are from one of our favorite movies, A Christmas Story, with thanks for many years of laughter.

The Red Ryders Baseball Team, in their capacity as a stadium owner, did not owe a duty of care to protect patrons from risks inherent to the activity of attending a baseball game. Like the plaintiff in *Petrongola*, Mr. Farcus was in his assigned seat when poked in the eye, and his injury was sustained during the course of the game. Further, Mr. Farcus' injury resulted from the fans' performance of the wave, an activity inherent to the sport. The wave is a cheer common to athletic events, and encourages participation from all fans because it is simple to perform. Moreover, the wave itself is an extension of a larger activity, cheering, which is inherent to all sporting events. Fans come to all sporting events with the specific purpose to watch the event and cheer. During the course of a game, it is expected that fans will stand, sit, and gesture with their arms and hands in a show of support for the teams and players. Also, the court in *Hughes* held that an activity comprises not just those specific acts that define the sport, but all acts incidental to the activity. Where moving from ski lift to slope is an incidental, but related, act of downhill skiing, the sport of baseball includes not just those activities occurring on the field of play, but the attendant cheering that is a part of every game.

The owner of a sports facility possesses no duty of care to protect a patron from risks of injury where the risks are inherent to the activities occurring on the stadium owner's property. *Jones*, 394 A.2d at 551. This "no-duty" rule, as defined by the Pennsylvania Supreme Court, is restricted to risks that are "common, frequent and expected" in the sport. *Id.* Where the court holds that the "no-duty" rule does not apply, the stadium owner will be held to a standard of ordinary care, requiring the landowner "to protect invitees from foreseeable harm." *Id.* at 552. However, the Pennsylvania Supreme Court held that where an "invitee assumes the risk of injury from obvious and avoidable dangers ... the possessor owes the invitee no duty to take measures to alleviate those dangers." *Carrender v. Fitterer*, 469 A.2d 120, 125 (Pa. 1983).

Mr. Farcus was aware prior to his entry to the stadium that the game was called "red, white, and blue day" and that flags would be distributed to all patrons. Mr. Farcus voluntarily entered the stadium, aware of the obvious dangerous condition on the property. Further, the waiver on the back of Mr. Farcus' ticket expressly warned him of the possibility of injury resulting from the reasonable activity of fans. The Red Ryders had no duty to protect Mr. Farcus from a risk of injury inherent to the game, nor were they obligated to protect him from an obvious dangerous condition on the property.

Additionally, the Pennsylvania Supreme Court extended the "no-duty" rule to a suit against a ski resort following a collision between two skiers at the base of a ski slope. *Hughes v. Seven Springs Farms, Inc.*, 762 A.2d 339, 344 (Pa. 2000). The plaintiff had finished her downhill run and was traveling away from the slope when she was struck by another skier. *Id.* The plaintiff argued that she had not been participating in the activity at the time of the collision, and thus her injury was not incurred during the course of the sport. *Id.* The court ruled that the plaintiff was sufficiently engaged in the activity, and that a collision at that location was an "all-too-common" occurrence for skiers. *Id.* The court held that the sport of skiing includes not just the basic act of traversing downhill on skis, but all activities incidental to the sport: riding ski lifts; skiing from the lift to the trail; and skiing from the base of the slope to the lifts. *Id.* The court stated that "[i]n order to accept [plaintiff's] argument, this Court would have to interpret ... the sport of downhill skiing, in an extremely narrow, hypertechnical and unrealistic manner." *Id.*

Should the court find, as it did in *Jones*, that the risk to Mr. Farcus was not common and expected, nor inherent to the activity, the Red Ryders will be held to have had a duty to protect Mr. Farcus from foreseeable risks. *Jones*, 394 A.2d at 551. The Pennsylvania Supreme Court held, however, that where a risk of injury is open and obvious to the invitee, the landowner will have no duty to protect the invitee from the dangers of those obvious risks. *Carrender*, 469 A.2d at 125. A condition is obvious when it is a risk that a "reasonable man, in the position of the visitor, exercising normal perception, intelligence, and judgment," would readily appreciate. *Id.* at 123. The court in *Carrender* held that the defendant, a chiropractor, owed no duty to protect a patient from a patch of ice located on the defendant's premises. *Id.* at 124. The plaintiff had parked her car in defendant's parking lot, and upon getting out, slipped and fell on the ice. *Id.* at 122. The plaintiff testified she perceived the icy surface prior to stepping from the car, was aware of the risks, and exited the car despite her awareness of the risk. *Id.*

The Pennsylvania Superior Court likewise failed to apply the "no-duty" rule in a case where a fan at a football game was tackled by an unruly mob of fans clamoring for a football. *Telega v. Sec. Bureau, Inc.*, 719 A.2d 372, 376 (Pa. Super. Ct. 1998). The plaintiff in *Telega* stood up from his assigned seat to catch a football that had been kicked into the stands. *Id.* The plaintiff caught the ball, but was injured when a group of fans attacked him in order to obtain the souvenir. *Id.* The fans attacked him in order to obtain the souvenir. *Id.* The fans causing the plaintiff's injury were not located near their assigned seats, and further, the stadium was aware of the fans' behavior but had done nothing to prevent it. *Id.* The *Telega* court echoed the *Jones* ruling, holding that the risk which led to the plaintiff's injury was not "common, frequent and expected," and that a fan does not "assume as inherent in the game the risk of being attacked by displaced fans." *Telega*, 719 A.2d at 376.

In contrast, the court in *Jones v. Three Rivers Management Corp.* affirmed the defendant stadium owner's liability for injuries sustained by the plaintiff after she was struck in the head by a baseball hit during batting practice. 394 A.2d at 553. At the time of her injury, the plaintiff Ms. Jones was located in the stadium's enclosed second-level concourse, which contained several large openings through which patrons could view the game. *Id.* at 548. The game had not yet begun, and Ms. Jones was standing with her back to the field when she was hit. *Id.* The *Jones* court refused to apply the "no-duty" rule in this case, holding that "the risk of being struck by a baseball while properly using an interior walkway" was not a risk inherent to attending a baseball game.

☑ Click Here to **Compare Your Response.**

——————

Checking Your Large-Scale Organization

Use the following checklist to evaluate your paper. Be sure to use a hardcopy of your draft and make notes in the margin as you move through your work. The instructions below are organized for evaluating an office memorandum, but they are easily adapted to a brief. This exercise is particularly effective because it requires a writer to re-envision completed text. Most of us write on a screen, and, even if we make notes and compose a rough draft on paper, by the time we are revising and editing we are scrolling through the document on a computer. We see it as a complete document, one page after another, which makes it difficult to see a gap in logic or where a component is incomplete or missing altogether. Using this checklist to examine your text will help you consider discrete elements of your writing separately, and that focus will allow you to see what you have written differently.

It is important to record the insights you have as they occur to you, but equally important not to get distracted by searching for the perfect word or phrase. Make small corrections as you edit, or just circle or otherwise mark places where you think a change may need to be made. Make those changes later; for now, keep moving through the components of your document as explained below.

The Header is:

- Complete (To, From, Date, Subject line)
- Error-free

The Question Presented:

- Refers to relevant rule of law
- Includes legally significant facts
- Does not draw legal conclusions
- Uses precise language, strong verbs, concrete nouns
- Reads easily

The Brief Answer:

- Predicts how the issue will be resolved
- Explains the prediction by referring to the rule of law
- Answers within the first few words
- Provides reader with your "bottom-line," particularly when read together with the question presented

The Fact Section:

- Includes all legally significant facts in a chronological narrative, if possible
- Provides necessary background information to orient readers
- Identifies client and the nature of the dispute
- States the facts accurately (neither adds nor deletes relevant facts)
- Expresses the facts objectively (does not judge or qualify the facts)
- Does not contain legal conclusions

The Discussion:

- Includes an opening or introductory paragraph that provides a prediction and the controlling rules
- States the rule by quoting or paraphrasing the common law rule or quoting the statutory rule
- States rules accurately and objectively
- Includes proper citation
- Breaks the discussion into subsections that set off the elements or subparts of the rule and applies each subpart of the rule to the client facts
- Uses an IRAC analysis in each subsection (Issue Prediction, Rule Statement in abstract and concrete form, Analysis of the facts of your case including the counter-analysis, Conclusion)

The Conclusion:

- Predicts how the issue will be resolved
- Summarizes your reasoning in more detail than brief answer
- Recommends how to proceed

The Memorandum uses:

- Standard formal English & grammatical patterns
- Proper citation form
- Readable font and typeface
- Page Numbers
- Proper closing ("Respectfully submitted" & signature)

———————

Examining the Small-Scale Organization: Paragraphs

Once the basic organizational structure of your document is in place, turn your focus to the components that make your writing flow: paragraphs, topic and thesis sentences, and word choice.

———————

Revising Paragraphs

A well-structured paragraph helps the reader stay focused. Paragraphs break your writing into manageable chunks. Ideally, they allow readers to follow your thought process as you move from one idea to the next. Paragraphs act as analytical tools in the sense that you, as a writer, must decide what it is that you are trying to prove. You should then state it at the paragraph's beginning. Paragraphs sharpen your focus on a small scale in the same way IRAC helps you to stay focused on a larger scale.

Read the paragraph below, and consider if it is a "good" paragraph. Do you like it? Is it doing what a paragraph "ought" to do? As you consider this paragraph, ask yourself what features make up a well-constructed paragraph.

[A] Under the "no duty" rule, the owner of a sports facility has a duty to protect patrons from those risks that are not inherent in the amusement activity. [B] A standard of ordinary duty of care exists for any conditions that are not inherent in the activity, but are foreseeably dangerous. [C] In *Jones*, the Pennsylvania Supreme Court adopted a "no duty" rule that applies to owners of places of amusement or sports facilities. [D] An owner of a place of amusement or sports facility that charges admission is not an insurer of its patrons' safety. [E] According to *Jones*, the owner will not be liable for risks that are "common, frequent and expected" to the activity of the establishment.

The paragraph above seems to satisfy one of the elements of a well-written paragraph. It is unified in its topic. The paragraph is about the duty of care a sports facility owner owes to its patrons. Paragraphs are easiest to read if they have a single focus; ideally, they should be about one subject or prove one proposition. However, a good paragraph needs more than unity of topic as the paragraph above demonstrates. The paragraph also needs an identifiable purpose, which in legal writing is usually expressed in a thesis or topic sentence at the start of the paragraph. It also needs a "logical flow," which is sometimes referred to as having coherence and cohesion.

If a paragraph lacks flow, it will appear to be a random collection of sentences on a topic, like the paragraph above. A paragraph also needs to be a readable length. Although this will vary, in legal writing, paragraphs tend to be short, between three and eight sentences, or about two or three paragraphs per page. Paragraphs that are shorter tend to feel incomplete to your reader. Longer paragraphs may contain too much information and will make it harder for your reader to determine the purpose of the paragraph, even where you have included a topic or thesis sentence. Based on these considerations, how might you revise the paragraph above?

Tell Me More

In the field of linguistics, coherence and cohesion are principles that identify how text is held together. In general, coherence refers to semantic meaning or the relationship in terms of ideas and the meaning of words and phrases. One important concept of coherence is to move from given information to new information. As a writer, you should try to start with the information that you expect that your reader shares. For example, place given or shared information at the start of the paragraph or in the subject position and put new ideas in the later part of the paragraph or in the object position. Cohesion refers to structural or grammatical connections such as the use of conjunctions or transitional phrases to show relationship between sentences.

Consider the following revision. If you change the order of the sentences and revise the subjects to focus on given rather than new information, you might be able to improve the flow:

[D] An owner of a place of amusement or sports facility that charges admission is not an insurer of its patrons' safety. [C] **As a result, the Pennsylvania Supreme Court adopted a** "no duty" rule that applies to owners of places of amusement or sports facilities. *Jones.* [E] According to *Jones*, the owner will not be liable for risks that are "common, frequent and expected" to the activity of the establishment. [A] Under **this** "no duty" rule, the owner of a sports facility has a duty to protect patrons from those risks that are not inherent in the amusement activity. [B] **However, a** standard of ordinary duty of care exists for any conditions that are not inherent in the activity, but are foreseeably dangerous.

The paragraph above is still missing a clear statement of purpose. A strong topic or thesis sentence will explain why a paragraph was written. For example, if the point of the paragraph above was to describe the "no duty" rule, the author might decide to begin with a sentence that states that in Pennsylvania the owner of a sports facility does not have a duty to protect patrons from the risks inherent to the facility, something like sentence [A]. A topic sentence introduces an idea. It is descriptive. However, many of the paragraphs you write in legal documents will be probative. In other words, you will be trying to prove or assert an idea and your sentences will need to directly convey that idea. For example, the above paragraph may be part of a larger document that is trying to prove a conclusion based upon a rule of law. In such a case, the paragraph might have a thesis sentence such as "The owners' of the Red Ryder baseball team did not have a duty to protect a fan who was injured in the eye after he was poked by another fan who was performing a cheer known as 'the wave.'"

As you saw with the IRAC structure, legal readers are trained to access information in a particular way. These readers need to know what the writer intends to prove before the proof begins. Your ideas will be challenged and require you to prove your assertions—paragraphs, beginning with a strong assertion of what each paragraph proves, is one of the analytical tools available to you to prove the strength of your analysis. In terms of IRAC, a thesis sentence asserts what you intend to prove. A paragraph with a strong thesis sentence, as opposed to a topic sentence, can help you to "prove" the meaning of your rule, the Rule section of IRAC. Thesis sentences are also helpful throughout the IRAC structure (to state the Issue and in the Application to facts) and elsewhere in the paper because they focus your readers and make your paper readable. A thesis sentence may appear in the subheading for an issue or in the first two sentences within a paragraph.

FYI

Thesis sentences and transitions are often forgotten in the early drafts of a brief or memo. Once the overall legal analysis is in place, look for them in each paragraph when you revise. Then, where necessary, draft the appropriate sentences.

You may not need a thesis sentence in every paragraph, but your writing will be clearer if you strive to identify and articulate the point of each paragraph. Thesis sentences also serve to orient and guide the reader—they move the discussion along; tie sentences together, and relate one idea to another. Thesis sentences have a positioning effect: A reader can jump to different sections and still not be lost. A paragraph is more likely to be effective if you and your reader know what the point of each paragraph is and why it appears in the paper in the position it does.

Make the Connection

Thesis sentences are used frequently in legal writing. The rule statement section of IRAC often acts as a thesis statement. Thesis sentences can also be particularly helpful to explain the rule. They can be used to help readers understand your synthesized rule. A thesis sentence can be used to tell the reader why you have selected these particular case examples.

Can you think of a thesis sentence for the following paragraph based on a student memo?

The court in *Rankin* determined that an officer had a voluntary assumption of care because after the plaintiff was stabbed, the officer took the plaintiff to a bench and told him that, "He would be alright." (cite) In *Dennis*, the court determined that no evidence of a voluntary assumption existed, even though the officer was able to ascertain that the decedent was inebriated. (cite) They held that, "a mere response by the police to a call for assistance," did not, "create a special relationship," as the officer did not volunteer any assistance either by words or actions. (cite)

☑ Click Here to **Check Your Response.**

Practice Pointer

Revising Paragraphs

Read the following paragraph from a student memo and decide whether the sentences should be reordered or revised. Citations have been omitted. As you read it, consider:

- What is the purpose of the paragraph?
- Is the paragraph probative or descriptive?
- Is the thesis or topic of the paragraph adequately expressed in the first two sentences?
- Are the sentences in a logical sequence? If not, how would you reorder them?
- Is the paragraph an appropriate length? If not, where would you divide it?

[A] In *Chicarelli*, the plaintiff was a tenant of the defendant. [B] The plaintiff was put on notice that she was effectively evicted from the premises. [C] The plaintiff did not leave the apartment so the defendant sent a police officer and several employees to the plaintiff's apartment to inquire as to why the plaintiff had not surrendered the premises. [D] The event took place without incident. [E] The court held that the plaintiff was not falsely imprisoned because she failed to show that the defendant intended to confine her. [F] "The confinement within the fixed boundaries by the defendant must be complete; if there is a known, safe means of escape, which would only involve a slight inconvenience, there is no false imprisonment." [G] Plaintiff did not indicate that she was confined, she was threatened or physically forced to remain, or even requested a desire to leave the apartment. [H] In *Cohen*, the plaintiff went into the defendant's department store. [I] The defendant's employee allegedly searched the plaintiff's person, finding no merchandise and forcibly grabbed plaintiff's arm to lead her to the manager's office. [J] The court held that if these allegations were true then the plaintiff had established a *prima facie* case of false imprisonment against the defendant. [K] A person has the requisite intent to confine another if "his act was done for the purpose of imposing confinement upon the other or with the knowledge that such confinement would, to a substantial certainty, result from it." [L] An actor is not liable by intentionally preventing another from going in a certain direction, which another has the right or privilege to go.

☑ Click Here to **Check Your Response.**

The first paragraph of the analytical section of your document is unique in that it presents the controlling rules of law and provides your reader with a guide to the full section. In the memorandum, this will be the first paragraph of the discussion. In the brief, it will be the first paragraph of the argument. The opening paragraphs often serve a different function from the paragraphs that set out your analysis. These paragraphs are often referred to as "roadmap" paragraphs. They provide a general introduction to the brief or memo as a whole. Review these paragraphs to be sure they include all necessary information, and edit to delete extraneous information or to add missing points.

In the following example, taken from a student memo, consider whether the roadmap paragraphs introduce the discussion section of the memo:

If the city does not grant Parr a permit to keep Dora, he will be likely to succeed in a discrimination claim against the city. To prove a *prima facie* claim involving a service animal under the ADA, the plaintiff must show: (1) the plaintiff is a qualified individual with a disability under 42 U.S.C. § 12131, (2) the animal is a service animal; (3) the plaintiff needs to use the animal as a service animal under the ADA; and (4) the public accommodation discriminated against the plaintiff in violation of 42 U.S.C. § 12132 by reason of plaintiff's disability. *Access Now, Inc. v. Town of Jasper*, 268 F. Supp. 2d 973, 979 (E.D. Tenn. 2003).

The first element is not in dispute. No Sixth Circuit case directly applies to Parr's situation, but cases from other jurisdictions provide more thorough definitions of service animals and will help Parr prove not only that Dora is a service animal, but that he needs it and that permitting it is a reasonable modification of the current No Pets ordinance. Thus, if the city refuses to grant his permit, this refusal will probably be considered as discrimination under the ADA.

After reading the introductory paragraphs, ask yourself:

- Does this paragraph provide a roadmap to the discussion that follows?
- Does it lead the reader through the steps necessary to reach the legal conclusion?
- Does it dispose of any elements of a test or a claim that will not be further discussed because they are not in dispute?
- Does it focus the reader on the precise issue?
- Does it present, without analysis, the legal issue prediction or conclusion?

Now, re-read your introductory paragraphs with the same questions in mind. Can the reader tell what you are writing about, what legal framework applies, and what you conclude the outcome will be?

Edit for Tone

Tone is the writer's attitude toward the reader. When drafting legal documents for different audiences, notice how your tone may differ and convey an attitude about your reader. You may be a bit more informal with your peers or immediate supervisors and that tone will convey familiarity or collegiality. However, you will adopt a formal tone in briefs to the court that will convey respect and deference. Examine the following notice to employees in a hospital by hospital counsel and the committee on hospital bylaws. See if you can determine the writer's attitude toward the readers. Could you rewrite this notice to communicate differently to the hospital employees?

Take note! This Hospital through the excellent work of the Bylaws Committee and Legal Council are exploring certain questions regarding bylaws about patients and their care. In The Committee's Expert Opinion, it has decided that requiring employee input might be helpful in this large task. Employees will be summoned if needed. If summoned, the employee will be considered clocked in, even if it is not the case. The Committee, under its Official mandate, charges employees to be looking for a summons in their hospital mailboxes, as employees will be called at the Committee's convenience.

————

Edit to Eliminate Extra Words

Lawyers are careful wordsmiths. When revising and editing a legal document, lawyers focus on writing clearly and concisely. Court rules impose page limits, so the word count in a legal document matters. Moreover, legal documents are written for judges and lawyers who are busy, skeptical readers. Thus, it is important to write so that your position is concisely stated and quickly understood.

FYI

For helpful information on concise legal writing, see RICHARD C. WYDICK, PLAIN ENGLISH FOR LAWYERS (5th ed. 2005). *See also* BRYAN A. GARNER, LEGAL WRITING IN PLAIN ENGLISH: A TEXT WITH EXERCISES (2001); TERRI LECLERCQ & KARIN MIKA, GUIDE TO LEGAL WRITING STYLE (5th ed. 2011); MARY BARNARD RAY & JILL J. RAMSFIELD, LEGAL WRITING: GETTING IT RIGHT AND GETTING IT WRITTEN (5th ed. 2010).

————

Eliminate Wordiness in Your Writing

Commonly used legal phrases often use extra words to make a simple point. Lawyers write "*ordered, adjudged, and decreed*," "*annul and set aside*" and "*full and complete*." Many lawyers continue to use such traditional phrases, but choosing one appropriate word will make your writing clearer and more concise. Lawyers may also use legalese. These words may sound important, but they add no meaning to your writing. Examples of legalese include: The *said* case; the *instant* case; the *aforementioned* facts; *heretofore; hereinafter*, and many other words and phrases. You can eliminate legalese without losing any of the content you are communicating.

When you revise, you should also identify and change other commonly used phrases that clutter legal prose. You may be tempted to write: *it was the fact that, in consideration of, is required to, during the time that*, and other wordy phrases. Be aware of these temptations and try to replace wordy phrases with single words, if possible.

Use Strong Verbs, Primarily in Active Voice

Another technique for writing more clearly is to avoid replacing strong verbs with nominalizations. A writer forms a nominalization when he or she turns a verb or adjective into a noun. Replacing a nominalization with the verb will make your writing stronger and more precise.

For example, the phrase "make a determination" uses a nominalization. It is correct grammar, but the effect is a cluttered sentence and less precise writing. Consider replacing it with the strong verb "determine."

> The following phrases are often used in legal writing. Can you identify the nominalization in each? How would you replace it with the verb?
>
> Make an objection to
>
> Makes an argument that
>
> Has a requirement of
>
> Has a provision that
>
> Has knowledge of

Make an objection to	Objects
Makes an argument that	Argues
Has a requirement of	Requires
Has a provision that	Provides
Has knowledge of	Knows

Active and Passive Verb Voice

A verb is either in active or passive voice. To quickly test your verb's voice, ask yourself this question: Is the subject of the sentence acting? If so, the verb is in active voice; if not, the verb is in passive voice.[1]

Examples

The plaintiff *took* the complaint to the prothonotary's office and *filed* it.

The complaint *was taken* to the prothonotary's office and *was filed* by the plaintiff.

Use the quick test on these sentences to check for active or passive voice.

Take Note

Exercise: For more practice with concise writing, revise the following sentences. Eliminate wordiness, and replace nominalizations with strong verbs, primarily using active voice. Keep in mind that shorter sentences often make your point more clearly and concisely.

1. Pursuant to the terms of the contract entered into between the parties, the defendant was required to make a delivery of the building materials within six months.

---

2.   For chapters and exercises explaining active and passive voice, *see* BRYAN A. GARNER, LEGAL WRITING IN PLAIN ENGLISH: A TEXT WITH EXERCISES 24 (2001); RICHARD C. WYDICK, PLAIN ENGLISH FOR LAWYERS 27 (5th ed. 2005).

2. As far as the involvement, both financially and non-financially, in the team by the employer is concerned, Pat, in her interview, stated that her employer, in addition to paying for the team membership, registration fees, and uniforms, allowed post-game festivities to be entirely paid for with a company credit card if clients of the firm were in attendance.

3. It seems, based on the aforementioned, that participation on the softball team was viewed favorably by the supervisor.

4. The injury would also not be considered, as a regular incident of the employment at the firm due to the fact that at that point in time playing softball was not part of the services of the firm.

5. In *Auto-Trol*, the plaintiff was awarded workers compensation, due to the fact that he was mandated by his supervisors to be in attendance of the picnic and to be a participant in the softball game.

6. In this case, the trial court denied compensation, which was also affirmed on appeal.

7. Several facts in the aforementioned statement demonstrate a substantial benefit enjoyed by the employer due to getting new clients.

8. The court made a determination that the defendant would be sentenced to 3 years imprisonment due to the fact that the statute required such a sentence.

9. The court must give consideration to the question as to whether the defendant is entitled to bail.

10. The facts of this case are very similar to those of our client's in that the games were held at a city park.

Revising exercise—This passage from a famous case is different from the original. It now contains overly long sentences, legalese and passive voice among other errors. Please rewrite it to be clearer and more concise. You need not correct the quoted language, and you need not strive to replicate the original. Review the case of _Hawkins v. McGee_ after you complete this exercise.

The plaintiff's skin, taken from his chest, was grafted, after removing scar tissue from the palm of his right hand, of which there was a considerable quantity, on to his hand in the place of the skin that was removed. About nine years before the transaction here involved, an electrical wire was caused to contact the heretofore mentioned hand and severe burning and the aforesaid scarring was the resulting injury. The trial evidence was presented effecting an event that occurred before the instant operation in which the plaintiff and his father and the defendant, in the defendant's office, discussed that, defendant stated "three or four days, not over four; then the boy can go home and it will be just a few days then he will go back to work with a good hand" while responding the defendant's father's question of "How long will the boy be in the hospital?" No justification can be found for a doctor to be contracting hospital treatment in three or four days or even with other testimony effecting the same information that the work could be resumed by the plaintiff in just a very few days following the time in the hospital. The probable construction of the heretofore mentioned statements would be as the opinion or prediction by said defendant and just because these predicted times were much longer in duration would not place the defendant in a position of liability for a breach of contract for making them. The plaintiff could have substantiality to his contract claim by his representation as testimony that before the operation was decided upon the statement made by said defendant was "I will guarantee to make the **hand** a hundred per cent perfect **hand** or a hundred per cent good **hand**." Defendant was alleged to have been in the plaintiff's presence at the time of this speaking and thus a warranty would have to have obviously been given if the utterances could have been proven and if they are to be taken as truth at their value on their face.

Revising exercise—Take this original language from a <u>famous case</u> from 1805, and write it as a court might write it today, using clear, concise, and plain language.

Pursuit alone gives no right of property in animals *feræ naturæ*, therefore an action will not lie against a man for killing and taking one pursued by, and in the view of, the person who originally found, started, chased it, and was on the point of seizing it. Occupancy in wild animals can be acquired only by possession, but such possession does not signify manucaption, though it must be of such a kind as by nets, snares or other means, as to so circumvent the creature that he cannot escape.

Now, read through your discussion paragraphs again, and this time circle words or phrases that you'll consider replacing. Revising to eliminate wordiness and replacing nominalizations with strong verbs in active voice will make your writing clearer and more concise.

————————

Peer Review: An Important Editing Skill for Legal Practice

This chapter has given you several approaches to revising and editing your own written work. However, your professor may ask you to review the work of another student, and may assign others in the class to assess and comment on your writing.

Although you may be anxious about having your peers review your work, giving and receiving such a critique is an important part of being a lawyer, and it is a skill worth practicing as you are starting your legal career.

For example, in your summer jobs and as a young lawyer, you will often be writing for other attorneys who will need to rely on your work. They will review it before using it to make a decision about a client's problem, and then may pass it on to others to review. You are likely to receive comments on your work, including requests for further analysis if yours is incomplete.

In practice, you will sometimes be assigned to write just part of a motion or brief, and to merge what you and others have written into a seamless document.

As a young lawyer you are also likely to review the work of summer associates and student interns. Knowing how best to help them write a well-structured and well-reasoned document is a valuable skill.

If you work for a judge, you will draft opinions, and other law clerks and the judge will review them. Each of them is likely to make changes in your text, and sometimes in your analysis, and you will be expected to revise your work according to their comments.

There is an art to critiquing another's work product without seeming to criticize the individual, and there is an art to learning to accept such a critique gracefully.

Your professor will give you guidelines for reviewing the work of your peers. However, here are some points to keep in mind:

- When reviewing a colleague's draft, read it as though you were the assigning partner who will use this analysis to make a decision about a client's problem.
- Ask what would make this a more useful document for you?
  - Is part of the analysis missing?
  - Is the analysis convincing? Are conclusions of law well supported?
  - Is any part of the analysis confusing? Is there any distracting or unnecessary content?

- ▢   Is there anything you still need to know?
- Review the headings. When read in sequence, do they logically organize the writer's position?
- Pay special attention to connecting sentences—to thesis or topic sentences, and to transitions between paragraphs. Does the writing make all necessary connections for the reader?
- Look for wordiness. Don't rewrite—but circle places where word choice interferes with a clear, concise analysis.

When you review a colleague's work, think about your own drafts of similar assignments. What kind of feedback would be most helpful to you? What problems are difficult to spot on your own? This is where an objective peer editor can be most helpful.

———————

Proofreading Your Document

When you have revised and edited the content of your legal document, one last task remains: Proofreading. Although you will have corrected spelling, grammar, and punctuation as you have noticed errors, creating a flawless brief or memo requires a final review specifically for these points. When proofreading, read each sentence carefully. Be especially alert to missing words, and to words that are spelled correctly but are not what you intended. Word processing will catch spelling errors, but it cannot know that you intended to write "firearm" but instead typed "fireman." Identifying and correcting such errors is the writer's responsibility, and the final step in assuring that your document is the work of a professional.

CHAPTER 10

Writing for Your Client

As an attorney, communication with your client will be a critical component of your practice. This is true not only at the initial stages of meeting and interviewing a client, but throughout your relationship. Effective communication helps to preserve and strengthen the relationship and will help you to attract new clients. Communication, however, is not just a good business practice. In law, it is also an ethical responsibility. Under the rules governing professional conduct, attorneys must maintain contact with their clients. Consider, for example, the American Bar Association's suggested rule for professional conduct:

American Bar Association

Model Rules of Professional Conduct

Client-Lawyer Relationship
Rule 1.4 Communication

(a) A lawyer shall:

　(1) Promptly inform the client of any decision or circumstance with respect to which the client's informed consent, as defined in Rule 1.0(e), is required by these Rules;

　(2) Reasonably consult with the client about the means by which the client's objectives are to be accomplished;

　(3) Keep the client reasonably informed about the status of the matter;

　(4) Promptly comply with reasonable requests for information; and

　(5) consult with the client about any relevant limitation on the lawyer's conduct when the lawyer knows that the client expects assistance not permitted by the Rules of Professional Conduct or other law.

(b) A lawyer shall explain a matter to the extent reasonably necessary to permit the client to make informed decisions regarding the representation.

Your objectives in most client communications include: Telling the client what the law is; explaining what you think the client should do; establishing and maintaining a relationship with your client; and building your professional reputation. You must provide your client with adequate information about the law so that your client can meaningfully consent to your suggested course of action. This means that you must explain to your client any material risks of your suggested course of action and any reasonable alternatives.

Consider your client in the implied warranty of habitability case. What information do you think this client needs to make an informed decision on the appropriate course of action? What level of detail do you think is appropriate? How might the language you use to explain the law to your client differ from the language you used to explain the law to your supervising attorney in the memo?

Often the substance of your client communications will be based upon the research and analysis that you have written in memorandum form. However, memos are rarely written in a way that clients will find helpful. Memos are written for legal audiences and are, therefore, too detailed and too inaccessible to fulfill most clients' needs. Memos do provide the basis for an effective client meeting, telephone conversation, letter or e-mail.

Again, consider your client in the implied warranty of habitability case. What form of communication would you use to convey the results of your research and analysis as to whether the stinkbugs constitute a material defect under the law of Massachusetts? What are the advantages and disadvantages of the various means of communicating with your client? Does your answer depend on whether you are delivering good or bad results?

───────────────

E-mail Correspondence

Increasingly, attorneys are using substantive e-mails to communicate legal advice.[1] These e-mails tend to take the form of an informal memo in that they include a statement of the issue, a recommendation, and the attorney's analysis.[2] Be careful. E-mail makes communication with a client extremely easy, but these e-mails are work-related. They constitute legal advice and should not be viewed casually. View these e-mails as professional correspondence: Edit them carefully and check them for accuracy. Moreover, perhaps because e-mail makes communication so easy, e-mail is easy to misuse. For example:

───────────

1.   *See* Kristen Konrad Robbins-Tiscione, *From Snail Mail to E-Mail: The Traditional Legal Memorandum in the Twenty-First Century*, 58 J. LEGAL EDUC. 32 (2008).

2.   *Id.* at 49.

- Hastily written e-mails can create confusion;

- a lack of proper greetings or closings may feel abrupt to the reader and may be interpreted as rude or unprofessional;

- the speed of e-mail exchanges can mimic face-to-face communication, but the absence of visual cues can easily lead to misunderstandings or emotional, even angry responses; and

- e-mails can be forwarded and compromise confidentiality.[3]

What follows is an e-mail exchange between a recent law school graduate and a well-regarded criminal defense attorney. As you read it, consider how e-mail facilitated this hostile exchange:[4]

——Original Message——

From: Dianna Abdala
Sent: Friday, February 03, 2006 9:23 PM
To: wak
Subject: Thank you

Dear Attorney Korman, At this time, I am writing to inform you that I will not be accepting your offer. After careful consideration, I have come to the conclusion that the pay you are offering would neither fulfill me nor support the lifestyle I am living in light of the work I would be doing for you. I have decided instead to work for myself, and reap 100% of the benefits that I sew. Thank you for the interviews. Dianna L. Abdala, Esq.

——Original Message——

From: William A. Korman
To: 'Dianna Abdala'
Sent: Monday, February 06, 2006 12:15 PM
Subject: RE: Thank you

Dianna—Given that you had two interviews, were offered and accepted the job (indeed, you had a definite start date), I am surprised that you chose an e-mail and a 9:30 PM voicemail message to convey this information to me. It smacks of immaturity and is quite unprofessional. Indeed, I did rely upon your acceptance by ordering stationary and business cards with your name, reformatting a computer and setting up both internal and external e-mails for you here at the office. While I do not quarrel with your reasoning, I am extremely disappointed in the way this played out. I sincerely wish you the best of luck in your future endeavors.—Will Korman

---

3.   For more information on using e-mail effectively, see Tracy Turner, *E-mail Etiquette in the Business World*, 18 PERSP.: TEACHING LEGAL RES. & WRITING 18 (2009); Anne Enquist & Laurel Oates, *You've Sent Mail: Ten Tips to Take with You to Practice*, 15 PERSP.: TEACHING LEGAL RES. & WRITING 127 (2007).

4.   http://www.theinternetpatrol.com/when-emails-haunt-you-the-saga-of-william-korman-and-diana-abdala/ (last visited 1/29/14).

——Original Message——

From: Dianna Abdala
Sent: Monday, February 06, 2006 4:01 PM
To: William A. Korman
Subject: Re: Thank you

A real lawyer would have put the contract into writing and not exercised any such reliance until he did so.

Again, thank you.

——Original Message——

From: William A. Korman
To: 'Dianna Abdala'
Sent: Monday, February 06, 2006 4:18 PM
Subject: RE: Thank you

Thank you for the refresher course on contracts. This is not a bar exam question. You need to realize that this is a very small legal community, especially the criminal defense bar. Do you really want to start pissing off more experienced lawyers at this early stage of your career?

——Original Message——

From: Dianna Abdala
Sent: Monday, February 06, 2006 4:29 PM
To: William A. Korman
Subject: Re: Thank you

bla bla bla

——Original Message——

From: William A. Korman
Sent: Friday, February 10, 2006 7:59 AM
To: 'David Breen'
Subject: FW: Thank you

Did I already forward this to you?

——Original Message——

From: David Breen
Sent: Friday, February 10, 2006 9:47 AM
To: 'William A. Korman'
Subject: RE: Thank you

OH MY GOD! Where to begin? First of all, how unprofessional. and secondly, it is "reap what you 'sow,'" now "sew". if she is going to use a cliché, couldn't she at least spell it right? And WTF is with her "bla bla bla"? Does she not read your e-mail about it being a small community?! So, finally, can I forward this along to some folks? I am sure they would love to see how the up-and-coming lawyers are comporting themselves! (Clearly she did not go to BU!!!) J

——Original Message——

From: William A. Korman
Sent: Friday, February 10, 2006 9:55 AM
To: 'David Breen'
Subject: RE: Thank you

You can e-mail this to whomever you want.

———————

Exercise 1: Tone

Read the e-mail below and consider how you think the recipient of this e-mail would react?

From: Unhappy student
Sent: On a bad day
To: Soon to be unhappy professor
Subject: Re: memos

I picked up my memo. Despite what I thought was having a good understanding of the material in class, I get a B-.

The comments say I should use more of the legislative history and the Act but say I give too many opinions and not enough explanation....

I think this paper was worth at least a B based on the criteria given unless everyone else's was so spectacularly great that their memo just glitters. I don't know if you have the rubric too and the breakdown of points?

Thank you.——

Student

JD Class of ****

How might you alter this e-mail?

———————

Exercise 2: Using E-mail to Communicate With a Client

a) Assume that you have received the following e-mail from your client in the landlord-tenant dispute that was the subject of your first memorandum. How might you respond?

From: Your client
Sent: Thursday, October 4, 2012
To: Junior Associate
Subject: My Apartment in Back Bay

Dear JA,

Thank you again for meeting with me last month. As you might imagine, I am anxious to know how my situation can be resolved and would very much appreciate any information you might be able to provide to this end. I look forward to hearing from you.

Sincerely,

Your Client

Consider both a) what information you need to communicate to your client and b) what form you will use to convey this information.

a) You have just completed a memorandum in which you evaluated this client's concerns. Based on your research, how might you answer the client's request for information? What do you think your client needs to know at this point? What level of detail is appropriate for this client?

b) You have several means available to communicate with your client. You could suggest a meeting in which you can convey information face-to-face. You might call your client, write a letter, or put the information into a reply e-mail. What are the advantages and disadvantages of each mode?

b) After evaluating the advantages and disadvantages, you have decided to summarize the key points of your memo and reply to your client by e-mail. What information would you include?

Please draft a short e-mail reply (no more than 250 words) to your client explaining the bottom-line of your research. Send this e-mail to your instructor as specified. Please include your name, the title of the document ("response to client"), and the name of your client in the subject line.

————————

Client Letters

There are many reasons why you might prefer to write a formal letter to your client instead of writing an e-mail or making a telephone call. A letter may be a better option if the answer to a client question is complicated, the content is more than a few paragraphs long, or if you anticipate that there will be other people reading the letter such as interested third parties, the opposing side, or future attorneys.

FYI The following letter addresses a complex subject and is the type of issue that would likely be shown to other readers:

Promising Junior Associate
3900 Forbes Ave.
Pittsburgh, PA 15260

December 10, 2012

Mr. Mayor and Mr. Chief of Wastewater Management
Mayor and Head of the Wastewater Management Department
City of Ehrendale
400 Green River Rd.
Ehrendale, PA 15210

Dear Mr. Mayor and Mr. Chief of Wastewater Management,

We have researched your questions regarding the discharge of phosphorous into the Green River. The law surrounding discharges into an impaired waterway is strict. Fortunately, there are positive action steps the City may undertake to ensure that it complies with the law and is insulated from citizen litigation or state enforcement penalties as Ehrendale constructs a wastewater treatment plant along the Green River. We have evaluated several scenarios that may arise during the construction and use of the new wastewater treatment plant, and we believe that the action steps stated in this letter offer practical ways to mitigate the potential liability that arises from discharging into an impaired waterway.

We caution, however, that after examining the law of impaired waterways, discharging into the Green River may contain hidden costs. Therefore, it may be cost-effective for the City of Ehrendale to investigate alternate locations for its new wastewater treatment plant. This is one course of action. The steps laid out in this letter proactively address the specific scenarios that could arise from discharging into the Green River. The City should be aware of all potential courses of action as it moves forward in the construction of a new wastewater treatment plant.

A Review of the Facts:
The Green River's Impaired Status

The City proposes to build a new state-of-the-art wastewater treatment plant along the Green River. However, even with the best technology available, the wastewater treated at the plant will produce phosphorous, a nutrient that contributes to low-dissolved oxygen levels in water bodies. Too much phosphorous in a river produces algae blooms and makes the river unsafe for fishing or swimming. From our research, it appears that phosphorous in the Green River currently is generated by two major pollutant sources, a wastewater treatment plant maintained by a nearby municipality and farms located upstream from the City of Ehrendale.

Due to the pollution from these two sources, Pennsylvania has classified the Green River as an impaired waterway for phosphorous. In other words, the state has declared that the Green River has reached its maximum saturation for the nutrient phosphorous, and a plan must be implemented to restore the low-dissolved oxygen in the river to a healthy level. One component of the plan will be a cap on the amount of phosphorous permitted to be in the water.

This cap is known as a Total Maximum Daily Load (TMDL): a specified daily amount of a pollutant permitted to be in the water body after dilution. It is unclear whether the state has developed the TMDL for phosphorous in the Green River. If the state is currently developing the TMDL, the City of Ehrendale is in a good position to advocate for its discharge needs before the TMDL for phosphorous has been set. However, if the TMDL is in place, the City's options may be more limited as it pursues a National Pollutant Discharge Elimination System (NPDES) permit for a phosphorous discharge from the PaDEP.

To better understand the unique challenges that the City will face at it pursues a NPDES permit for its wastewater treatment plant, we will give a brief overview of the relevant regulatory scheme surrounding impaired waterways.

The Clean Water Act and What It Means for Green River

The overarching goal of the Clean Water Act (CWA) is to eliminate all pollution in the nation's waterways. As an interim goal, the CWA seeks to restore the nation's waterways to a level that is fishable and swimmable. To accomplish this, the CWA prohibits the discharge of pollutants like phosphorous from a point source without a NPDES permit. For a waterway that has been classified by a state as an impaired waterway, it is difficult for new dischargers to obtain a NPDES permit. To better grasp the reasons for this challenge, an overview of the impaired waterway regulatory scheme is articulated below.

Total Maximum Daily Loads (TMDLs):

Once a water body has been classified as impaired, the state must develop a plan to return the water body to a water quality standard sufficient for its classified use. As part of the plan, the state must set a Total Maximum Daily Load (TMDL) for each pollutant that has contributed to the water body's impairment. A TMDL is the amount of a particular pollutant allowed to be in the entire water body on any given day. There are several criteria considered when the state sets a TMDL for an impaired waterway. The important thing is that once TMDL is set, it is very difficult to have it revised.

In setting the TMDL for a pollutant such as phosphorous, the state will evaluate all of the current sources of the pollutant in the river. There are two categories of pollutant sources: point sources and non-point sources. A wastewater treatment plant is a point source. A farm is a non-point source of pollution. The CWA only regulates point sources, but in calculating the TMDL for phosphorous in the Green River, the DEP will take into consideration the total amount of phosphorous generated by both point and non-point sources. Once the DEP estimates the amount of phosphorous generated by non-point sources which it cannot regulate, it will then designate the balance of the TMDL pollutant load to be regulated under NPDES permits for point source phosphorous dischargers.

Functionally, TMDL allocations place a cap on the amount of a particular pollutant allowed to be discharged into an impaired waterway by each point source with a current NPDES permit. This cap is implemented by the effluent limitation permitted to the point source. Fortunately, once a NPDES permit has been issued to a point source discharger, as long as that point source does not discharge more of the pollutant than is designated by its corresponding effluent limitation, it is shielded from both citizen suit liability and state sanctions. In the next section, we evaluate the potential legal scenarios the City may face as it pursues a NPDES permit for discharging into the Green River, an impaired waterway.

Receiving a NPDES Permit to Discharge Phosphorous Into the Green River:

The proposed Ehrendale wastewater treatment plant does not currently have a NPDES permit. Because the Green River has already been declared an impaired waterway, the Ehrendale wastewater treatment plant is considered a "new discharger" under the DEP's regulations for impaired waterways.

In order for a new discharger to receive a NPDES permit to release a pollutant into an impaired waterway, it must show that not all the TMDL pollutant allocation loads have been distributed. In other words, once the TMDL has been set for phosphorous, new dischargers to the Green River will have to prove that there is enough undistributed load allocation within the phosphorous TMDL to allow them a permitted load allocation. After examining the unique circumstances surrounding Ehrendale's proposed treatment plant, we anticipate that there are three potential scenarios which may occur as Ehrendale pursues a NPDES permit. The three scenarios are described below:

Scenario 1: The TMDL is set, but there are unassigned phosphorous load allocations:

The first scenario occurs if the DEP has set the TMDL for Green River's phosphorous, but the TMDL load allocations for phosphorous have not yet been entirely apportioned to dischargers through current NPDES permits. In order to receive a NPDES permit for phosphorous, Ehrendale will have to show two things. First, Ehrendale will have to show that the DEP has reserved the necessary pollutant load allocation that if permitted to Ehrendale, would be enough to meet its phosphorous discharge needs. Second, Ehrendale will have to show that the upstream wastewater treatment plant that currently has a permit to discharge phosphorous complies with the state's water quality improvement plan for Green River. If Ehrendale satisfies both of these requirements, the DEP may issue a NPDES permit with a phosphorous effluent limitation to Ehrendale.

Scenario 2: The TMDL is set, but the entirety of the phosphorous load allocations is assigned to the upstream wastewater treatment plant:

The TMDL allocations set aside for point source dischargers may be entirely apportioned to the nearby municipality's wastewater treatment plant. If this is the case, it would be absolutely illegal for Ehrendale to discharge phosphorous into the Green River, with one potential exception: it may be possible for Ehrendale to bargain with the existing wastewater treatment plant to obtain a portion of the current discharger's pollutant load of phosphorous. Ehrendale could then use the portion of the TMDL that it bargained for from the upstream plant as proof that the remaining unassigned pollutant load allocation is sufficient to allow for Ehrendale to discharge phosphorous. If Ehrendale also proved that the upstream discharger is compliant with the water quality plan for Green River, the DEP may issue a NPDES permit to Ehrendale.

Scenario 3: The TMDL for Green River's phosphorous has not yet been determined by the DEP:

It is also possible that the Green River's TMDL for phosphorous has not yet been set by the DEP. Under this scenario, it would still be illegal for Ehrendale to discharge phosphorous into the Green River without a NPDES permit. Yet under this scenario, the City would be in a good position to advocate for a larger portion of load allocations to be calculated into the TMDL for point source dischargers, therefore increasing its likelihood of receiving a NPDES permit to discharge phosphorous into the impaired Green River.

Again, TMDLs allocations are designated after accounting for all of the sources of pollutants: both point and non-point sources. The main sources of Green River phosphorous pollution are the existing upstream wastewater plant and farms. The City could negotiate with these sources to decrease their phosphorous discharge levels, and then advocate to the DEP to allocate a sufficient portion of the phosphorous TMDL to "new dischargers." Negotiations with the farmers may include incentivizing farmers to use best management practices for nutrient run-off. If the City demonstrates that non-point source polluters cause less pollution, then more of the TMDL may be allocated to point source dischargers. Since there is only one other known point source discharger on the Green River, the higher the TMDL allocation for point source dischargers, the more likely some of that allocation will be set aside for new dischargers. In this instance, once the TMDL for Green River phosphorous is set and the City demonstrates that the other point source dischargers are compliant with the water quality plan for Green River, the DEP may issue a NPDES permit to Ehrendale.

Liability Shield and Action Steps

It is not lawful for the City of Ehrendale to discharge phosphorous into the Green River without a NPDES permit. Any illegal discharge would expose the City to a citizen suit or government penalties. However, if the City receives a NPDES permit as a new discharger and then discharges within its effluent limitation for phosphorous, the City would be shielded from liability.

In conclusion, if the City of Ehrendale successfully bargains and advocates for a NPDES permit with a sufficient effluent limitation for discharging phosphorous into the Green River, and the City remains within that limitation when discharging into the impaired waterway, the City will remain free from exposure to citizen suit or government penalties. However, due to the impaired status of the Green River, the City may still be exposed to future hidden costs, including potential litigation or the high cost of new and updated phosphorous treatment technology. Therefore, the City should investigate other locations for its new wastewater treatment plant. If this is not possible, a comprehensive understanding of the law surrounding impaired waterways will insulate the City from a windfall citizen suit. We hope this letter has offered an overview of impaired water body law, the scenarios that may arise as the City pursues a NPDES permit for discharging into the Green River, and some practical action steps that the City may undertake in order mitigate potential liability and costs associated with discharging into an impaired waterway.

Thank you for your inquiries into this important issue. Please do not hesitate to contact our firm with any questions regarding this letter or the scenarios presented within the letter. We hope to remain continually useful to the City of Ehrendale as it moves forward in constructing its new wastewater treatment plant.

Sincerely,

/s/

Promising Young Associate

————

You might also select to send a letter if you want to distance yourself from the reader, for example in a situation where you do not have an attorney-client relationship.

 Notice how the following letter provides instruction without misleading the recipient as to the author's status.

April 2, 2013

Mr. Mitch and Mr. Carl
Dazzle
1 Grant Street
Pittsburgh, PA 15234

Dear Mr. Mitch and Mr. Carl:

It was a pleasure meeting with both of you to discuss the potential of your new business, Dazzle, and where you hope to take it in the future. I understand that you need recommendations on how to legally form your business. I hope my suggestions will be of use to you as you continue with launching and growing Dazzle.

First, I must emphasize that I am not a lawyer, only a law student; therefore I am not authorized to give a legal opinion or practice law. This letter is intended to only serve as a loose guide of the potential issues you should consider as you move forward in forming a formal business entity. I recommend that you seek legal counsel in regards to all matters discussed here.

There are four kinds of business entities for a new business to consider: C Corporation (C Corp), S Corporation (S Corp), Limited Liability Corporation (LLC), and Sole Proprietorship. Given that you are a new and upcoming business that seeks to grow and hopes to pursue venture capital, I recommend you form as a C Corp. There are six things to take into account when choosing an entity: liability, flexibility in ownership and use, venture capital favorability, the inclusion of foreign nationals, initial public offering (IPO) favorability, and taxation.

A C Corp may be the best option for Dazzle. Under a C Corp, shareholders are typically not liable for the business' actions, which is an important benefit of legally forming the company. To establish a C Corp, you are required to register with the state, pay a fee, and file by-laws and annual reports. There must also be an elected board of directors or officers who manage the company, annual meetings, and annual reports filed. While this is not the most flexible operating scheme for a budding business, a C Corp offers many other benefits. For example, stocks in a C Corp are easily transferable. When capital needs to be raised, shares of the company can be sold. It also allows for flexible profit sharing between the owners. If you want to easily sell the business and want the earnings to stay in the business, a C Corp is a good choice.

A C Corp offers many other favorable features. A C Corp permits the use of venture capital. Given that you expect to seek out venture capital investments, this is of paramount importance. C Corps allow foreign nationals to own stock. If you anticipate soliciting foreign investment, this is an important consideration. Moreover, if you foresee Dazzle considering an IPO (offering stocks to the general public), a C Corp extends that availability.

The tax structure of a C Corp is also beneficial for a new business. With a C Corp, the company is taxed at the corporate rate. It is also subject to "double taxation." If dividends are distributed to individuals, those dividends are taxed, as well. While this may be a drawback, a C Corp offers a great benefit to the business owners. It has favorable Section 1202 tax treatment. Under Section 1202 of the tax code, individual small business owners may qualify for special capital gains tax breaks netted from small business stocks. A C Corp offers the best combination of all the necessary components of forming a business for Dazzle.

Another reasonable formation option for Dazzle would be an S Corp. It has many features similar to a C Corp. An S Corp has the same liability structure; forms in the same way; requires the same organizational structure; possesses the same stock options; offers the same ease in selling the business; and is excellent for keeping the money in the company. It differs, however, in several important aspects. It is venture capital friendly but is not as amenable as a C Corp. An S Corp does not permit foreign investors or allow for an IPO. The taxes are also substantially different, though not necessarily in a way that disadvantages the company. The S Corp avoids the "double taxation" of the C Corp with what is called "pass through taxation." With this, there is no tax at the business level. The income is passed to the shareholders who then pay taxes on it. An S Corp, however, does not have the same favorable Section 1202 treatment as a C Corp. An S Corp may be considered for Dazzle, but ultimately a C Corp is most likely the best route for the company.

I would not recommend forming as an LLC in this case. An LCC is not amenable to venture capital. You should take into account that an LLC offers great flexibility for a fledgling business. To form an LLC, all a business has to do is register with the state. There is no mandated management structure to steer and watch over the company. Members can set up the business structure as they wish with an Operating Agreement. Members are also typically not liable for the business' actions. Given, however, that you foresee the use of venture capital, an LLC is likely not the best business formation for Dazzle.

I would also not suggest that Dazzle form as a Sole Proprietorship. Under a Sole Proprietorship, there is unlimited personal liability to the business members. One of the great benefits of legally forming your business is the lifting of personal liability. You do not want to sacrifice that with a Sole Proprietorship.

Given all of these factors, I recommend that you form as a C Corp. This allows for the best use of venture capital. As individuals and a new business, you would benefit from a C Corp tax formation. This also allows for the most future flexibility, opening up the possibility for foreign investors and an IPO. I would like to reiterate that you should seek legal counsel regarding this recommendation and in moving forward as you form your business. As previously stated, I am not a lawyer and am not authorized to provide a legal opinion. I wish you best of luck with the further development and success of Dazzle.

Sincerely,

/s/

Promising Junior Associate

————————

Client letters are business letters and follow the same format with a few special features. First, remember your reader is likely to be a layperson, unfamiliar with legal vocabulary, legal concepts, or legal reasoning. Even if your reader is a lawyer, he or she will not be as familiar with the complexity of the law that you have researched and, importantly, the reader does not need to be this familiar. Do not devote space to explanations that your reader will find confusing and unnecessary. Include what the client needs to make an informed decision: "A lawyer shall explain a matter to the extent reasonably necessary to permit the client to make informed decisions regarding the representation." ABA rules of PC 5(a) page 147.

While a legal memorandum will often form the basis for the content of your letter, because your reader has different motivations for reading the letter than your supervisor has for reading your memorandum, the content and style of the letter will vary from the memorandum.

Make the Connection

Memorandum	Client Letter
Heading	Name, address, salutation
Question presented/issue	Introductory paragraph, which states the issue
Brief answer	Opinion
Statement of the facts	Summary of the facts
Discussion	Explanation suitable for client
Conclusion & closing	Advice & closing

The client letter is meant to answer the client's concerns by informing him or her of the controlling law and explaining exactly what the client should do or what you will do on behalf of your client. While the letter is meant to inform, it also has a persuasive function in that you may need to convince your client to follow a certain course of action. It is also meant to demonstrate that you have listened to and heard your client's concerns and to show that you are able to express the law in language they can understand and easily access. The letter should provide sound advice. Do not make promises that you cannot keep. Also, maintain a professional demeanor by writing in a timely fashion, carefully editing your document and using a direct, businesslike tone.

Format and Style: Client letters typically include the following elements in the following order.

- Name and address of the recipient and a file reference;

- Salutation ("Dear ____,");

- Introductory paragraph;

- Your opinion (if the news is favorable);

- Summary of the facts upon which the opinion is based;

- Explanation of your opinion;

- Advice (if the news is unfavorable, you might hold stating your opinion until this point in the letter);

- Closing ("sincerely," and your signature).

The introductory paragraph should establish the appropriate relationship with your reader. Try to personalize the letter in some way. You can do this in many ways including using precise language so that the reader knows you understand his or her particular issue. If you have met with the reader, you may want to acknowledge this meeting or if you have discussed a particular issue, acknowledge this. You should define the issue or indicate the scope of the letter in the first or second sentence. If you have an answer to a particular question or an opinion that is favorable, you should state this opinion and then explain your advice. This explanation should include how the reader should proceed. If the news, however, is unfavorable, you may need to prepare the reader for your opinion. In this case, your introductory paragraph may summarize the facts or law briefly to lay a foundation for what will follow. If the letter is detailed, you should also include a roadmap.

FYI

Notice how this author has used two questions in the introductory paragraph to serve as a roadmap:

"It was a pleasure meeting with you last week and thank you for contacting our offices to provide you with assistance. There are several circumstances to consider regarding the opening of a new wastewater treatment plant in relation to the Clean Water Act. I understand that this is an incredibly complicated process involving funding, regulations, labor, etc. I will provide the necessary legal implications based on the facts that we currently know in order to provide you with the ability to make informed decisions. The purpose of this letter is to examine the specific questions that we discussed in our meeting: 1) What are the legal standards related to new discharges into an impaired waterway? 2) Will the new facility be subject to a citizen suit or subsequent state enforcement?"

Your letter should also include an explanation of your opinion. This may be placed before or after the statement of your opinion. This explanation must be shorter and more client-specific than the explanation contained in a legal memorandum. Although the level of detail will depend on the issue subject matter, and the client, generally you do not need to include the text of the statute or references to cases. Summarize these references generally in a way that does not require citations to authority. Focus particularly on how the law impacts your client. In terms of IRAC, this means focus on the "A" or the application portion of your analysis. You will probably need to only briefly touch on counter-arguments if you touch on them at all. The reader of a client letter will typically be concerned with the bottom-line and the steps he or she should take in the future, according to your advice.

The client letter should also explain the implications of your opinion. In other words, you should advise your client. Be sure to clearly articulate how the client should proceed. If there is more than one possible course of action, describe and evaluate these options. Tell your client which option you believe to be in his or her best interests.

As with your introductory paragraph, your concluding paragraph should be tailored to the particular situation. Avoid canned conclusions. Some firms include a statement that the opinion is based on current law and specified facts and that the opinion would differ given different facts or law. Some law firms believe this sort of disclaimer sets the wrong tone. Be sure to clarify your supervisors' expectations. Finally, close as you would any business letter: "Sincerely," or "Sincerely yours," and your signature.

Edit the letter carefully. Check your overall organization and your organization at the paragraph level. Use thesis or topic sentences. The point of each paragraph should be clear to you and your reader. Examine the sentences within each paragraph to make sure that they support the thesis or topic sentence. The relationship between ideas and from one sentence to another should be explicit, either through a choice of language that links ideas or by using transitional phrases.

At the sentence level, check to see if you have used concrete subjects, active verbs, and relatively short sentences. Remove grammatical and typographical errors, and be sure to get the client's name right. Assess the tone of your letter as well. You should strive for a professional, direct tone, but you will also want to appear approachable and accessible.

FYI How does the letter deliver difficult advice to the client? How would you describe the tone? What language or organization does the author use to create this tone?

[HOSPITAL LETTERHEAD]

CONFIDENTIAL AND PRIVILEGED PEER REVIEW

March 12, 2011
[name]
[address]

Re: Letter of Counsel

Dear Dr. _____:

Thank you for meeting with the Executive Leadership Committee on March 10, 2011 to discuss a complaint regarding your interactions with a nurse in the Emergency Department on Feb. 14, 2011. We appreciate your professionalism in speaking with us about these difficult issues.

We recognize the ED can be an extremely stressful environment. However, we counsel you to remember that everyone who works in the ED feels that same stress. In such a setting, a person may say something that sounds harsher than intended, and the recipient of the statement may perceive it more negatively than intended.

Accordingly, as a leader in the ED, you must set the example by striving to maintain a professional demeanor at all times. If occasionally an interaction does not meet this standard, remember that a simple apology can go a long way in maintaining effective working relationships with your colleagues.

Also, remember that there are always channels by which you can raise concerns about the quality of a nurse's work. If the head nurse is unable to address the issue, please inform nursing administration. If the issue is still not resolved, please go directly to the President of the Medical Staff or the Chief Nursing Officer.

A copy of this letter will be placed in your confidential file. You may file a written response if you wish, and that response will be maintained along with this letter.

Thank you for your efforts on behalf of the Hospital. We look forward to continuing to work with you to provide care to our patients.

Sincerely,

/s/

Attorney's name

Take Note

An effective client letter should consider the following elements:

I.   Organization:
   - Letter contains an introductory paragraph, opinion, summary of the facts, explanation, advice, and concluding paragraph;
   - Information is logically arranged.

II. Content:
   - The introductory sentence identifies the topic and establishes the appropriate relationship with the client;
   - The opinion is sound and adequately explained on the basis of an accurate understanding and assessment of the controlling law and facts;
   - The explanation provides adequate information for the client both to understand the opinion and advice and to make an informed decision as to the course of action;
   - Options are explained and advice is explicit.

III. Writing:
   - The letter is well written in terms of tone, paragraphing, sentence structure, word choice, and editing.

Client Presentations

You might also decide to present information to your client in person or by telephone. Even when informal, this interaction will likely be more efficient if you prepare talking points. As with an e-mail and letter, your memorandum will provide the content you will need to cover, but as with written correspondence, the client will require less detail or less nuanced explanation of the law. Begin your preparation by rereading your memorandum. Consider next if you can organize your thoughts into three major points. You may, of course, have more or less than three points, but you will often be able to cover a great deal in three points. Limiting the amount of information to three points will also help your listener to follow your presentation. For example, you can touch on background information, your opinion, and your advice in three points. In selecting precisely what to go over, try to anticipate what questions or concerns your client might have. Imagining how you might express this information in spoken form is also a useful way to consider what your written correspondence might include. Even if your communication with your client will be exclusively written, thinking about how you would articulate these ideas in a colloquial yet professional manner will help you to adopt the proper written tone.

———————————

Communication With a Supervisor

As a junior associate, much of your communication will be with colleagues, for example a senior partner, a person senior in command, or another attorney. You would be wise to think about these colleagues in much the same way you think about your clients. This means that you should communicate with them with the same level of formality and professionalism as you would with a client. Be respectful, responsive, and meticulous with your analysis and presentation of that analysis. The effort you put forward at the start of your career will help you to not only develop good habits, but also to establish your reputation, advance in the legal profession, and avoid negative interactions and unnecessary confusion. This advice extends to all communication with colleagues, including short conversations, e-mails, informal and formal presentations.

———————————

Exercise: Presentation to a Supervisor

Working in small groups, prepare a 10-15 minute presentation for your supervising attorney. In this presentation, you should explain the analysis of your client's case under the Massachusetts law defining the Implied Warranty of Habitability, and advise your client of your findings. The content of this presentation should be based upon your completed memorandum. Also discuss whether we should consider other actions on behalf of our client.

This is a group presentation; you may divide the work as you like, provided that the work is evenly distributed among your group members. If the members of your group reached different conclusions, you should consider how to incorporate these differences in a way that provides your supervisor with a coherent explanation of the law and a consistent application of the law to the client's facts. For example, differences could potentially be incorporated as counter-analysis.

One member of your group should be in charge of recording the process your group used to complete this task. This person should submit a one-page summary describing this process and should explain each member's role in the group. This report should also evaluate the effectiveness of your approach and explain how you resolved any difficulties you encountered.

Your supervisor will be interested in learning the results of your research and will also be assessing the accuracy and depth of your legal analysis, the clarity of your explanation, your organization, creativity, communicative skills, and your ability to work effectively as a group. The supervisor may ask questions during and at the end of your presentation.

Take Note

Consider the following elements as you prepare your presentation:

I.   Analysis

- Issues concisely framed;
- Argument clearly and accurately supported;
- Relevant authority thoroughly and objectively considered;
- Solution insightful and original;
- Client's needs understood.

II. Style

- Well organized/logically presented;
- Appropriate and fluent use of terms and concepts;
- Effective use of verbal and nonverbal communication;
- Creative;
- Within time limit.

III. Team Roles

- Equivalent roles/balanced contribution.

CHAPTER 11

Introduction to Advocacy

In the first part of this text, you learned how to draft a document that predicts the answer a court might give to a legal question. To predict, you must examine statutes, precedent cases, and other authorities and evaluate answers on both sides of the legal question. Predictive writing reaches a conclusion, but does so only after a thorough examination of the issue from all perspectives.

You will now focus on writing persuasively. In persuasive writing, you focus on legal analysis and arguments that benefit your legal conclusion. However, first you must examine the legal issue dispassionately and predictively to determine the arguments that you will face and to determine how to rebut those arguments. Writing persuasively, however, you will not expound on the arguments on all sides of the issue, as you did with the counter-analysis in predictive writing.

Practice Pointer

In practice, before writing a brief or other persuasive document, many attorneys will write a predictive memorandum examining all of the issues before the court and the arguments that would support a decision in favor of each party. Judges will often have their clerks draft bench memos examining all the arguments on both sides of an issue and proposing the best legal solution under existing law.

Persuasive Argument

Attorneys write advocating for certain results in many different situations. They write motions and briefs in each level of court representing the interests of their clients and requesting rulings from the court or decision-maker. Lawyers also advocate in letters to opposing counsel and sometimes to their clients arguing for a particularly well-advised course of action. Judicial opinions are also pieces of advocacy as judges write to persuade multiple audiences, including the parties, other courts, and the legal community.

Knowing your audience is very important when you write persuasively. Your arguments are tailored to the particular person or group of persons who will read and decide on the issue you present. The tone of written advocacy often is more formal than that of predictive memoranda, as you are asking for a particular result from the reader, and many times the reader is a formal decision-maker such as a judge, justice, or arbitrator. If you are writing as a judge, the tone is formal because the work may stand as precedent and will be read by the bench, bar, the parties and other lay people.

To advocate well, the lawyer must persuade the reader to agree with the propositions made in the document. In order to persuade, writers use many different techniques. Some focus on language: word choice as well as word placement are tools of persuasion for the legal writer. Others may persuade through the weight of authority that supports a certain legal conclusion. Still others focus on factual similarities and differences in the case or rely on the work of legal scholars. Some use all of these techniques.

To write persuasively, you must first understand all of the controlling law, including constitutional provisions, applicable statutes, regulations, and cases. Then, you should understand how those authorities can be understood to support or to possibly undermine your argument. In essence, you need to be able to know the information that would be in a predictive memo before you begin to write a persuasive document.

Persuasion

Think for a moment about something you recently were persuaded to do. Perhaps you responded to television coverage of those whose homes were destroyed in a hurricane, and you made a donation to a relief organization. If so, you were persuaded by an emotional appeal, or pathos. Or maybe you decided to purchase a particular phone after comparing statistics on cost, service, and user satisfaction. In that case, you made a decision based on logic, or logos. You may have made a decision to vote for a candidate after hearing her speak, and being convinced by her candor, thoughtfulness, and honesty. There, you were persuaded by credibility, or ethos.

Persuasive argument by pathos, logos, and ethos was identified by Aristotle, and lawyers and others continue to base their arguments on one or, more often, a combination of these classic categories. Judges rely on these principles as well. In the U.S. legal system, judges are neutrals, not advocates, but as discussed in the next chapter, a judge writing an opinion is also writing to persuade.

A brief or opinion will use logos to indicate its logic and consistency, based on legal support. Advocates demonstrate logos with documents that follow a logical structure and present well-supported legal conclusions based on the controlling law.

Additionally, to persuade a court or a jury to decide in favor of your client, you must prove yourself to be a credible source of information. In other words, you should provide ethos to your argument. You must be an expert in the field of law about which you argue and you should make your arguments well-based in prevailing law, reasonable, and believable. Lawyers may lose credibility with the court and other attorneys by failing to follow court rules or making arguments that are not grounded in current law.

Finally, many well written legal arguments provide an element of pathos. Pathos is an emotional appeal to win the heart of your audience. While appellate briefs and judicial opinions are usually not full of emotional language, they often appeal to the goodness of their audience and a

> **FYI**
>
> To read more about Ethos, Pathos and Logos in argumentation, *see* IRENE L. CLARK, THE GENRE OF ARGUMENT 73, 87-91 (1998).

sense of fairness while using professional language and tone, and applying the controlling law.

Exercise

Bring to class an example of something that persuades you. It can be a legal or non-legal source. Be prepared to explain why it persuades you using the theories of ethos, pathos and logos and how similar reasoning might be helpful in a legal document.

Persuasion in Appellate Practice

To be persuasive to an appellate court, an appeal must follow the rules of appellate procedure for the federal courts or for an individual state. Attorneys

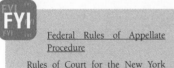

> **FYI**
>
> Federal Rules of Appellate Procedure
>
> Rules of Court for the New York Court of Appeals (the state's highest court): http://www.nycourts.gov/ctapps/techspecs.htm

need to know and follow any court rules which control the format and submission of a particular document. These rules will often limit the arguments that you can raise with the court and will, therefore, also limit the types of arguments that will be persuasive to an appellate court.

When appealing to an intermediate appellate court in the United States, the losing party has an appeal as of right. If you follow all the procedural requirements and can present an error of law preserved for the court's review, the court must accept the case.

An appeal to the highest court must start with a timely request for the court to hear the case as highest courts have discretionary review. This means the court can choose the cases that it hears. In the United States Supreme Court, the request for review is called a Petition for a **Writ of *Certiorari***. This request has different names in different states. Your case will only be heard on the merits, or the issues you are appealing, if the court first accepts your case for review and grants the petition.

An attorney appealing in either level of appellate court must also consider the scope and standard under which that court will evaluate the issues raised. The arguments you use to persuade the court must satisfy both the scope and standard of review. The standard of review gives the court the procedure it must use to decide the case. The scope of review determines how much of the record is available for the court to review. Although many courts use these terms interchangeably, they are separate concepts, and we will address them individually so that the distinction is clear to you.

When appellate courts review the decisions of the lower courts, the scope of review states the portions of the record a reviewing court can consider. The record will include all documents filed in the case thus far. Questions of law are reviewed under the *de novo* scope of review, which is also called plenary review. Under this standard, the court can review the entire record and need not accept any legal conclusions of the court below.

However, as mentioned in chapter Two, appellate courts are reluctant to review findings of facts. When addressing an argument based on facts, the appellate court gives great deference to the trial court and reviews only for clear error under the <u>abuse of discretion</u> scope of review. A reviewing court will overturn a finding of fact only when the record shows that the finding was clearly erroneous.

The standard of review is often based on the procedural posture of the case and directs the court on how it should review the record. For example,

Make the Connection

When writing to persuade an appellate court, the advocate primarily should consider presenting issues and errors of law for the court's review. Appellate courts will almost always accept the findings of fact from the trial court, except under the most exceptional of circumstances. *See* Alex Wilson Albright & Susan Vance, *Ten Practical Tips for Making Your Case Appealable*—Tip 10, 38 LITIGATION NEWS, ABA SECTION ON LITIGATION (Spring 2013).

if a case comes before an appellate court on a motion to dismiss for failure to state a claim under <u>Rule 12(b)(6)</u>, the appellate court is reviewing only the Complaint (the first document filed by the plaintiff in a civil case) to see if has put forth a legal claim. The standard of review tells the court how to review the Complaint. As you can see in the example below, the standard gives the court precise guidance on the procedure for reviewing and deciding the case.

Take Note

Here is an example of the standard of review on a motion to dismiss:

For a defendant to prevail on a motion to dismiss under Federal Rule of Civil Procedure 12(b)(6), it must appear beyond doubt that the plaintiff can prove no set of facts in support of his claim which would entitle him [or her] to relief. *Conley v. Gibson,* 355 U.S. 41, 45-46 (1957); the purpose of a motion under Federal Rule 12(b)(6) is to test the formal sufficiency of the statement of the claim for relief in the complaint. *Rutman Wine Co. v. E. & J. Gallo Winery,* 829 F.2d 729, 738 (9th Cir. 1987). It is not a procedure for resolving a contest about the facts or the merits of the case. In reviewing the sufficiency of the complaint, the issue is not whether the plaintiff will ultimately prevail but whether the plaintiff is entitled to offer evidence to support the claims asserted. *Scheuer v. Rhodes,* 416 U.S. 232, 236 (1974). Since the motion raises only an issue of law, the court has no discretion as to whether to dismiss a complaint that it determines to be formally insufficient. *Yuba Consolidated Gold Fields v. Kilkeary,* 206 F.2d 884, 889 (9th Cir. 1953). *** The complaint should be construed in the light most favorable to the plaintiff, and its allegations are taken as true. *Scheuer,* 416 U.S. at 237. (Some text and cites omitted.)

Click case name to read <u>California v. Credit Managers Association</u>, the case from which this standard was excerpted.

Often, the scope and standard of review are discussed in the appellate brief. The rules for most courts indicate where to place the statement of the scope and standard of review. A well-written brief may refer to the standard of review when advocating for the court to rule in a particular way, and may frame its arguments according to the standard.

For more information on the scope and standard of review, including standards used to review agency decisions, see MARY BETH BEAZLEY, A PRACTICAL GUIDE TO APPELLATE ADVOCACY (3d ed. 2012).

Exercises

1. Research the Rules of Court for the United States Supreme Court. Where did you find them? Which rules must an attorney writing a Brief on the Merits follow in formatting his or her brief for the Court?

2. Review and bring to class a well-written court decision, and examine the format the court uses in writing its opinion. Be prepared to explain why the format of the opinion helps to persuade the reader. Also be prepared to explain other persuasive techniques that the court uses.

CHAPTER 12

Writing as the Court

There are several reasons for including an understanding of judicial writing as one of the foundational skills you learn during this first year of law school. Right now, you may never think you will be a judge; however, all judges were law students at one time and your desire to work as or for the court may grow over time. Judicial writing is persuasive writing, and the tools of persuasion that you have been learning and practicing are also part of a well-reasoned judicial opinion. Now that you have an understanding of using persuasive techniques to support a legal argument, you will be able to recognize the courts' more subtle use of persuasion in opinions, and may better understand how and why each opinion is structured as it is.

In addition, many students work for judges, both during and after law school. Most state and federal judges have unpaid law student interns during the school year or during the summer. This is an invaluable experience, as it provides insights into the adjudicative process as well as opportunities to observe lawyers in the courtroom. Most judges (or their law clerks) assign student interns parts of judicial opinions to draft. Students often find it challenging to write in a context that affects actual parties using a judicial voice with an authoritative tone. Practicing this skill will make a student law clerk more comfortable when presented with the task of drafting a judicial opinion.

Finally, many of the key components of judicial opinions were first written by the attorneys in briefs and legal memoranda submitted to a court. Judges rely on the parties' written arguments. In the U.S. common law legal system, lawyers frame the issues the court will decide, research and make the arguments that support their client's position, explain why the court should not be persuaded by the arguments of the opposing party, and show the court how to use precedent to decide in their client's favor. Legal briefs give the court alternate ways to decide a legal problem, and these frameworks are first conceptualized and written by the lawyers. The task of writing briefs is quite common, so recognizing the impact of the brief on the judicial opinion is important. Therefore practicing drafting judicial opinions or bench memos will help you to appreciate your brief writing from the perspective of your audience.

Bench Memos and Judicial Opinions

This chapter addresses the types of writing that judges—and those working for them—compose. Judges rely on their law clerks and student interns to help prepare them for a wide variety of judicial tasks. Law clerks frequently summarize the parties' arguments or research the current state of the law in a document you have already learned to write: a legal memorandum. Although a judge may prefer a particular format, the memos you have practiced researching and writing this year have prepared you well for such an assignment.

The focus here is on two other documents you may find yourself drafting if you work for a judge: a bench memo and a judicial opinion. The first of these, a bench memo, is written by a law clerk for an appellate judge. Much as a memo prepares a judge for a conference with counsel or to hear argument on a trial motion, a bench memo prepares an appellate judge for oral argument.

———————————

Writing a Bench Memo

A bench memo summarizes the case on appeal. Using the parties' briefs, the writer summarizes each side's position on each issue. The focus is on the actual dispute. The bench memo will address where the parties disagree and how legal rules may support each position. It identifies strengths and weaknesses in each party's arguments, and it indicates significant policy implications for the court. A well written bench memo is a great asset to an appellate judge. It is an internal document that is designed to be *used*, and the judge is likely to refer to it before, during, and after oral argument.

A bench memo must include the writer's recommendation on the procedural disposition of the case. The writer's recommendation is such an important component that most judges expect it to be presented twice. The recommendation will typically appear in a brief introduction at the start of the memo, and again at the end of the document. It may appear in bold type for emphasis.

———————————

Bench Memo Format

Although an individual judge may have a preferred format, a bench memo will generally include the following components:

I.   Introduction: a short opening paragraph summarizing the parties and the claim, and including the writer's recommendation. This may include a brief statement of the procedural posture, so the judge knows precisely why it is before the court.

II. Brief facts or background, including procedural posture if not already explained, and a statement of the appellate court's jurisdiction.

III. A statement of the issues or questions presented. This should include the standard of review.

IV. Discussion or Analysis. Similar to the discussion section of a research memorandum, the discussion component of a bench memo should follow a logical format, and be broken up with headings and subheadings where appropriate. The judge should be able to quickly move through the discussion of an issue and clearly understand the actual dispute, and each party's argument.

V.   Brief conclusion, repeating the recommendation.

See It

The following Introduction is from a student bench memo summarizing the briefs in *Perkins v. McQuiggin*, 670 F.3d 665 (6th Cir. 2012).

Introduction

This case concerns whether Respondent Floyd Perkins, an inmate in a Michigan correctional facility, can bring an untimely habeas corpus petition under the Antiterrorism and Effective Death Penalty Act of 1996 where the petition is based on a claim of actual innocence and was not pursued with reasonable diligence. Petitioner, Greg McQuiggin, a Warden of a Michigan correctional facility, appeals from the Sixth Circuit decision allowing Perkins's habeas corpus petition to be heard in the district court. The Sixth Circuit held that reasonable diligence is not a requirement for pursuing a writ of habeas corpus when actual innocence is the basis for the petition.

Recommendation: Affirm

The following Discussion is part of a student bench memo summarizing the briefs in *Perkins v. McQuiggin*, 670 F.3d 665 (6th Cir. 2012). As you read this component of the bench memo, remember that the purpose of a bench memo is to summarize the case for the judge and make a well-supported recommendation. Put yourself in the judge's robe, and ask yourself the following questions: What precise legal

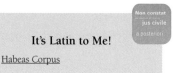

It's Latin to Me!

Habeas Corpus

question is before the court? What are each party's positions on that issue? Do you think the writer summarized the arguments so that they are easy to understand? Why or why not? What position does the writer take? Does the writer do a good job explaining the reasons for this recommendation?

See It

Discussion

To decide whether Perkins can bring a petition for a writ of habeas corpus based on his new evidence of actual innocence, this Court must interpret 28 U.S.C. § 2244(d)(1)(D) (2012). In 1996, Congress enacted this statute to "streamline the federal habeas review process 'without undermining basic habeas corpus principles and while seeking to harmonize the new statute with prior law.'" *Perkins v. McQuiggin*, 670 F.3d 665, 674 (6th Cir. 2012) (*citing Holland v. Florida*, 130 S. Ct. 2549, 2562 (2010)). The statute balances the need for finality and the ability to litigate fresh issues against the defendant's interest in being released from incarceration, especially improper incarceration. Pet. Br. 7.

Under 28 U.S.C. § 2254(d), a habeas petitioner may obtain relief for a state-court conviction in limited circumstances. However, the petition must be filed within one year from the latest of four possible dates. 28 U.S.C. § 2244(d)(1). At issue here is the new evidence provision. 28 U.S.C. § 2244(d)(1)(D). Pursuant to § 2244(d)(1)(D), a habeas petitioner must file a habeas corpus petition based on new evidence within one year from "the date on which the factual predicate of the claim or claims presented could have been discovered through the exercise of due diligence." 28 U.S.C. § 2244(d)(1)(D). This provision, however, does not address whether there is an exception to the one-year statute of limitations period when the petitioner claims actual innocence. *Id.*

The Warden argues that the plain meaning of the statute and equity dictate that an actual innocence exception does not exist when a habeas petitioner files based on new evidence, and that reasonable diligence is always required. Pet. Br. 17-18, 26-27. Perkins, on the other hand, submits that the past use of and the precedent surrounding the actual innocence exception indicates that the exception is included in § 2244(d)(1), despite the statute's silence. Resp. Br. 17-25.

A. This Court should find that there is an actual innocence exception.

Petitioner and Respondent disagree about whether 28 U.S.C. § 2244(d)(1) (D) incorporates an actual innocence exception to its new evidence statute of limitations. Under the relevant provision, a habeas corpus petitioner must file for relief one year from the date on which new evidence could have been discovered through reasonable diligence. The Warden argues that both the plain meaning and context of the statute show that no actual innocence exception to § 2244(d)(1)(D) exists. Pet. Br. 17.

The Warden first notes that the statutory language is unambiguous and that the statute does not list an exception. *Id.* at 17-18. Additionally, in context of the successive petition provision, 28 U.S.C. § 2244(b)(2)(B), the actual innocence exception for new evidence is unnecessary. *Id.* at 17. Section 2244(b)(2) (B) allows a defendant to file a second motion for habeas relief if the defendant has new evidence that was not discovered before the first habeas motion. *Id.* Therefore, if Perkins were permitted to file an untimely first habeas petition based on new evidence, this would render the new evidence exception to successive petitions useless. *Id.* at 18. For instance, the Warden notes that with an actual innocence exception to the new evidence limitations period Perkins could file a habeas petition at any time after discovering new evidence—even as much as fifty years after discovery. *Id.* Instead, the Warden suggests that the successive petitions provision indicates that Congress intended a habeas petitioner to file the first petition within a year of discovering the new evidence, and if necessary, he or she could then file a successive petition after discovering additional evidence. *Id.*

Perkins, however, argues that Supreme Court case law, specifically this Court's holding in *Holland*, illustrates that the statute's limitation period recognizes the actual innocence exception. Resp. Br. 26. In *Holland*, this Court, interpreting a different statute of limitations, held that a "nonjurisdictional federal statute of limitations is normally subject to a 'rebuttable presumption' in favor of 'equitable tolling.'" *Id.* (quoting *Holland*, 130 S. Ct. at 2560 (citation omitted)). Furthermore, this Court stated in *Holland* that "where 'equitable principles have traditionally governed,' it has refused to 'construe a statute to displace courts' *traditional equitable authority* absent the clearest command.'" *Id.* at 27 (quoting *Holland*, 130 S. Ct. at 2560). Therefore, statutory silence regarding the actual innocence exception does not foreclose the exception's existence but rather indicates its presence. *Id.* at 27-28.

In fact, the dense history surrounding habeas practice shows that the actual innocence exception is an example of traditional equitable authority. *Id.* at 28-29. Initially, federal courts hearing habeas petitions did not utilize procedural limits, such as a statute of limitations, when deciding the issue. *Id.* at 18. Instead, procedural barriers did not exist for habeas petitions, so that courts could consider the defendant's detention. *Id.* However, eventually Congress and the courts began to develop some habeas corpus petition procedures. *Id.* Still, the procedural limits balanced the interests of finality and administrative ease with the individual's interest in his or her detention. *Id.* at 19.

In addition to habeas petitions' history, Perkins also argues that the courts have traditionally recognized the actual innocence exception. *Id.* at 20-25. For example, traditionally, new evidence could overcome procedural barriers if the petitioner could show that "that it was more likely than not that no reasonable juror would have convicted him in the light of the new evidence." *Id.* (citations omitted). Also, this Court has previously recognized the actual innocence exception despite procedural limits imposed by Congress, the courts, or the states. *Id.* at 21-25.

Perkins's argument about the history of this Court's jurisprudence surrounding habeas petitions is persuasive. He correctly notes that the statute is silent regarding the actual innocence exception. However, this silence does not make the statute unambiguous; instead, the silence leads to ambiguity. It is possible that if Congress intended an actual innocence exception to § 2244(d)(1)(D), it could have clearly written so. However, the rich jurisprudence surrounding habeas petitions and the actual innocence exception suggests that, despite the statute's silence, "traditional equitable authority" should govern "absent the clearest command." *Holland,* 130 S. Ct. at 2560.

Furthermore, the Warden's argument regarding the successive petition provision is not persuasive. While that provision allows one to file a petition based on actual innocence, it does not render an actual innocence exception to § 2244(d)(1)(D) unnecessary. Instead, if the habeas petitioner can only file a first habeas petition based on an actual innocence exception, then the successive petition will never even be possible if the first petition cannot be filed. Consequently, the Warden's argument about successive petitions is unavailing. Overall, Perkins's arguments are more sound. This Court's jurisprudence and the rich history of habeas petitions implies that § 2244(d)(1)(D) contains an actual innocence exception.

Tone and Audience

A judicial opinion may be read as a persuasive document, but a bench memo is more of a hybrid. It must be an objective and candid assessment of the arguments for each party on every issue. At the same time, the writer must make a recommendation and logically support it through persuasive reasoning. It should help the judge understand the case, and it should supply reasoning for the suggested outcome.

The audience for a legal document always affects the voice in which a lawyer writes. For most documents written for a court, lawyers must adopt a formal, respectful tone. A bench memo must be complete in addressing all legal issues raised by the parties. It should also be professional in tone and appearance. However, this document will be internal to the judge's chambers. and typically only the judge and his or her staff will read it.

An appellate judge may use the bench memo to help to fully understand the case and to prepare for oral argument. After argument, the panel of judges will confer and generally determine how the case will be decided and who will be writing the majority opinion. The clerk writes a bench memo with the final opinion in mind. A judge may use entire sections of a bench memo in the opinion, including factual background, statement of jurisdiction, and procedural facts.

Final Considerations

Practice Pointer

When writing a bench memo, keep the following questions in mind:

- Have you given the judge all the information needed to make a decision?
- Have you clearly and concisely explained the parties' arguments?
- Have you identified any weak points in the parties' arguments?
- Have you made a recommendation and supported it?
- Have you identified the proper standard of review?
- Have you organized the memo logically, using headings and subheadings, so that it is easy to follow?

Bench Memo Exercise

After reading the briefs of the <u>appellant</u> and <u>appellee</u> in *Commonwealth v. Brunson*, draft a bench memo to summarize the parties' arguments for the appellate court. Follow the format for the bench memo discussed above.

Drafting Judicial Opinions

Shortly after the completion of oral arguments, the court convenes to discuss the case. At this stage, the likely disposition emerges, and a judge is assigned to write the opinion of a unanimous court or the majority decision. Sometimes judges will draft their own opinions, but often law clerks or legal interns also will draft opinions or parts of opinions. Therefore, experience in drafting judicial opinions is a useful skill for students to acquire.

Judges must write for multiple audiences. They write for the parties to the dispute. An opinion decides the underlying conflict between the parties, at least until the losing party appeals to a higher court. Judges decide who prevails and who does not. They also write for judges and lawyers in future cases. Applying law to new facts, judges develop the common law or interpretive case law and set precedent to be followed in subsequent cases in that jurisdiction. An appellate judge writing a majority opinion or a concurrence is also writing for current colleagues, and trying to convince other members of the panel to join the opinion's rationale or outcome. And, particularly in cases which decide controversial policy issues, judges write for the public.

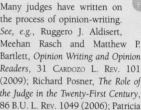

Many judges have written on the process of opinion-writing. *See, e.g.*, Ruggero J. Aldisert, Meehan Rasch and Matthew P. Bartlett, *Opinion Writing and Opinion Readers*, 31 Cardozo L. Rev. 101 (2009); Richard Posner, *The Role of the Judge in the Twenty-First Century*, 86 B.U. L. Rev. 1049 (2006); Patricia M. Wald, *The Rhetoric of Results and the Results of Rhetoric: Judicial Writing*, 62 U. Chi. L. Rev. 1371 (1995).

────────

Judicial Opinions Are Persuasive Writing

Judges write to convince the reader that the case has been correctly decided—whether the reader is a party to the case, other judges and lawyers, or the general public. To achieve this result, courts use persuasive language, and may strategically place it at the beginning or end of a sentence or paragraph. A court also writes persuasively when it:

- Uses logical organization and reasoning;

- Addresses and refutes the arguments it will reject;

- Analogizes and distinguishes case precedent;

- Uses citations to show that the decision is grounded in precedent;

- Tells the reader that a majority of courts that have considered the same issue have agreed with the rationale this court is using;

- Includes policy as part of the rationale for the decision.

────────

Opinion Format

As with many legal documents, such as the case brief, an opinion follows a generally predictable pattern.

An opinion will usually include the following components:

Make the Connection

Review the case briefing material in Chapter 3.

Introduction

An opinion will usually begin with an introductory paragraph or two. This information sets the stage: after reading it, the reader knows who the parties are, why they are in court, what precise issue is being decided, and how the court rules. It is also common to include the procedural posture of the case.

Review of the Facts

Just as lawyers do when drafting the statement of the case for a brief, judges often include the facts on which the underlying analysis is based. The opinion may state the procedural facts here, if not already stated. The authoring judge tells the story that supports the conclusion reached in the court's analysis and that supports its theory of the case.

Standard of Review

The court will usually present its standard of review prior to beginning its analysis to frame its view of the record and the procedure it will use for its analysis.

Analysis

Courts often use the persuasive IRAC format when crafting their analyses. Usually, the opinion will give its legal conclusion on an issue, state the abstract precedential rule on which the analysis relies, discuss the important cases that put the rule in factual context, apply the rule to the case, and then conclude the analysis. Some courts use variations of this format, but if you read carefully, you will find all the pieces of the IRAC format.

Conclusion

This is the decision of the court. Often, the court uses procedural language, such as, "We affirm the decision of the trial court." If the deciding court has further directions for the lower court, it often includes them here.

Consider the Sixth Circuit opinion in *Perkins v. McQuiggin*, 670 F.3d 665 (6th Cir. 2012).

The bench memo evaluated the arguments of the parties. Now consider this opinion. What information do you find in the introductory paragraph? Does this give you a good sense of what the case is about? After reading the factual and procedural background, try to explain the precise issue before the court and the relevant facts. Where does the authoring judge put the standard of review? What is the standard? How does it affect what the court must decide? The Sixth Circuit spends much of the opinion explaining what it CANNOT decide. Why do you think this is? What important issues are NOT before the court of appeals?

What conclusion does the court reach? How is this conclusion supported? What persuasive techniques does Judge Cole employ? Do you think they are effective? Do you think the court successfully distinguishes adverse authority?

> **FYI**
>
> The United States Supreme Court overruled the Sixth Circuit. *McQuiggin v. Perkins*, 133 S. Ct. 1924 (2013). As you read that opinion, think about the arguments that persuaded the majority of the Court to reverse. How does Justice Ginsburg support the decision to reverse? What is the basis for the dissent?

Opinion Checklist

After you have drafted and revised an opinion, read it with the following questions in mind:

- Does your format include all necessary components in a logical order?

- Have you started with a helpful introduction?

- Have you clearly stated the issue or issues before the court?

- Have you included all legally significant facts?

- Have you included the facts on which your decision relies?

- Have you included the facts supporting the losing party?

- Have the arguments of the losing party been adequately addressed?

- Are your conclusions supported by relevant legal authorities?

- Have you clearly explained the rationale for your decision?

- Is the court's ruling clearly stated?

- Are your citations in proper format?

- Have you properly cited any quotations?

- Have you proofread carefully? Is the opinion free of grammar and punctuation errors?

Notice that much of the language in the judicial opinion—the reasoning, legal conclusions, cases used, even specific language—first appeared in the attorneys' written submissions to the court. Lawyers recognize an exception to plagiarism when courts adopt—usually without attribution—the words and reasoning from a submitted brief. This is the goal of each lawyer in writing a brief. The lawyer should give the court the language, the reasoning and the precedent it needs to decide in his or her client's favor.

Opinion Writing Exercise

Review the briefs for the <u>appellant</u> and <u>appellee</u> and your bench memo in *Commonwealth v. Brunson*. Draft an opinion in the case using the format discussed above. In class, get together in three-judge panels and discuss your predicted outcome in the case. Then, vote to see if you will write a majority opinion or a dissent. When writing the majority opinion, you are writing in the formal voice of the court. You will write in the first person plural (we). When writing the dissent, you are expressing your own views as a jurist as to how the court should have reasoned in the case and will thus write in the first person singular (I). After your vote, revise the draft of your opinion in the case as if you were writing for the court or in dissent.

After completing your opinion, compare it with the one written by the <u>intermediate appellate court in *Commonwealth v. Brunson*</u>. Would you have joined the majority in that case or would you have written a dissent? Why?

CHAPTER 13

Writing the Appellate Brief

You will be drafting an appellate brief as part of your exploration of persuasion and advocacy. Attorneys draft briefs as their primary document explaining the issues on appeal to the court. The document must present all of the issues that the court will address on appeal and should educate the court about the precedential authority. Then, the brief demonstrates how the court can use the legal authorities to arrive at a conclusion that benefits the attorney's client.

The goal in brief writing is to win the case for the client. The audience, the appellate court, may remedy errors of law, apply existing law, and in the case of the highest court, develop new legal doctrines. Appellate courts typically are not concerned with mistakes of fact, but usually accept the facts as found in the trial court. Appellate briefs should focus on important errors in interpreting or applying the law or in the highest court, advocate for a change in the law or for new legal doctrines.

The well-written brief presents every issue firmly supported with legal authority. It will also demonstrate how the court can use or change legal precedents to arrive at a legal conclusion on each issue. The brief advocates for the client's legal view of the issues, but if primary mandatory authority directly contradicts the client's perspective on the legal issue, the brief should also persuasively present and explain why that authority should not alter the legal conclusion proposed in the brief.

Each brief must follow all the formatting rules required by the court. While each court has its own rules as you learned in the last chapter, the format of most appellate briefs is similar. Rules also differ somewhat between state and federal appellate courts.

Once the case is on the appellate court docket, the court will give the parties a schedule with dates by which they must submit the briefs. Typically, the schedule provides for responsive briefing with appellant filing first, and the appellee filing a brief that responds to that of the appellant. Then, the appellant may file a reply brief. When in the highest court, the parties may be called the petitioner and respondent.

You will be drafting a brief to the United States Supreme Court.

———————

Format of the Brief

In general, most briefs include the following sections. The following examples are drawn from student briefs in the U.S. Supreme Court case of *Windsor v. United States*, 699 F.3d 169 (2d Cir. 2012).

> **Go Online**
>
> The United States Supreme Court website is http://www.supremecourt.gov/. On this website, you will find the rules of court that guide every attorney's interactions with the court and the formatting of briefs attorneys submit to the court.

———————

Cover Page

The parties use the cover page to give important identifying information about the case. The cover page usually displays the name of the court, the docket number, the names of the parties and their procedural designations, the title of the document, some reference to the order or the proceeding that gives rise to the appeal, and the name and identifying information of the attorney on appeal. The Rules for the jurisdiction may require the cover to be a particular color. The Rules of the Court for the Supreme Court and many other courts have color requirements. No page number appears on the cover.

Here is a student example of a cover page to the U.S. Supreme Court:

No. 12-307

IN THE SUPREME COURT OF THE UNITED STATES

UNITED STATES OF AMERICA

Petitioner

v.

EDITH WINDSOR

Respondent

ON WRIT OF CERTIORARI TO THE U.S. COURT OF APPEALS
FOR THE SECOND CIRCUIT

BRIEF FOR RESPONDENT EDITH WINDSOR

Excellent Student

Counsel for the Respondent

ID #41413

3900 Forbes Avenue.

Pittsburgh, PA 15206

Light red   (412) 555-5555

Question Presented for Review

This first page of the "front matter" of the brief presents the court with the legal question it will answer. If there are multiple issues, there should be a question for each issue. The Question should detail the precise legal issue in its general factual context, and should be persuasive. The answer to the Question Presented should be "yes" in favor of the party drafting the brief. This and all pages in the "front matter" should be numbered with small roman numerals. The Appellate Rules and Rules of Court for each jurisdiction dictate the exact format and placement of the Question Presented.[1]

Here are examples of Questions Presented from student briefs on the same issue to the U.S. Supreme Court:

Does a federal statute that distinguishes between legally married couples based on their sexual orientation require the Court to use heightened scrutiny in its Fifth Amendment equal protection analysis, and, is the statute unconstitutional under both heightened scrutiny and rational basis review?

Does Section 3 of the Defense of Marriage Act violate the equal protection guarantee of the Fifth Amendment of the Constitution as applied to same-sex couples that are lawfully married under the laws of their state?

Student Exercise

How might you draft the Questions Presented if you represented the government and were defending the constitutionality of the Defense of Marriage Act?

Table of Contents

The Table of Contents lists the formal divisions in the brief, and outlines the legal issues as argued in the brief. Each section of the brief and the page number on which a reader can find the first page of each section is included. Each point heading and subheading appears verbatim under the Argument section in the Table of Contents with the page numbers on which one can find each legal argument.

The Table of Contents may be the first place where the court sees the outline of the legal argument in the case. Persuasive and clear point headings and subheadings here can begin to advance the client's legal argument.[2]

---

1. Rules 14.1 and 24.1(a) dictate the placement and form of the Question Presented in the Supreme Court.
2. Rule 24.1(c) details the table of contents.

Here is an example of a Table of Contents:

TABLE OF CONTENTS

Table of Authorities

This section lists every legal authority in the brief. The formatting is guided by the Rules of Appellate Procedure or the Rules of Court.[3] This section lists cases in alphabetical order, statutes, constitutions and rules, and then any other authorities. The table indicates all pages on which each authority is found. It is the last section of the "front matter of the brief." Each of these pages is numbered with small roman numerals. The Table of Authorities gives the court a view of the quality of the research contained within the brief.[4]

Here is an example of a Table of Authorities:

TABLE OF AUTHORITIES

CASES

---

3.   The Rules of Court for the Supreme Court rules 24(1) and 34(2) dictate format and content in briefs to the U.S. Supreme Court.
4.   Rule 24.1(c).

CONSTITUTIONAL PROVISIONS

STATUTES

MISCELLANEOUS

The following sections of the brief may appear on the same page.

Opinions Below

This section cites to the cases in the procedural history of the case under review.

Statement of Jurisdiction

This section begins the numbered pages of the brief and indicates which statute gives the court power to hear the case.[5]

Constitutional Provisions, Treaties, Statutes or Regulations Involved

In this section, the portions of the Constitution or Statute in question in the case are set out verbatim. If the authorities are extremely lengthy, only the relevant material should appear. List only those authorities that go directly to the question presented. Headings should separate different types of authorities in the same order as found in the Table of Authorities.[6]

Here are examples of the above sections:

OPINIONS BELOW

The decision of the United States District Court for the Southern District of New York is reported as *Windsor v. United States*, 833 F. Supp. 2d 394 (S.D.N.Y. 2012), *aff'd*, 699 F.3d 169 (2d Cir. 2012), *cert. granted*, 133 S. Ct. 786 (U.S. 2012). The decision of the United States Court of Appeals for the Second Circuit is published at *Windsor v. United States*, 699 F.3d 169 (2d Cir. 2012), *cert. granted*, 133 S. Ct. 786 (U.S. 2012).

STATEMENT OF JURISDICTION

The United States Court of Appeals for the Second Circuit reached its decision on October 18, 2012. *Windsor v. United States*, 699 F.3d 169 (2d Cir. 2012) *cert. granted*, 133 S. Ct. 786 (U.S. 2012). The United States Supreme Court granted a writ of *certiorari* on December 7, 2012. *Windsor v. United States*, 133 S. Ct. 786 (U.S. 2012) (granting writ of *certiorari*). The jurisdiction of this Court is conferred by 28 U.S.C. § 1254(1) (2012).

CONSTITUTIONAL PROVISIONS AND STATUTES

The Fifth Amendment of the United States Constitution provides: "No person shall ... be deprived of life, liberty, or property, without due process of law." U.S. Const. amend. V.

---

5.   Rule 24.1(e) dictates the substance of jurisdictional statements in briefs to the U.S. Supreme Court.

6.   Rules 24.1(f) dictate the form and substance of this section of U.S. Supreme Court briefs.

The Fourteenth Amendment provides that no state shall "deny to any person within its jurisdiction the equal protection of the laws." U.S. Const. amend. XIV.

1 U.S.C. § 7 provides: "In determining the meaning of any Act of Congress, or of any ruling, regulation, or interpretation of the various administrative bureaus and agencies of the United States, the word "marriage" means only a legal union between one man and one woman as husband and wife, and the word "spouse" refers only to a person of the opposite sex who is a husband or a wife." 1 U.S.C. § 7 (2012).

Statement of the Case

In the Statement of the Case, you should write both the procedural and substantive facts of the case. In many jurisdictions, the Statement of the Case lists the procedural history of the case first, and then lists the substantive facts of the case.[7] The U.S. Supreme Court does not indicate in which order the facts should be placed. However, most briefs detail the substantive facts first and lead into a discussion of the procedural facts.

The Statement of the Case should persuade the court of the legal merits of the case by recounting the facts in a persuasive way. It should include only those facts that are in the record.[8] Properly cite every fact to the record. The cites in the Statement of the Case must be the basis for any arguments in the brief that rely on facts.

Include all relevant facts in the Statement of the Case, including both positive and negative facts for each party. Chronologically order the all facts. The Statement must be completely accurate; however, it can relate the facts in the light most beneficial to each party. Do not include in the Statement any legal arguments or factual inferences.

> **FYI**
>
> Look at some actual Supreme Court Briefs at this site: http://www.americanbar.org/publications/preview_home/alphabetical.html.

Here is an example of a student written Statement of the Case:

---

7. Supreme Court Rule 24.1(g) dictates form and content of the Statement of the Case in U.S. Supreme Court briefs.

8. The record contains all official documents filed in the case. In a case appealed after a trial, it will include all notes of testimony.

STATEMENT OF THE CASE

Edith Windsor commenced her relationship with her deceased spouse, Thea Spyer, in 1963 upon meeting in New York City. *Windsor v. United States*, 833 F. Supp. 2d 394, 397 (S.D.N.Y. 2012). The two shared their lives together through sickness and in health, entering into a domestic partnership in 1993 once New York recognized such a legal status. *Id.* As Thea's health began to deteriorate in 2007, the two sought a more formal recognition of the bonds they shared and legally married in a Canadian jurisdiction. *Id.* The state of New York recognized the couple as legally married. *Id.* at 399. Thea succumbed to multiple sclerosis and a heart condition in 2009, and left her entire estate to her committed partner Edith. *Id.* at 397. The federal government refused to recognize the marriage between the two under the Defense of Marriage Act ("DOMA"), disqualifying Edith from receiving an unlimited marital deduction pursuant to 26 U.S.C. § 2056(a)(2012). *Id.* Thus, Edith was required to pay an estate tax in the amount of $363,053. *Id.* Forced to recognize her devoted life-long spouse as nothing more than a stranger in her life, Edith appropriately paid the estate tax in her capacity as executor of Thea's estate. *Id.*

Edith filed suit in the United States District Court for the Southern District of New York in November 2010 seeking a refund for the tax levied on Thea's estate. *Id.* Edith argued that DOMA's denial of federal benefits to same-sex couples violates the equal protection guarantee of the Fifth Amendment. *Id.* The court granted her motion for summary judgment, ruling DOMA "unconstitutional as applied" and awarding Edith her refund of $363,053 plus interest. *Id.* at 406. The Bipartisan Legal Advisory Group ("BLAG") appealed to the Court of Appeals for the Second Circuit, which affirmed the district court ruling that DOMA is unconstitutional. *Windsor v. United States*, 699 F.3d 169, 188 (2d Cir. 2012). The Supreme Court granted Edith's petition for a writ of *certiorari* on December 7, 2012. *Windsor v. United States*, 133 S. Ct. 786 (U.S. 2012).

Student Exercise

How might you write the facts differently if you were drafting the Statement of the Case for the Government?

Summary of the Argument

The Summary of the Argument encompasses the substance of the argument in one or two pages. Usually, this section summarizes the substance of the arguments, but does not repeat the point headings and subheadings.[9]

Here is an example of a student written Summary of the Argument:

SUMMARY OF THE ARGUMENT

The Court of Appeals for the Second Circuit properly held that Section 3 of DOMA violates the equal protection guarantee of the Fifth Amendment of the United State Constitution and thus is unconstitutional. Additionally, the Court of Appeals for the Second Circuit properly determined that classifications based on sexual orientation constitute a quasi-suspect class and warrant a heightened form of scrutiny.

As articulated in *Lyng v. Castillo* and *City of Cleburne v. Cleburne Living Center*, the Supreme Court has considered four factors when determining whether heightened scrutiny applies to a classification. These factors include: (1) whether the group has suffered a history of discrimination; (2) whether the characteristics distinguishing the group are unrelated to the ability to perform or contribute to society; (3) whether members of the group exhibit obvious, immutable, or distinguishing characteristics that define them as a discrete group; and (4) whether the group is a minority or is politically powerless. An application of these factors to classifications based on sexual orientation demonstrates that heightened scrutiny is the appropriate standard of review.

In applying a heightened form of scrutiny to Section 3 of DOMA, the statute fails to offer any justifications that substantially further an important governmental objective. Should this Court determine that rational basis review is the appropriate analysis, DOMA similarly fails to offer sufficient justifications that rationally relate to a legitimate government interest. The legislative record associated with DOMA's enactment supports this conclusion, as it contains numerous examples of moral disapproval and animus-based thinking against which the equal protection guarantee of the Constitution seeks to protect.

Argument

The Argument is where you present your legal analysis to the court.[10] It presents each legal argument completely. To keep the issue distinct and for the ease of the reader, the Argument is divided into subsections called point headings

---

9. Rule 24.1(h).
10. Rule 24.1(i).

and subheadings. These subsections act as a guide through the substance of the legal argument. The point headings are the legal grounds for relief on the issues, and are required in every jurisdiction. Subheadings are subdivisions in each issue, and you, the brief writer, decides how best to use them. Typically, the brief will begin by generally introducing the legal issues and giving a brief guide to the reader as to the subsections that follow.

Within each issue argument, the brief should persuade the court of the correctness of the client's position through clear, concise writing and through good organization. As in the memo, you will use the IRAC format separately for each legal argument and each subsection of each argument:

Issue—Here, you should place your persuasive issue statement advocating for the relief your client desires. This should be one or two sentences.

Rule—**a)** First discuss the **abstract rule** or the controlling legal principle for the issue you are discussing. This rule may come from the constitution, statute or case. Then, cite to the authority.

b) Next, in the **concrete rule**, discuss the cases that contextualize the rule and apply it in different factual situations. Give the facts, holding and reasoning of enough cases to fully educate the court about this particular legal issue.

Analysis—**a)** After fully discussing the cases, **apply** them and the legal rule to your case **to support your assertion**. Compare the facts in precedent with the facts of your case. Consider the similarities between your case and those you would like the court to follow. Through analogical reasoning discuss why the reasoning in precedent should guide the court's reasoning in your case. Similarly, distinguish or find dissimilarities between your case and those cases the outcome of which harms your client's interests. Explain to the court why the reasoning of the opposing precedent does not apply or should not apply to your case. Fully explain why the cases you have selected would best guide the court in its decision-making here. Where primary authority is missing, you may rely on law reviews or books to explain the rationale or public policy that you wish the court to adopt.

b) Counter–analysis—Here, you should rebut any remaining adverse argument or precedent that you have not addressed in your primary argument. You need not address every possible argument against your position, but do address those that may cause harm to your client's interests if left unaddressed. Do not fully explain the opposing argument as you did in your objective memo. Rather, you should disqualify the opposing authorities or arguments by explaining why they are not useful to the court in this case, if you can.

Conclusion—Summarize the reasoning and analysis that supports your assertion for this issue. Try to do this in one sentence.

Repeat this format for each issue or sub-issue you address.

The Argument should be as brief and clear as possible. Edit each sentence and paragraph to eliminate wordiness, legal jargon or ambiguity. You will then present the court with a fine and easily readable legal argument.

Here is an example of a portion of a well written student Argument section:

A. DOMA does not promote responsible procreation and child-rearing.

Congress' interest in enacting DOMA to promote responsible procreation and child-rearing is unrelated to what DOMA actually does. Even under a rational basis standard, there has been an insistence on "knowing the relation between the classification adopted and the objective to be attained." *Romer v. Evans*, 517 U.S. 620, 632 (1996).

In *Baker*, same-sex couples alleged that a Vermont statute prohibiting same-sex couples from marrying was unconstitutional. *Baker v. State*, 744 A.2d 864, 868 (Vt. 1999). The court found the statute unconstitutional and entitled same-sex couples to the same benefits and protections as opposite-sex couples. *Id.* at 889. The court found no logical connection between procreation and child-rearing and denying same-sex couples marriage benefits. *Id.* at 881.

In *Goodridge*, seven same-sex couples sued the Massachusetts Department of Health claiming that the denial of their marriage licenses was unconstitutional under state law. *Goodridge v. Dep't of Pub. Health*, 798 N.E.2d 941, 950 (Mass. 2003). The court struck down the marriage statute finding no rational basis in the legislative rationales of providing a "favorable setting for procreation" and ensuring an optimal setting for child-rearing. *Id.* at 968.

Similar to the statutes in *Baker* and *Goodridge*, DOMA does not encourage responsible procreation or promote child-rearing. As recognized in *Baker*, many heterosexual couples marry for reasons unrelated to bearing children. *Baker*, 744 A.2d at 881. DOMA does not encourage procreation as it merely denies same-sex couples federal benefits, offering no incentives to heterosexual procreation. Further, *Goodridge* recognizes that restricting marriage to heterosexuals does not protect the welfare of child development. *Goodridge*, 798 N.E.2d at 963. The American Psychological Association supports this proposition, concluding that empirical evidence shows that children of same-sex couples are as likely as those of heterosexual couples to flourish in adolescent development.

David J. Herzig, *DOMA and Diffusion Theory: Ending Animus Legislation Through A Rational Basis Approach*, 44 Akron L. Rev. 621, 670 (2011). Further, the application of DOMA actually deprives same-sex couples from receiving financial resources that could aid in a child's development. Thus, no rational relationship exists between denying same-sex couples federal benefits and encouraging responsible procreation and child-rearing.

Take Note

Notice the use of IRAC format and the forceful and persuasive use of language in this argument. See that it differs from the more objective use of language in an objective memorandum. In a brief to the highest court, the use of secondary authorities, as you see here, can persuade when case law is lacking to support a developing area of law.

Student Exercise

After reading the Second Circuit decision in this case, construct a portion of an opposing argument to the one presented here, writing as the government attorney defending the Defense of Marriage Act. Remember to use IRAC.

The Conclusion

The Conclusion section of the brief contains one sentence that requests procedural relief from the court.[11] This Conclusion is unlike the conclusion in a memo, because it does not summarize the legal arguments in the brief. It merely asks for the court's procedural disposition in the case.

Below the Conclusion, the attorney's name, designation and contact information should appear and the attorney should sign the brief.

———————

11. Rule 24.1(j).

Here is an example of a student written Conclusion and signature section:

CONCLUSION

This Court should affirm the judgment of the Court of Appeals for the Second Circuit holding that Section 3 of DOMA denies equal protection of the law as applied to Edith Windsor, as it lacks justification in support of a government interest and thus is unconstitutional.

Respectfully Submitted,

Excellent Student
Counsel for the Respondent Edith Windsor
ID# 12345
3900 Forbes Avenue
Pittsburgh, PA 15206
(724) 555-5555

Practice Pointer

Tips for Writing the Appellate Brief

- Check the Rules for your Jurisdiction and ensure that your brief complies with them in style and format.
- Check your organization section by section. Each sentence in each section of your brief should advance your argument for your client.
- Check your argument section for its use of point headings and subheadings and its organization within each subsection. Review use of strong thesis sentences to guide the reader through your argument.
- Check accuracy and form of citations to authority.
- Edit each sentence and paragraph for clarity and use strong verbs and persuasive language.
- Proof read, remembering that spell-checking programs may not check text written in all capital letters. Leave enough time to thoroughly review your document for errors in substance, style, citation or editing.
- Ensure that your document is professional in appearance as it is a representation of you and your ability to communicate as a professional. Your documents will leave an impression with its readers about you.

Make the Connection

Review Chapter 6 and its review of the 18 thesis sentences in the sample memo and how they guide the reader through the analysis. Your thesis sentences in each section of your brief should guide the court through your argument.

Student Exercise

Review these briefs for the U.S. Supreme Court.

- What arguments does each side advance?
- How do they support the arguments?
- On what authority does each party rely?
- Does each party anticipate the questions the court might have about the case?
- Do the parties address counter-analyses raised by their opposing counsel?
- What questions do you have for the parties after reading these briefs?
- Does the writing in the brief, its formatting, or its use of language affect how you feel about the legal issue in question?

Fisher v. University of Texas-Brief for Petitioner

Fisher v. University of Texas-Brief for Respondent

Chapter 14

Oral Advocacy

Your opportunities to advocate for your client before an appellate court may continue after you have submitted your brief. In many appellate courts[1] and all highest courts,[2] the attorneys may present their arguments orally to the court. Of course, every argument you wish to present to the court must be preserved for review in your brief, but you will have limited time[3] at oral argument to answer the court's questions about the legal issues you present and your client's perspective on those issues. Therefore, while you must know your entire case well, it is best to choose the most important or contested issues to be the focus of your oral argument.

The purpose of oral argument is to educate and persuade the court of the correctness of your legal position or proposal. You should know the details of your case[4] better than the court, and should be able to explain the nuances of how the case fits in or differs from prior precedent. To be effective in this role of oral educator and persuader, you must fully prepare yourself by reading both briefs, the important cases and by preparing and practicing your oral argument many times, ideally with different audiences.

Oral argument is not a speech you give to the court about your case. Rather, it is a formal conversation between the advocate and the court. You should have a prepared outline or text in case you face a "cold" court, or one that asks few questions. However, in law school and in actual courtrooms, most appellate courts are "hot," or well-prepared to engage in a dialogue about your case. When a court is engaged, the judges will pose numerous questions to the attorneys trying to clarify their understanding of the case and its implications in other factual scenarios. The attorneys must anticipate the questions that the court might ask and be prepared to answer those questions.

---

1. <u>Fed. R. App. Pro. 34</u>.
2. *See, e.g.,* <u>Rule 28 of Rules of Court for the U.S. Supreme Court.</u>
3. In the U.S. Supreme Court, each side is given one half hour. In the Pennsylvania Supreme Court there is no time limit.
4. Know the entirety of the record. The record is every document that has been filed in the case.

The court's questions may appear to be hostile, but actually the court is testing whether your legal theory will stand as good precedent. In other instances, a judge may ask friendly questions to place your argument in the best light in order to convince his or her colleagues on the court of the correctness of your position. You must be able to recognize the nature of the questions posed in order to answer them most effectively.

Preparing for oral argument may cause you some anxiety, especially if you are not used to public speaking, but the key to decreasing your anxiety is preparation. If you know the record, the lower court opinions, the briefs, have notes on the most important cases, and you review these materials, you will feel as if you are prepared to discuss your case with court. Practicing your oral presentation with others interrupting you with questions, especially those questions that you least wish to answer, will also prepare you well for your time before the court. Know that every attorney who will give oral argument to an appellate court will practice many times before actually walking into the court room. So the preparation you do for your oral argument experience will prepare you for court after law school. It will also prepare you for every oral presentation you may need to give, such as briefing a senior partner or an important client. The process will be quite similar.

————————

Oral Argument: The Details

1. Dress like a lawyer. Men should wear a dark suit with a white shirt and neutral tie. Women should wear a dark suit or business dress, with long hair tied back and little or no jewelry. Remember that you are the vehicle for your client's argument; therefore, your appearance should not be distracting to the court.

2. Arrive at the courtroom on time, prepared with all materials you might need, such as your outline or notes for presentation, briefs, lower court opinions, portions of the record, and a notepad and pen.

3. When your case is called, the counsel for appellant or petitioner will approach the lectern and introduce yourself to the court:

    "Good morning, Your Honors, my name is_____, and I represent the petitioner, _____, in this case."

    The counsel for appellant or petitioner may then request the court for a small amount of time (1 or 2 minutes) for rebuttal, which the court will usually grant. Then, counsel should immediately introduce the issues before the court and number them if there are more than one. For example:

"I have two issues to present to the court today. First, _____;
Second, _____."

You should then present the first issue in an engaging and interesting way.

4. If the court would like a statement of the facts of the case, be prepared to give a very brief rendition of the facts.

5. Continue through your argument in an organized way, standing still, making eye contact with the court, and speaking in a clear, moderately loud voice.

6. The court may start asking questions at any time, and you should welcome the court's questions, as they indicate an interest in the issue you are discussing. When the court asks a question, you should:

    A. Be prepared to stop talking; notice if it looks like a judge or justice is going to ask a question. Never speak over the judge or justice.

    B. Carefully listen to the question. You may take notes, if needed. Try to understand if the question is friendly or is testing your legal theory.

    C. Take a moment to reflect on the question, compose your answer and take a breath.

    D. Give a definitive answer, if possible. Start with, "yes, Your Honor" or "no, Your Honor," and then explain your reasoning, relying on precedent to support your answer.

    E. After answering completely, return to your argument at a logical point.

7. Your argument will be timed, and you should pay attention to the time cards. When you have about 1 minute remaining in your argument, you should think about concluding. State the holding or rule you would like the court to put forth and the procedural relief you request. If the end of time card is presented while you are answering a question, stop, and indicate that your time has expired and ask if you may have an additional minute or so to complete your answer to the question. Try to finish quickly. Ask for your desired procedural relief. Thank the court, and sit down.

8. The argument will proceed in the same way for the appellee or respondent, except you will not ask for or receive rebuttal time. You, therefore, should rebut any of your opposing counsel's arguments during your argument time.

9.　If the appellant or petitioner chooses to rebut, that argument should directly address a point made in the appellee or respondent's argument. The rebuttal should be as direct and to the point as possible. You should never use rebuttal time to discuss legal issues that you hoped to raise in your primary argument, but didn't have time to address.

10.　Lastly, take a deep breath, be yourself and relax. Most students enjoy oral argument once it begins, and the anticipation is over. The time passes quickly, and you will know that you were well-prepared and gave your best effort on behalf of your client.

For More Information

To read more about oral argument, try RUGGERO J. ALDISERT, WINNING ON APPEAL 293-341 (1996); JOHN T. GAUBATZ & TAYLOR MATTIS, THE MOOT COURT BOOK A STUDENT GUIDE TO APPELLATE ADVOCACY 81-109 (1994); BRADLEY CLARY ET AL., ADVOCACY ON APPEAL 97-133 (2000); DAVID FREDERICK, THE ART OF ORAL ADVOCACY (2003).

See It

Here is a <u>transcript</u> of a recent U.S. Supreme Court Oral Argument indicating types of questions asked by the justices.

Hear It

Listen to the Supreme Court Oral Argument in <u>Miller v. Alabama</u>.

Student Exercise:

You will recall hypothetical 2 from Chapter 4. Now use that case, reprinted below, as the basis for oral argument. Half the class will be customs office attorneys, while the other half will represent ABC Importers. Work together with your colleagues to prepare arguments based on the facts, the statute, cases and definitions. Take turns individually presenting responsive arguments to each other in class. While this is not how a formal argument is presented, this format will give you a chance to think spontaneously and consider answers to arguments you hadn't anticipated, and it is a bit less stressful and more relaxed. Have fun!

ABC Importers, Inc. ("ABC") imports golf sets for children. ABC imports this item from a country with which the United States maintains "Normal Trade Relations." The golf set consists of a nylon carrying bag, two plastic regulation-size golf balls, and three metal golf clubs with Puppy designs. The nylon bag is twelve inches high and has an opening large enough to hold three golf clubs and a side zipper pocket to hold the balls. The three golf clubs are representative of a full golf set, and each is seventeen inches long. The clubs include: one driver, one iron, and one putter. ABC sells only a right-handed set and imports these items for sale to retail toy stores.

The United States Customs Service (Customs) is charged with classifying imported items under the Harmonized Tariff Schedule of the United States (HTSUS) for purposes of assessing the tariff rate. Customs classified ABC's New Puppy Putters Golf Club Set under Chapter 95 of the HTSUS, heading 9506 "[a] rticles and equipment for . . . outdoor games . . . ," subheading 9506.31.00 "[g] olf clubs and other equipment; parts and accessories thereof: golf clubs complete" which are taxed at 4.4% *ad valorem*. Harmonized Tariff Schedule of the United States, Ch. 95, § 9506, 19 U.S.C. § 1202 (2003). ABC argues that the correct classification of this item under Chapter 95, heading 9503 "[o]ther toys; reduced-size ("scale") models . . ." under which the New Puppy Putters Golf Club Set would be imported duty free. Harmonized Tariff Schedule of the United States, Ch. 95, § 9503, 19 U.S.C. § 1202 (2003).

ABC Importers, Inc. is appealing the decision of the U.S. Customs Service, arguing that it can import the Puppy Putters duty free. Consider the following authority to formulate your arguments for this case.

1. The statute: The Harmonized Tariff Schedule of the United States, HTSUS

2. Relevant case law:

    a. Schulstad USA, Inc. v. United States, 240 F. Supp. 2d 1335 (CIT 2002);

    b. R. Dakin & Co. v. United States, 752 F. Supp. 483 (CIT 1990).

3. **Dictionary Definitions:**

    • **Golf**: game played on a large open-air course, in which a small hard ball is struck with a club into a series of small holes in the ground, the object being to use the fewest possible strokes to complete the course.

- **Model:** a three-dimensional representation of a person or thing or of a proposed structure, typically on a smaller scale than the original: *a model of St. Paul's Cathedral [as modifier]: a model airplane.*

- **Toy:** an object for a child to play with, typically a model or miniature replica of something.

and

4. **Trade Association Rules: The United States Golf Association,** http://www.usga.org/Rule-Books/Rules-of-Golf/Appendix-II/.

Civil Law Appellate Briefs and Advocacy

In the civil law tradition, persuasion does not depend on the weight of case authority upon which the advocate relies either in briefs or oral arguments. Because there is no doctrine of *stare decisis*, advocates carefully review the language of the code and rely on the analysis provided by scholars or professors in that particular field of law. While briefs cite to prior cases as examples, the court will not be bound to follow them. Therefore, the common law methods of reasoning by analogy will not be as persuasive to judges in civil law countries. Each case decided settles the dispute for the parties but will not set precedent. Common law lawyers practicing in civil law countries should learn the persuasive techniques that can succeed in each jurisdiction. *See, e.g.,* Sabrina De Fabritis, *Lost in Translation: Oral Advocacy in a Land Without Binding Precedent;* Declan O Dempsy, *Litigating Before the European Court of Justice: Practical Issues to Consider. See also* this brief to the European Court of Human Rights.

Chapter 15

Mindful Lawyering

For more than 2500 years, cultures around the world have been using mindfulness to guide their daily interactions with each other, to acknowledge their feelings about themselves and each other, to moderate the stress and anxiety of their lives and to enjoy life more fully in all its aspects. To be mindful is to keep one's mind in the present moment focused on whatever the present activity is, rather than dwelling on past mistakes or worrying about what will happen in the future. A mindful person is one who is living in the moment and concentrating only on the present events. To be able to achieve this state of mind requires determination and/or practice in meditation, deep relaxation or a mind/body practice such as yoga or qi gong.

In the mid-twentieth century, the practice of secular mindfulness began to make its way into U.S. life and culture in small ways.[1] Near the end of the last century, psychologists and physicians began to notice that the use of mindfulness with their patients could lead to profound insights on the nature of mental and physical illness and could provide healing to those patients who practiced mindfulness methods.[2] While mindfulness practices began to grow in the healing professions, they were still viewed by many in the United States as part of Eastern religions, or cult practices and were not widely accepted.[3]

During the last part of the twentieth and now in this century, lawyers began to recognize that the stress associated with modern law practices was becoming unmanageable for many.[4] It led to substance abuse and depression for members of the profession, so much so that many bar associations formed groups to help

---

1.   See RONALD D. SIEGEL ET AL., MINDFULNESS: WHAT IS IT? WHERE DOES IT COME FROM? (2008), for a nice discussion of the movement of mindfulness from a religious to secular practice. For a discussion of insight meditation or mindfulness meditation origins in the United States, see also Gil Fronsdal, Insight Meditation in the United States: Life, Liberty, and the Pursuit of Happiness (1998); CHÖGYAM TRUNGPA, THE SACRED PATH OF THE WARRIOR (1984) (the author began teaching meditation in the United States in 1976).
2.   See, e.g., Center for Mindfulness in Health Care, started in 1979.
3.   See, e.g., Steven C. Hayes & Chad Shenk, Operationalizing Mindfulness Without Unnecessary Attachments, 11 CLINICAL PSYCHOL. SCI. PRAC. 249-54 (2004).
4.   James J. Alfini & Joseph N. Van Vooren, Is There a Solution to the Problem of Lawyer Stress—The Law School Perspective, 10 J.L. & HEALTH 61 (1995).

with these problems.[5] While bar associations gave support for avoiding harmful behaviors, not much was offered to actually aid lawyers in managing their stress, anxiety and aggressive feelings toward themselves and others. In addition, the law has continued to be a high-pressure profession, despite the emergence of non-litigation dispute resolution practices.[6]

Recently, however, those teaching, practicing and learning about the law are beginning recognize the value of mindfulness training.[7] To be mindful, one need only to sit and let the mind and body be comfortable, yet aware. Then, the meditator may concentrate on the breath and will observe thoughts as they arise and leave the mind without following any one thought or train of thoughts. If one practices meditating with some regularity, the mind may become calmer and more relaxed over time. This calm and relaxed attitude may then stay with the lawyer throughout other parts of the day. The mindful lawyer will be awake and aware of what is required of him or her in the present moment. The lawyer's attention to each task or personal interaction should be focused, yet kind and compassionate personally and toward others. Mindfulness does not include self-aggression over work that is due or not proceeding as well as planned, but rather helps the lawyer to focus on what is needed to improve performance on the task with a calm awareness. Lawyers and judges are beginning to realize that this ability to be calm and focused is useful for them to be effective in their daily work and can also help to eliminate feeling of stress.

Legal education is often the place where lawyers start to feel the pressure, competition and conflict that will often increase as they take their place

Take Note!

Even Supreme Court Justices <u>meditate</u>.

See It

See Jack Kornfield's blog on <u>The Gifts of Mindfulness and the Law</u> (quoting a judge's mindfulness instructions to the jury), March 15, 2012.

---

5.   *See, e.g.,* <u>Lawyers Helping Lawyers, Virginia Chapter.</u>

6.   *See generally* Leonard L. Riskin, *Further and Beyond Reason: Emotions, the Core Concerns, and Mindfulness in Negotiation,* 10 Nɛv. L.J. 289 (2010).

7.   *E.g.,* Charles Halpern started the mindfulness movement for law schools and lawyers at The City University of New York Law School and then at the University of California, Berkeley Law School which established the Berkeley Initiative for Mindfulness in Law. *See* Charles Halpern, <u>*The Mindful Lawyer: Why Contemporary Lawyers Are Practicing Meditation*</u>, 61 J. Lɛɢ. Eᴅ. 641 (2012), for an example of Professor Halpern's work on Mindfulness. He has been followed in teaching mindfulness by Professor Leonard Riskin at the University of Florida Levin College of Law who also directs that institution's Initiative on Mindfulness in Law and Dispute Resolution and many others. *See, e.g.,* Leonard L. Riskin, <u>*Awareness and the Legal Profession: An Introduction to the Mindful Lawyer Symposium*</u>, 61 J. Lɛɢ. Eᴅ. 634 (2012) (one of Professor Riskin's many articles on mindfulness).

in the working world. Law schools in large part have failed to recognize the need for or to teach, as one commentator calls it, "emotional competence."[8] She defines this term as encompassing, self awareness, self management, social awareness and relationship management.[9] While a full discussion of emotional competence is beyond the scope of this chapter, one way to be fully aware of each of its required components is through mindfulness practice. Law professors have recognized the need for stress relief, emotional competence and self-awareness in their students and have begun to offer mindfulness practice to their students.[10] Students have responded eagerly and found that mindfulness helped them in many ways that they never expected.[11]

When practicing mindfulness, you gain the ability to focus on the work at hand without the lost time of a wandering mind. While mindfulness practice does not seek to eliminate the wandering mind, it allows you to notice more quickly when the mind wanders and bring it back to the present task and to see the task more clearly. The ability to be mindful may help you and other students in class when reading long assignments, and when preparing challenging written documents. You can also interact with more thoughtful presence with your fellow students, teachers, and potential clients.[12] In addition, staying the present moment helps to alleviate worries about the future that plague many students, such as their performance in class or the grade for documents they are writing. You may also find that meditation or other mindfulness techniques assist with the anxiety that is often part of the competitive world of law school. Taking a few minutes each day to sit quietly and reflectively helps put your place in the world in better perspective, and may help you to become more resilient by realizing that you are whole, complete and good despite what might be unsettling circumstances around you. There is also some indication that being mindful helps practitioners to react thoughtfully to their experiences, rather than reflexively (and sometimes aggressively), and may promote more ethical behavior.[13] Therefore, you may be the beginning of a more caring and thoughtful work and school environment for yourself and others through your mindfulness practice.[14]

---

8. Robin Slocum, *An Inconvenient Truth: The Need to Educate Emotionally Competent Lawyers*, 45 Creighton L. Rev. 827, 830 (2012).

9. *Id.* at 833.

10. *See supra* note 7.

11. *See, e.g.,* Katherine Larkin-Wong, *A Newbie's Impression: One Student's Mindfulness Lessons*, 61 J. Leg. Ed. 665 (2012).

12. *See, e.g.,* Deborah Calloway, *Using Mindfulness Practice to Work with Emotions*, 10 Nev. L.J. 338 (2010); Jan L. Jacobowitz, *The Benefits of Mindfulness for Litigators,* 39 Litigation 27 (Spring 2013).

13. *See* Jacobowitz, *supra* note 12; David DeSteno, *The Morality of Meditation*, N.Y. Times, July 7. 2012, at Sunday Review.

14. DeSteno, *supra* note 13.

Meditation Instruction

See It—Hear It

Here are examples of meditation or mind/body instruction from the <u>Mayo Clinic</u>, <u>Shambhala</u>, <u>Bell Meditation</u> from the On Being blog, and <u>Qi Gong</u> instruction from the Berkeley Mindfulness Initiative with Professor Halpern. The purpose is to relax and calm your body and mind. There is no one right way to meditate.

Meditation leads to mindfulness. Here are some instructions for sitting meditation. You can practice meditation and mindfulness anywhere.

1. Find a comfortable position in a chair or on the floor. Sit with upright, uplifted posture with a straight, but relaxed back and relaxed shoulders.

2. You may meditate with your eyes open or closed or half closed. Choose what is comfortable for you. Be kind and compassionate to yourself.

3. Begin to notice your breath without changing it. Keep your focus on your breath. Notice the effortless nature of the breath and how soothing it is to focus your attention on this natural process.

4. You will notice that thoughts will enter your mind, sometimes with great rapidity. This is natural. Notice the thoughts, but try not to follow a train of thought or build a story around a thought. Just notice that the thoughts will arise and pass and then return your attention to the breath. If you find that you have followed a thought, just notice and return your focus to the breath. Be kind to yourself. Having your mind wander, noticing that it has, and returning to your focus of meditation is part of successful meditation. After becoming a more seasoned practitioner, you will notice that your mind will become calm and less filled with thoughts as you meditate, but the elimination of thoughts is not the goal.

5. Sit with this practice for 5 or 10 minutes as you begin to meditate once or twice a day. You may lengthen the time of your sitting practice as you desire over time.

6. As you return to your day, bring the calm, peaceful and compassionate attitude with you to your everyday activities. Bringing present awareness to your writing will help you stay focused at each stage of the writing process.

CHAPTER 16

Beyond Law School

Throughout your legal career, you will use and develop the skills you have begun to learn in this text. In the summer after your 1L year, you may have a chance to write objectively or persuasively in a summer job, internship or clinic. Working in a legal setting will help you to hone your writing and editing skills. You will also see that a different pace may be required in the work setting from the relatively long periods of time during which you wrote your initial memoranda and briefs in law school. Your supervisor may expect you to focus on your assignments and complete your writing quickly. This is a reasonable expectation of law students or lawyers in any legal setting, and you will soon adjust to it.

You will have to take responsibility for your writing and other work products. Remain engaged and mindful as you continue to learn. Ask questions; look for ways to expand your understanding of the writing process and seek writing projects. See your work efforts as opportunities to learn from your exposure to new people and personalities, new subject matter, different formats that your work setting may require for documents, and the editing you will receive from your supervisors. When you return to law school in your second year, your first year and summer writing experiences will help you to be confident in your writing, and will allow you to succeed in more complex classes with more complex assignments. Reflect on all you have learned knowing you have the foundation you need to solve problems as a lawyer.

We wish you every good fortune on your path in law school and beyond.